Deviational Syntactic Structures

Bloomsbury Studies in Theoretical Linguistics

Bloomsbury Studies in Theoretical Linguistics publishes work at the forefront of present-day developments in the field. The series is open to studies from all branches of theoretical linguistics and to the full range of theoretical frameworks. Titles in the series present original research that makes a new and significant contribution and are aimed primarily at scholars in the field, but are clear and accessible, making them useful also to students, to new researchers and to scholars in related disciplines.

Series Editor: Siobhan Chapman, Reader in English, University of Liverpool, UK.

Other titles in the series:

Agreement, Pronominal Clitics and Negation in Tamazight Berber, Hamid Ouali
Contact Linguistics and Corpora, Cedric Krummes
Deviational Syntactic Structures, Hans Götzsche
First Language Acquisition in Spanish, Gilda Socarras
Grammar of Spoken English Discourse, Gerard O'Grady
A Neural Network Model of Lexical Organisation, Michael Fortescue
The Semantic Representation of Natural Language, Michael Levison, Greg Lessard, Craig Thomas, and Matthew Donald
The Syntax and Semantics of Discourse Markers, Miriam Urgelles-Coll
The Syntax of Mauritian Creole, Anand Syea

Deviational Syntactic Structures

Hans Götzsche

BLOOMSBURY

LONDON • NEW DELHI • NEW YORK • SYDNEY

Bloomsbury Academic
An imprint of Bloomsbury Publishing Plc

50 Bedford Square
London
WC1B 3DP
UK

175 Fifth Avenue
New York
NY 10010
USA

www.bloomsbury.com

First published 2013

British Library Cataloguing-in-Publication Data
A catalogue record for this book is available from the British Library.

ISBN: HB: 9780826457387
eBook: 9781441144973

Library of Congress Cataloging-in-Publication Data
Götzsche, Hans.
Deviational Syntactic Structures / Hans Götzsche.
pages cm.
Originally published as author's Ph.D. thesis, Göteborgs universitet, 1994 under the title Deviational syntactic structures : a contrastive linguistic study in the syntax of Danish and Swedish.
Includes bibliographical references.
ISBN 978-0-8264-5738-7 (hardcover)– ISBN 978-1-4411-4497-3 (ebook) 1. Grammar, Comparative and general–Syntax 2. Language and languages–Syntax. 3. English language–Syntax. 4. Danish language–Syntax. 5. Swedish language–Syntax. I. Title.
P291.G668 2013
415–dc23
2012041630

Typeset by Fakenham Prepress Solutions, Fakenham, Norfolk NR21 8NN
Printed and bound in Great Britain

To my wife and my family

In the beginning
Words were made
To make us forget
That we are alone.
Hans Götzsche, 2011

Contents

Preface

This book is about syntax. In contemporary English and other languages the word *syntax* is used in a number of ways, for instance, in programming languages referring to the combination of characters in the kind of code specific for each of these languages, but this book is about the structure of sentences in natural languages like English, Danish and Swedish. It is intended, first of all, for the specialist in syntax, but also linguists in other sub-fields, students in linguistics, and readers in other fields may find its approach interesting.

Scholars in Theoretical Linguistics may ask: who needs another book on syntax? My spontaneous answer will be that I do. A standard reference book on theories on syntax like Brown and Miller (1996) claims that there are 64 acknowledged theories on syntax – depending on how you count them; some of them may be considered versions of some of the other ones – but none of them seem to be able to satisfy certain specific criteria in description and explanation. Their shortcomings are of three kinds: first, there seem to be data that cannot be easily handled by these descriptive apparatuses; second, there seem to be theoretical inconsistencies in many conceptual frameworks; and, third, there seem to be, in some of them, implied unduly complicated conceptual systems or unduly complicated processes set up in order to handle relatively simple data. The essential opposition can be characterized as the one between descriptive ambitions: 'we want to know everything about these bits and pieces', and rational ambitions: 'we want to keep our minds clear'. The outcome is that today traditional philologists may find it hard to communicate with Chomskyan tree-diagram theorists, and the sad story is that sometimes they do not want to. I will not claim that no one has ever made generative analyses of excerpts of historical languages but such efforts have not always been fascinating topics to philologists.

My own ambition is an attempt to contribute to – not effect a reconciliation between – an adequate unification of the conceptual frameworks of descriptive work and theoretical work respectively. Basically, it is a personal ambition, because I am interested in formal syntax in parallel with a passion for the Gothic language, for Icelandic sagas, for Swedish poetry and for Danish biblical translations in the sixteenth century; combined with an urge to seek answers to basic philosophical questions, sometimes in the history of linguistics. This is reflected in the *modus operandi* of this book: I set off with a historical retrospective: where do my own ideas come from?; then I offer a formal theory of syntax that I have spent quite many years creating, developing and elaborating; and then I try to apply it to some language data from Danish and Swedish. The format of the book is based on my 1994 Swedish doctoral thesis, and the content is, to a certain – but limited – extent, a revised version of the thesis. This applies to Chapter 1 on three Danish grammarians. Chapter 2 on Chomskyan linguistics is written for this book, whereas the thesis' chapters on style and translation, and on the theoretical notion of 'word' have been left out. Instead, Chapters 3 and 4 are entirely revised presentations of the so-called EFA(X) theory in the framework that I now call Formative Grammar. Most of the basic assumptions are the same as in 1994, but the theoretical rigour has been improved, the formalisms have been updated, checked and extended with new suggestions, and a number of solutions to theoretical and analytical problems are being discussed. Finally, some perspectives concerning the adequacy of the theoretical model in the field of cognitive linguistics have been outlined.

Both my diverse interests and my way of doing things will possibly make it easy for my learned colleagues to find things in the following that they would have done otherwise. There may be theoretical inconsistencies, and the line of reasoning in the conceptual transition from formalisms to detailed accounts of the patterns of some data may have its weak points. My answer to this is that the content of this book is not an alleged ultimate and supreme set of ideas, purified to perfection and with total formal rigour. What is now known under the label Epi-Formal Analysis in Syntax (EFA(X)) is a theoretical project set up in order to try to solve some of the basic problems in the understanding of how expressions that constitute languages work, and it is now part of a research programme – henceforth called Formative Grammar (FoG) – that also aims at proposing alternative theoretical solutions to basic problems in semantics, pragmatics and phonology.

When trying to make things look – or make them understood – in alternative ways, one basic thing is integrated in this kind of endeavour: either you suggest new definitions of traditional words or you come up with new ways of using words from the daily lives of people; or, in the last resort, you invent new terms. I do all of these things. One of my predecessors in the line of linguists, and someone with high theoretical ambitions, Louis Hjelmslev, also offered new terms; in his case a huge amount of innovations in linguistic nomenclature. In this perspective my own terminological modifications are modest, and I hope that my reader will tolerate them as a legitimate way of thinking about the subject matter of linguistics.

It should be acknowledged that the format of this book is not the minimalistic (Chomsky:) *Syntactic Structures* style. Rather it is the (Chomsky:) *Cartesian Linguistics* style, incorporating quite a lot of notes expressing reservations or explanations. The background is the general characteristics of an academic piece of work: on the one hand, it presents a consistent line of reasoning, and, on the other, it demonstrates that not much has been ignored in the train of thought. Both of these things have been essential to the end product.

Introduction to the topics of the book

Linguistics in the late twentieth century: a personal view

In the theoretical landscape of twentieth-century linguistics the most salient feature was the discrepancy between descriptive analyses and formal theories, and the next most salient feature was continuous controversies about how to identify and precisely delimit the scientific object of language.

It is a well-known fact that the science of linguistics has a fairly short history – but so have many other sciences – and that, when the scientific approaches in linguistics were established in the nineteenth century, it was the descriptive historical perspectives that founded the theories and analytical methods. Partly as a response to this, some twentieth-century linguists suggested that languages should be regarded as systems, and, furthermore, that it would be plausible to elaborate formal theories to describe and explain the systematic nature of languages. Some of the prominent figures representing these efforts were Ferdinand de Saussure, who – so the story goes, cf. Chapter 3 – proposed the systematic synchronic view of language as one kind of social semiotic system among others, Louis Hjelmslev, who invented an abstract formal system for the description of the totality of language, and Noam Chomsky, who offered a formalistic theory of the grammar of the English language (called Generative Grammar) and of the innate Universal Grammar. By an irony of fate de Saussure's semiotic proposal has been largely employed by people working outside the field of linguistics, for instance, in literary and cultural studies, and his basic point of view, that, if language is a system, then it is a system combining expression and meaning, has to some extent been ignored by formalistic approaches, which have in general concentrated on linguistic form. It is also an irony of fate that the linguist who tried to elaborate a theoretical model describing the system of language assumed by de Saussure, Louis Hjelmslev, became quite famous among fellow scholars and linguistic descendants, but never contributed, in a significant way, to the improvement of linguistic analysis. Presumably one of the reasons for this is the fact that the central parts of his work were written in Danish and in French, and that reading Hjelmslev can be a challenging task. The opposite fact is true about Noam Chomsky and his Generative Grammar. He is not famous in the traditional sense of the word; one could say that he is extremely well known, because everybody in linguistics knows his work – more or less profoundly – and his theoretical grammatical models have, justifiably, had an enormous influence on linguistic analysis. This is also an irony of fate, because, apart from those who are 'members of the team', quite many linguists are sceptical of the adequacy of the Chomskyan theories.

So the situation in the late twentieth century[1] was, on the one hand, that people carried on with the descriptive work of recording all expressions and meanings of languages, and on the other hand other people carried on with attempts to establish formalistic theories about how the internal systems of these languages work. Furthermore, linguistics was taken up from many other perspectives, because language use is one of the more important keys to knowledge about psychological, cultural and social phenomena. In this situation it is, in fact, an irony of fate that sometimes, on more or less official occasions, these people still find it difficult to communicate, although the topic of the conversation apparently is the same for all the interlocutors.[2]

Maybe the problem is that it is not quite clear what the topic of the conversation is, and this has to do with the question: what is language?[3] And if one wants to discuss linguistic matters, then a number of ideas are presupposed, and these ideas, in turn, presuppose a number of basic choices that may lead one in different directions.

One possibility is to conceive of language 'as it is'. In that case one tries to find linguistic phenomena and then characterize them, and maybe also characterize their interrelations. This could be called the naïve naturalistic[4] approach, i.e. there are a number of linguistic categories because of the nature of language and the nature of the world – cf. the philosophical notion of 'natural classes'. One only has to unveil and conceptualize these categories. Thus it makes no difference whether one scrutinizes isolated linguistic items in a historical, geographical or social context, or whether one investigates relations between elements in abstract combinations. The point of view is merely immanent; and it contains some work under the labels 'phonetics and phonology' and 'syntax and morphology', and as long as one agrees with other linguists upon what the relevant data are and what the unmistakably identifiable classes are, one may be working in any specialized field of immanent linguistics.

A path apparently followed by some people is to see language as something else, i.e. as something that is not linguistic expressions. Then linguistic patterns are not especially interesting, and a language is conceived of as symptoms of some fundamental entities that can only be found by understanding the meanings of the words of language use. Since people may disagree on what these fundamental entities are, meanings may differ substantially, and severe disputes may arise over which interpretations are the correct ones. I am inclined to call this the approach of mystification, and it is found in some kinds of literary interpretation and media and culture studies, sometimes seen from the perspective of the tradition of psychoanalysis (cf. Kristeva 1989).[5] The paradox embodied here is, that one of the most frequent terms in the nomenclature of this approach is derivations of the word *language*, but only little linguistically significant is said, except for presentations of potential interpretations of words and texts.

The last option is an attempt to connect linguistic phenomena with other phenomena from the realm of individual or common experiences. If one chooses that aspect of language, then one's main interest is most likely to be the frame within which certain kinds of discourse are taking place. I suggest this approach is called the approach of human concern. What is significant for this approach is the fact that the internal linguistic patterns are not the focus, sometimes not even the relations between such patterns and individuals or groups, but what is the focus is the way in which the use of words is interpreted by individuals and groups under specific circumstances, and accordingly how it can be assumed that these words are used for various purposes in different kinds of psychological and social processes. During the second half of the twentieth century this approach has flourished under labels like 'discourse analysis', 'language and gender', 'speech act theory', etc., depending on whether the perspective is more or less political, whether it is the uncovering of universal conditions of discourse, or it is correlations between ways of talking and gender. The position of this third approach might be said to be one between the first and the second approach, but this is not quite fair because the accepted interpretations are often strictly limited, since they are almost always arrived at within the setting established by the persons and the situations one examines.

One might say that there is one more dimension in linguistics, namely, the fields of 'language acquisition', 'linguistic dysfunctions', 'language teaching', 'literacy studies', etc. I agree that these are linguistic fields, which are, in the tradition covered by the label 'psycholinguistics', but in general such studies are carried out as larger multi-disciplinary projects involving linguistics, psychology, the psychology of perception, pedagogy, and other fields contributing to the knowledge about human language and psychology. The achievements may say something significant about languages or particular languages, but sometimes the results are relevant only for special parts of linguistic patterns.[6]

The linguistics in this book

Many years ago, in the 1970s, when I was a student at Odense University, I attended a course in what was called 'psycholinguistics'. The course book was a monograph entitled *Aspects of the Theory of Syntax*. Admittedly, the book was a hard read, and at the first lecture there were only two students, but the next time there was only one student (me); and it stayed that way for the rest of the course. The teacher was the late Carl Erik Lindberg, a Swedish linguist with a profound knowledge of the subject matter of linguistics, and I am, as I told him on several occasions, deeply indebted to him. If it had not been for his enthusiasm, I would not have been in linguistics and this book would not have been written. But, obviously, as I attended the lectures, I did not have the option of not having read the pages required for each lecture because I was the only student and I was sometimes asked about my opinion on this and that. As a frame of reference, I had read Diderichsen's 'grammar' and I was (not well but fairly) acquainted with Hjelmslev's thoughts – and I had heard about Brøndal – but my time with Carl Erik Lindberg and the way he meticulously made clear the deeper implications of *Aspects* mark the foundation of my own thoughts on languages and the theoretical and analytic issues I have, since then, tried to address. The following is to be understood in this perspective.

I would like to thank Professor Staffan Hellberg, Stockholm University, for having checked the grammatical analyses, and I also want to thank my learned colleague Dr. rer. nat. habil. Norbert Endres for having checked my formalisms and for inspiring discussions over the years.

Technical Information

In the following I use different characters for special kinds of text:

1 Specific technical accounts of syntactic theory and analyses (i.e. formal definitions, symbols, formulae and annotations (including the analysed text)) are written in Courier black, extensively using '#' to mark sections and paragraphs.
2 General technical accounts, for instance arguments in formal logic, are written with the same typeface as the body text.
3 Linguistic excerpts and examples in Chapters 3 and 4 are written in Courier black.
4 Analyses are written below the examples in Courier 10 gray.

Capital letters (letters in the upper case) are used for Concepts (e.g. 'PETER TRAINED THE DOG').

1 Initial Capital Letters (letters in the upper case) are used for names and labels (e.g. 'the Classical Danish Tradition in Grammatical Analysis'),
2 SMALL CAPITAL LETTERS are used for technical terms (e.g. 'CONSTITUENT', 'TOPOLOGICAL SIGNIFICATION') when they are introduced or in contexts where they may be confused with non-technical terms.
3 Abbreviations written in SMALL CAPITAL LETTERS are used for frequent technical terms (e.g. 'CST', for 'CONSTITUENT').

Italics is used for:

1 Titles of published references (journals and books).
2 Linguistic forms cited in the body text.

Bold is used for emphasized forms in the linguistic examples (e.g. han **fik repareret** sin bil) and in instantiated parameters in a calculus.

Asterisk '*' is used for:

1 The marking of artificial or unorthodox terms when they are introduced (e.g. *CONJECTION).
2 The marking of ungrammatical forms.

Punctuation is made according to standard conventions. Single quotation marks are used for:

1 unpublished references;
2 quotations in English;
3 translations into English of quotations in other languages;
4 meanings of words or phrases (not in syntactic analyses);
5 paraphrases;
6 metaphorical, unorthodox or non-technical use of words and expressions;
7 technical terms (not in SMALL CAPITALS) when they may be confused with a non-technical meaning.

Definitions of technical or more important terms in the body text are in general marked by the use of a colon after the term and a semicolon after the definition (e.g. government: 'CST-external multiple MORPHOLOGICAL SIGNIFICATION;'). Formulae may be separated in a similar way.

In Appendix A there is a Glossary of technical terms, and the definitions and formalisms of the EFA(X) theory are presented in Appendix B.

The Birth of Linguistics

When the Danes came

Sproget er det redskab hvormed mennesket former tanke og følelse,
stemning, stræben, vilje og handling, det redskab hvormed han paavirker
og paavirkes, menneskesamfundets sidste og dybeste forudsætning. Men
ogsaa menneskeindividets sidste uundværlige redningsplanke, hans indhold i
ensomme stunder, hvor sindet brydes med tilværelsen, og konflikten udløses i
digterens, tænkerens, grublerens monolog.

Language is the instrument by means of which man shapes his thoughts,
mood, feelings, endeavour, will and acts, the instrument by means of which
he affects and is affected, the last and indispensable precondition of human
society. But it is also the last and indispensable hope of the individual human
being, his comfort in lonely hours, where his mind struggles with matters
of existence, and when this conflict evokes the monologue of the poet, the
thinker, the contemplator.[1]
(Louis Hjelmslev, Omkring sprogteoriens grundlæggelse *([1943], 1966: 5)*

The Classical Danish Tradition in Grammatical Analysis

Christiern Pedersen did not create modern Danish linguistics, neither did Jens
Pedersen Høysgaard, nor did Rasmus Kristian Rask, but it is generally acknowl-
edged that they are among the major contributors to the conceptual background
of the scientific notion of language that was expressed by Jespersen, Brøndal,
Hjelmslev and Diderichsen in the first half of the twentieth century, and which
I shall call the Classical Danish Tradition in Grammatical Analysis.

If one accepts the broad view that grammar, in a broad sense, includes the
physical linguistic manifestations described in phonetics and orthography,
then Christiern Pedersen (ca. 1480–1554) can be said to have had a certain
influence on the expressional structure of Danish grammar, namely, that of the

orthography of Danish after the Old Danish period, i.e. after 1500 (cf. Skautrup 1947: 176, *et passim*). He was the linguist of his time. His first book was printed in 1510 (a Latin–Danish dictionary: *Vocabularium ad usum dacorum* (cf. also Skautrup 1947: 148 *et passim*)). He was a clergyman at the time of the Danish Reformation. He was an author, a translator and a publisher, and for a period he was also a canon at the Cathedral of Lund in Scania, which was then a part of Denmark. His major achievement was his contributions to the translation of the biblical texts into Danish, and it has been argued that he also made, or largely contributed to, the 1550 edition (cf. Molde 1950; Skautrup 1950) of the Bible known as *Christian III's Bibel,* after the Danish king who initiated its publication, but the claim is most likely not one that can be substantiated (cf. Götzsche 2007). Besides adapting the ecclesiastical conceptions of the Reformation into a more straightforward vernacular, Christiern Pedersen was able to make systematic proposals concerning the spelling of words in Danish, so that it became, to a higher degree, nationally unitary, systematic and consistent. As a result of language change, pronunciation and other spoken language features had changed substantially during the Old Danish period, and Christiern Pedersen's suggestions were so ingenious that since then only limited systematic changes were made up until the end of the nineteenth century. This was achieved in a spirit of 'determination, effort, hard work, and intellect', characteristics which are also ascribed to Rasmus Rask, Vilhelm Thomsen and Holger Pedersen by Louis Hjelmslev, in his inaugural lecture on his appointment in 1937 to the Chair of Comparative Linguistics at the University of Copenhagen (cf. Hjelmslev 1959: 9), and which can be said to be those which characterize some of the most outstanding Danish contributions to linguistics.

These personal traits would also characterize Jens Pedersen Høysgaard (1698–1773),[2] who never received an appointment worthy of his linguistic skills. He worked as a caretaker at the University of Copenhagen and as a bell ringer at churches administered by the university (Trinitatis Kirke and Vor Frue Kirke). He took part in the ongoing debates about Danish orthography, but his most impressive contributions were in the fields of phonetics and grammar. He offered the first systematic account of the nature and the distribution of the Danish glottal stop (in Danish, *stød*), and these results and his description of the Danish grammatical system in the framework of a kind of 'dependency' grammar were mainly offered in his publications of 1747: *Accentuered og Raisonered Grammatica,* and 1752: *Methodisk Forsøg til en Fuldstændig Dansk Syntax.*[3] Høysgaard's achievements can hardly be overestimated, since the quality of grammatical description and explanation concerning the Danish language was (according to Skautrup 1953: 13–16) not surpassed until the twentieth century.

Høysgaard's work was in fact surpassed in the nineteenth century, not in the field of Danish language, but in the discipline of comparative linguistics. Rasmus Kristian Rask (1787–1832) can be regarded as the founder of the philological study of these Scandinavian languages by pointing to the genetic relationship between the languages with Old Icelandic as the representative of a prototypical origin (Rask 1818). He also studied quite a large number of foreign languages, both Indo-European and other languages. Rask, more or less in line with the Germans Franz Bopp and Jacob Grimm, founded the scientific discipline of comparative linguistics (cf. Götzsche 2007). To him, the current theoretical notions of genetic language relationship vs. typological similarities were not clear, but he contributed to the groundwork that led to later clarifications. His urge to systematize, which led him to a continual rearranging and regrouping of the grammatical and phonetic systems, has been an inspiration for succeeding generations of Danish linguists. It has been an inspiration in two ways: first, by entertaining an awareness of the need always to question the established scientific paradigms; second, by encouraging an awareness of the need always to clarify the analytical concepts, theories and methods, an effort which led Hjelmslev to characterize Rasmus Rask as one of the initiators of twentieth-century structuralism (cf. Diderichsen 1960: 135–45; M. Bjerrum 1959). Hjelmslev describes this 'untraditional tradition' of Danish linguistics as: 'The study of the methods and results of their predecessors has never been an education in dependence to Danish scholars, but training in independence' (Hjelmslev 1959: 12).

Rask's last contribution to linguistics was his proposal for a revision of Danish orthography (Rask 1826). His main principle was that the conventions of writing should reflect the pronunciation, but the changes that would follow from his recommendations were so radical that they were not approved in his own lifetime. Some of them were introduced in the last part of the nineteenth century, and the last one was adopted in 1948.

Apart from scattered remarks below, I am not going to mention other 'great Danes', among them Karl Verner, Vilhelm Thomsen, Holger Pedersen and Kristian Mikkelsen (cf. Mikkelsen 1911).

In the following I shall not tell the story of the life of Viggo Brøndal and his work – nor shall I tell that of the lives of Otto Jespersen, Louis Hjelmslev and Paul Diderichsen – and I do not summarize the history of the 'Copenhagen

School of Linguistics' (Le Cercle Linguistique de Copenhague) in the first half of the twentieth century. To certain extent, further information about these individuals can be found in Bandle et al. (2005) and the series *Acta Linguistica*. The main purpose of my description is to account for the conceptual, theoretical and methodological ideas and principles characteristic of the most salient approaches in Danish grammatical analysis in this period – in accordance with the way these themes are accounted for in the central works of the grammarians – and this inevitably is bound up with the people who developed the ideas and principles: Brøndal, Hjelmslev and Diderichsen. My account is intended to demonstrate that they had some characteristics in common, i.e. the structuralist approach and the striving to go back to the foundations of theoretical reasoning, and that there were also things that distinguished them, i.e. the nature of the basic scientific assumptions in linguistics and the kinds of theoretical systems they created. But hopefully my account will also demonstrate that what unites their approaches is an endeavour to achieve clarity and logical consistency in dealing with fundamental linguistic problems.

It is now widely acknowledged that linguistic problems are more than grammatical problems, and it is also widely acknowledged that grammatical analysis is more than finding morphological paradigms or diagramming sentences. Nevertheless, investigation of the expressions of language still lies at the heart of linguistic theory, and in this account the notion of grammatical analysis will cover any attempt to conceive of and explain the expressional phenomena of languages, both in general and in their instantiations. Thus, grammatical analysis means both conceiving theories about the more or less universal categories that linguistic expressions are divided into, and finding the particular units that represent the categories, and so Brøndal's word classification, Hjelmslev's Glossematics and Diderichsen's sentence topology all come under the term 'Classical Danish Tradition in Grammatical Analysis'.

Jespersen on language

Otto Jespersen is well known among contemporary linguists, first of all for his contributions to descriptions of the English language, but he also made acknowledged advances in our understanding of phonetics, in language education and in the philosophical basis of linguistics, and his work clearly belongs to the Classical Danish Tradition in Grammatical Analysis. His achievements have been accounted for in detail elsewhere, and I shall only touch on briefly what is relevant to the model of syntax that I propose in Chapters 3 and 4 of this book.

It is noteworthy that in a standard reference work on syntax like Brown and Miller (1996), Jespersen is only mentioned on two occasions (on pp. 77 and 80 (the bibliography of the entry), 166 and 168 (the bibliography of the entry), in both places as a reference to his *Analytic Syntax* (1937). In this, he makes 'An attempt ... at devising a system of succinct and in part self-interpreting syntactic formulas' (Jespersen 1937: 13). So, 20 years before Chomsky's *Syntactic Structures,* Jespersen tried to offer a formal syntactic theory, which he thought 'So far as I know, this is the first complete attempt at a systematic symbolization of the chief elements of sentence-structure' (1937: 98).

I shall not go into how Jespersen's formal approach is evaluated today, only mention that the entry 'Descriptive Grammar and Formal Grammar' by F. Stuurman in Brown and Miller (1996: 75–80) takes up the issue of whether Jespersen's system is more or less formal, and also Chomsky's perception of Jespersen's views, but it is noticeable that the other reference to Jespersen (1937) is found in the entry 'Generative Grammar' by the late James D. McCawley (1996: 164–9), and in that context as a remark on some details concerning auxiliary verbs.

What Jespersen did in his formal syntax is that he made it 'possible to denote all the most important interrelations of words and parts of words in connected speech ... By means of letters, chiefly initials of ordinary grammatical terms, numerals, and a few more or less arbitrary signs' (Jespersen 1937: 13).

When compared with my approach in Chapters 3 and 4, one may find some similarities to this. For instance, Jespersen has symbols for 'Subject', 'Object' and 'Predicative' (1937: 16), but he also has symbols for things like 'Agent-substantive' and 'Recipient' (*ibid.*), and this broad conceptualization sits uneasily between syntax as structures of sentences and scenarios that sentences may depict; in a kind of role-semantic fashion. No doubt, Jespersen's approach to formal syntax must be seen as a first – and, admittedly, diligently elaborated – attempt to purify a descriptive system to analyse syntax in the manner of sciences such as mathematics, logic and chemistry (which he discusses on p. 13) but, in my view, the basic problem with his approach is that he takes as his point of departure words and word meanings. By doing so, he seems to assume that traditional transferred goods from logic such as 'subject' and predicate (as 'predicative') combined with word class categories like 'Verb' and 'preposition' and with morphological paradigms like 'Infinitive' and 'Gerund' (1937:

16) – and furthermore furnished with some semantic roles – would make a coherent system. As is well known today, it is not quite as easy to put together symbols in a formalised system if they refer to phenomena that seem to belong to different 'natural classes' or conceptual domains, and even though Jespersen (1937) has been an inspiration to me in creating the theory below – for instance, concerning his ideas about 'nexus' and 'rank' which to a certain extent correspond to my ideas about how to analyse sentences and phrases – I have not been able to use his insights in formal syntax, except for a number of minor details (cf. Chapters 3 and 4).

Brøndal's theory of word classes

Jespersen seems to have held Brøndal in high esteem since he mentions (Jespersen 1937: 98–101) the Brøndalian word class theory (Brøndal 1928) and Brøndal's contemplations on morphology and syntax (Brøndal 1932) with much enthusiasm, but for Brøndal (1928), language is made out of words, and once this is accepted (a view that he finds quite uncontroversial), if out of chaos one wants to create order, then one must divide the set of objects under investigation into groups, depending on the nature of their properties. Thus the full title of his (1928) account of his theory of language is: *Ordklasserne. Partes Orationis: Studier over de sproglige Kategorier* ('The Word Classes. Partes Orationis: Studies in the Linguistic Categories).

His project was not only one of linguistics. He also refers (pp. vi–vii) to the nineteenth-century debate as to whether or not there are 'psychological' or 'logical' differences between the humans of 'lower' and 'modern' societies respectively, and he points to the potential of solving this controversy by investigating the linguistic categories of the languages of the peoples of the world. If there can be said to be universal language categories, then it can be inferred that human minds are basically identical (cf. also Brøndal 1928: 63). In this way, his work turns out to be a philosophical, a psychological, a sociological and anthropological as well as a linguistic project. He summarizes the purpose of his investigation as three problems concerning the number of word classes and their nature (1928: 2): (1) 'is there a minimum number of word classes; and is there also a maximum?'; (2) 'do word classes form systems, how and why?'; and (3) 'is there a common logical base of all or some languages?'. He points to the fact that the European paradigm of word classes originates in Ancient Greece (except for the class of interjections that was invented by the Romans), and that this classificatory system has turned out to be unsatisfactory when applied to more 'exotic' languages. Then, consequently, he traces the conceptual and terminological development of the current theoretical paradigm (1928, pp. 3–55) in its historical context and origin to see if there can be found any theoretical import in the tradition.

His answer is that there can be found both terms and notions that can be utilized to build a universal theory of words and their classes, and the basic theoretical concepts are explained on pp. 55–73. He knew, of course, that the classical categorizations, which had survived from Classical Greece until the nineteenth century, were driven by other motives than those of modern science, namely by normative and prescriptive ideals. Yet, he is convinced that the classificatory achievements of the traditions of antiquity and their followers do imply some kind of scientific perception of the problems, and in his elaboration of the classical concepts his point of departure is the linguistic doctrine of 'semiological structuralism' (cf. Götzsche, 'Structuralism', in Chapman and Routledge 2009: 219–25), a notion, whose theoretical meaning in the modern European tradition of the humanities is ascribed to Ferdinand de Saussure (cf. de Saussure 1916: 24: 'système [linguistique]'; 25: 'La langue, au contraire, est un tout en soi et un principe de classification'; 33: 'sémiologie'; 97: 'signe linguistique', *et passim*):

According to Brøndal:

Hvis sproget er et system af Tegn, maa klasserne paa ethvert givet Sprogtrin danne et Hele, hvori hvert Led kun faar Eksistens og Værdi ved sit Forhold til alle de øvrige.

If language is a system of signs, then the classes at any stage [of development] must create a [unified] whole in which every single part achieves existence and value only by means of its relation to all the other [parts].

(1928: 55)

Then he points to the fact that the criteria that have been used since antiquity, when people have been trying to make systematic arrangements of word classes, have been of a morphological, syntactic or logical nature. He summarizes the morphological attempts and rejects the syntactic approaches.[4] Then he offers a detailed summary of the options for logical solutions, and he arrives at the conclusion that there seem to be a number of basic concepts that are maintained throughout the history of philosophy. Labelled as 'categories', they are considered central to formulating and solving philosophical problems, and Brøndal adopts these concepts as basic linguistic categories:

1   Substans (cf. Egenavne)
2   Kvantitet (cf. Talord)
3   Kvalitet (cf. Adverbier)
4   Relation (cf. Præpositioner).

(Brøndal 1928: 65)

Thus the four fundamental concepts in describing the word classes are (1) 'Substans' 'substance'; (2) 'Kvantitet' 'quantity'; (3) 'Kvalitet' 'quality'; and (4) 'Relation' 'relation', and each of them is closely linked to one apparently basic word class ('Egenavne' 'proper names', 'Talord' 'numerals', 'Adverbier' 'adverbs' and 'Præpositioner' 'prepositions' respectively).

It is important to admit, first, that the main source of these categories is the Aristotelian scheme of categories (which appears in different versions with different numbers of categories to a maximum of 10), second, that the ones chosen are: 'hos ARISTOTELES ... de, der nævnes först' 'by Aristotle ... the ones that are mentioned first' (p. 65), and, third, that the nature of the categories is not made quite clear by Brøndal.[5] Thus, they can be conceived of as metaphysical notions, i.e. entities or properties functioning as conditions or as a fundamental background for the existence of the physical world (presumably the Aristotelian view), they can be conceived of as basic ontological entities, i.e. elements, the aggregation of which make up the other entities of the world, or they can be understood as epistemological categories, i.e. basic human concepts employed in knowing and understanding the world, which is the view held by Kant.[6] So it follows that it is not evident what the starting-point for Brøndal really is, whether it is a number of more or less accurately expounded philosophical classifications used to characterize classes of words, or whether it is a more or less intuitive classification of four types of words functioning as the basic ones, underpinned by philosophical investigations into conceptual structures. This is not contradicted by Brøndal's attempt to claim that the categories can be derived from the conceptual apparatus of traditional logic (for instance, by saying that 'substance' can only be the subject of a well-formed proposition, while the other three categories can only be predicates (p. 65)), because then we are left with the problem of the philosophical (ontological) status of logic. Nor is it contradicted by the claim that the categories are to 'be stripped of any metaphysical and absolute character' (p. 68), based on the argument that 'language is a system of signs' (p. 69), because it is not thereby justified that the categories reflect properties of this system of signs.

But such difficulties are commonplace in scientific theories; and from this point onwards Brøndal develops a formalistic theory of word classes that both includes all the traditional word classes (and would include any word class one could imagine), and is able to account for all the words in the languages known by him, in one system.

The first step in developing the formalistic system is the production of the expressions that signify the properties of word classes and the combinations of which are stipulated to be assigned to each specific word class. Through a series of contemplations, all of which are not quite transparent, and a piece of text, which is by no means lucid, he makes the connection between the basic categories mentioned and the formal concepts. Thus 'substance' is characterized as 'Genstand for Relation' 'object of relation' (p. 70) and is labelled as '*Relat*' ('das Bezogene')', i.e. an entity or a property implying the ability to establish relationships, while 'quantity' is characterized as 'Genstand[e] for Beskrivelse' 'object of description' (p. 72) and is labelled as '*Descript*', i.e. an entity or a property implying the ability of being described. Out of this emerges a distinction between 'Genstandsarter' 'kinds of objects' (entities, properties or elements: 'Relat' and 'Descript') and 'Funktionsarter' ('kinds of functions' (relations and descriptions)), and:

> *Det foreslaaes da at betragte disse fire Begreber og kun dem som fundamentale. De antages – efter den foregaaende Begrundelse – at være Sprogets faste Kategorier, de eneste nødvendige og tilstrækkelige til at definere et hvilketsomhelst Sprogs System af Ordklasser.*

> It is proposed, then, to consider these four concepts, and only them, as fundamental. They are supposed to be – according to the previous argument – the fixed categories of language, the only necessary and sufficient ones [i.e. concepts] in order to define the system of word classes of any language.
>
> (Brøndal 1928: 72)

The corresponding symbols are derived from the chosen terms:

> *Det foreslaaes endvidere paa det relative Omraade at betegne Forbinder eller Relator ved* **r**, *Genstand eller Relat ved* **R**, *– og parallelt paa det descriptive Omraade Beskriverelement, Kvalitet eller Descriptor ved* **d**, *'Formkapacitet', Kvantitet eller Descript ved* **D**.

> It is further suggested in the relative field to label connective or relator with **r**, object or relating entity with **R**, – and in parallel in the descriptive field describing element, quality or descriptor with **d**, form-capacity, quantity or described entity with **D**.
>
> (Brøndal 1928: 72)

By this, it is implied that any word class can be defined by being assigned one of these symbols, or a specific combination of two or more symbols, and if the result is empirically plausible, i.e. if it is an adequate description of all (or most) of the data, and if it furthermore builds an aesthetic pattern, then there is a strong inclination to believe that it is also a true description.

So Brøndal sets out to demonstrate that word classes can reasonably be defined and characterized by this formalistic system. The first problem to solve is to answer the questions 'which combinations are possible at all' (p. 74, '1°'), and 'which combinations are possible at the same time' (*ibid.*, '2°'), and Brøndal strongly rejects the suggestion that an empirical method should be adequate, because it would always be based on special facts, and these would create arbitrary limitations (p. 75). As a quite different approach, he suggests two principles called the 'principle of continuity' and 'the principle of symmetry' respectively (*ibid.*). The former implies that 'differences and contrasts should always be neutralized by connecting links and transitions' and the latter implies that 'in any kind of totality ('Helhed'), there will always be established some equilibrium' (*ibid.*). At the basis of these principles his 'combinatorial system' comprises four levels: on the first level (p. 76, 'I'), there are four classes that are assigned one symbol each and which are called 'abstract classes' ('r, R, d, D'); at the second level (*ibid.*, 'II'), there are six classes that are called 'concrete classes', and each class is assigned two symbols ('rR, Dd' = the 'homogeneous group'; 'Rd, rd, RD, rD' = the 'heterogeneous group'); at the third level (*ibid.*, 'III') we find four classes as combinations of three symbols ('Drd, DRd, rDR, rdR') that are called the 'complex classes'; and at the fourth level (*ibid.*, 'IV') only one class remains, namely, the combination of all the symbols ('rRDd'), a combination which is called the 'undifferentiated class'. This is regarded as the absolute maximum of word classes in any one language (in total, 15 classes), and if one calculates the possible combinations of word classes found in the languages of the world, then there is a maximum of 32,767 different languages (p. 77), but since the 'principle of symmetry' is applied, then some dependences or 'solidarities' between the occurrences of word classes are established and the actual number is assumed to be much smaller.

Up until this point the procedure has not been much different from that of creating some kind of logical system according to clearly defined rules to manipulate the symbols, and in that sense it is quite speculative as a scientific theory. The verification[7] of the theory will not be established until it has been demonstrated that it matches the facts, and Brøndal thus makes an evaluation of a number of words from different languages as interpreted by the theory. The four basic word classes are of no special interest, since they are more or less part of the defining apparatus, but it should be observed that, according to Brøndal, relatively few languages have genuine prepositions (p. 79), if they are defined as being only abstract conveyers of relation, and an example of a preposition that satisfies this definition is the French word *de*.[8] It should also be noted that the class of proper names corresponds more or less to the classifications in traditional grammars (pp. 81–5), and that the class of numerals is indisputable (pp. 85–90) while it appears to be more difficult to find genuine adverbs (pp. 90–5). But it is interesting, actually, that Brøndal is able to define the four traditional Aristotelian word classes of nouns ('Nominer', p. 97), verbs ('Verber', p. 104), pronouns ('Pronominer', p. 109) and conjunctions ('Conjunctioner', p. 113) as two-symbol classes. Thus nouns are defined by the properties 'Rd', which means that the class is allowed to contain only words that denote an 'object or substance' and words 'describing content or quality'. Intuitively, we find this to be true of nouns and adjectives in the Western European languages, and Brøndal mentions examples of nouns like Danish *Sæk* 'bag', which can be traced back to Phoenician *saq*, and found as a loanword as Finnish *sekki*, and in the adjectives Danish *stor* 'big' (Arabic *kabir*, Finnish *iso*). The word *Sæk* has to refer to something, and we know that the thing has some specific properties, and the word *stor* refers to a property, but we cannot imagine the property without something having the property. According to Brøndal, it is only the Indo-European, the Semitic and the Finno-Ugrian languages that can be said to have clearly definite sets of nouns, while the other languages of the world display classes of nouns that have a more complex or blurred semantics. The same principles are, by Brøndal, applied to the other three word classes with more or less the same result; only pronouns do not quite fit into the model because only demonstrative and indefinite pronouns are accepted as genuine members of this class. The two 'homogeneous' classes ('rR, Dd') are used to account for possessive pronouns (p. 124) and personal pronouns (p. 129) respectively, and after having illustrated the adequacy of his theory with samples like these, then Brøndal passes the symbolic elements on to the three-symbol classes.

The wider aspect of the implementation of the theory is the interesting fact that Brøndal produces not only an account of all the traditional word classes and their sub-classes, e.g. the class of nouns that can be divided into substantives and adjectives as a consequence of the significance (marked by letters in bold) of the elements of the combination (thus 'R**d**' (nouns), '**R**d' (substantives) and 'R**d**' (adjectives), p. 97 seqq. and 'Synopsis'). But he is also able to account for more subtle morphological categories (all symbolized by 'Drd'): the gerund;

the two supine forms of Latin ('venio *questum*' 'I come to complain', '*facile dictu*' 'easy to say' (p. 107)); two of the Finnish infinitives (p. 137), (Finnish infinitive 1: basic form like *ostaa* 'buy', translative like *sanoakseni* 'I having the intention/ purpose of saying', and Finnish infinitive 2: in the inessive case like *sanoessani* 'I saying'). Or he is able to account for, for instance, complex numerals by the elements 'rDR' (p. 145). The procedure does not stop until he has exhausted all the logical and empirical options inherent in the languages known to him and he arrives at the final combinatorial option of 'rRDd', which he applies to the class of interjections (p. 155).

The last part of the theory is a presentation of universal exemplars ('Universalier' 'universals', p. 164 seqq.) of each of the word classes. Brøndal's basis for this is the way he handles three kinds of expressions that he has not yet defined: 'articles' ('Artikler'), 'genitive-particles' ('Genitivpartikler') and 'answering-words' ('Svarord'), (pp. 162–3). In his view, they are abstract forms of other word classes (p. 163) and through a number of deliberations, which are not all quite perspicuous, he comes to the point where he claims that all the words within a word class are ordered according to their degree of abstractness (p. 164), and that there may be a most abstract representative of any word class: a universal exemplar. Then the interesting thing for Brøndal is whether these phenomena are actually found in different languages and to what extent the distribution of them is a characteristic feature of particular languages.

His answer to this enquiry is typical for him: only French (it may be mentioned that he was a professor of Romance Languages), and to a very limited extent English, have the universals of the 'abstract' (one symbol) and the 'concrete' (two symbols) classes, e.g. French '*chose*' is the universal proper name ('R') and French '*on*' is the universal noun ('Rd'), (p. 165), while the Scandinavian and other Germanic languages are abundantly represented by three-symbol universals (pp. 168–75). The last question to be answered is, then, whether or not there are universal representatives of the sub-classes of the undifferentiated class of interjections – sub-classes which emerge on the basis of the emphasis on one or more of the aggregated elements – and the result is that such abstractions are actually found primarily in the Western European languages. It is an intrinsic characteristic of Brøndal's line of reasoning that these findings confirm the hypothesis about a connection between the manifes- tation of the different word classes in actual languages, the existence of abstract universal exemplars of word classes in actual languages, and the ability to create abstractions as a mental property. Thus, the evidence mentioned:

*vil da kun findes, hvor Abstraktionsevnen paa det paagældende Felt har naaet sin
höjeste Udvikling.*

will be found only where the faculty of abstraction in the actual [subject] field
has reached its highest [level of] development.

(Brøndal 1928: 180)

This convergence of linguistic and anthropological generalizations is then
discussed further in the third chapter of the book: 'Konsekvenser' 'consequences' (p. 181).

In his last chapter, before the Conclusion, Brøndal deals with the link
between word classes and linguistic variation, i.e. 'Sprogtyper' 'language types',
'Nationalsprog' 'national languages' and 'Dialekter' 'dialects', the last item also
including the phenomenon of stylistic variation (p. 182). The primary purpose
of his reflections on dialects and style is the underpinning of his general theory
concerning an axis of abstractness, and the final and general question is:

*Hvilket Forhold er der mellem Sprogtyper og Ordklassesystemer og mellem disse
og Mentalitetstyper?*

What kind of relationship is there between language types and word class-
systems and between these and types of mentality?

(Brøndal 1928: 207)

It may come as no surprise that the answer is that only the Indo-European and
Semitic Languages contain all of the advanced word classes, i.e. levels 'I', 'II'
and 'III', with one, two and three symbol assignments respectively (and French
seems to be the most advanced language of them all, cf. p. 215). These languages
have obtained:

den största for Mennesker mulige Alsidighed eller Fuldstændighed

the greatest versatility or completeness for human beings.

(*ibid.*: 209)

and all other languages are judged '*Reduktioner eller enklere Former heraf*'
'reductions or simpler forms thereof' (*ibid.*). There are, of course, languages that
are less perfect than the advanced types without being 'primitive or standing
on a lower logical level' (p. 211) and in this case the logical possibilities are
exclusively 'I' or 'II' type languages, or a combination of 'I' and 'II'. It is not easy
to find type 'II' or type 'I, II' languages, but some examples are mentioned on
p. 212, and the only instance of a type 'I' language is Chinese. Brøndal refers

to Chinese (pp. 212–15) with much respect because it represents 'en Grad af Analyse, hvortil intet Sidestykke kendes' 'an unparalleled degree of analysis' (p. 215), by which is meant that the logical capacities are eminent. Consequently, Brøndal accords the Chinese culture the highest esteem (*ibid.*). For Brøndal, it is, accordingly, evident that culture and language types (in the Brøndalian sense as word classes) correspond (p. 216), and this conceptual paradigm is the hallmark of the concluding remarks.

In his Conclusion (pp. 217–19), he answers his initial questions: there is no word class (except for interjections), or no group of word classes, such that it necessarily exists everywhere. As a minimum, a language has to consist of at least two correlating word classes (apart from the interjections), and a maximum of word classes seems to Brøndal to be his 15 basic word classes, the defining principles of which have been presented above, but depending on the nuances and the emphasis on the different properties, the real number may be considered to be much larger. Furthermore, Brøndal claims, on the basis of this investigation, that 'a language is always divided into classes and classes always form systems' (p. 218), but the systems always vary, and what is 'constant are not the combinations but the elements which are combined' (*ibid.*), i.e. the 'four basic concepts of substance, relation, quantity and quality' (*ibid.*). Finally, and as a consequence of this, Brøndal claims that the 'logical basis of all languages is the same' (p. 219), and thus the variation depends on the combination and the accentuation of the basic categories. So, summarizing the Conclusion, it is evident that he provides us with positive answers to all his hypotheses, and an evaluation of Brøndal's theory ought to start at this last point. To Brøndal, it was obvious that all human languages and all mental activity had the same logical basis, namely, the four categories, and in that respect all human beings are basically the same, but it was equally obvious to him as a linguist that human languages have major differences, and it was also obvious to him as a representative of Western European civilisation that there were cultural differences between societies. To conceive of this linguistic and cultural multitude in relation to the relatively modern idea of all mankind being equal, he created his system as a minor number of elements with some specific 'combinatorial' rules and a theoretically almost infinite number of combinations. In this way all humans are basically the same, but the greater the number of combinations and the more obscure the system, the more primitive the culture and the people.

Judged on their own premises, Brøndal's views were not especially peculiar, and most accounts in the field of natural language linguistics presuppose relations between a language and the culture of a society. Therefore, the main question is whether Brøndal illustrates some of the early twenty-first-century problems in theories of language.

First of all, he actually carries out a critical assessment of the traditional grammatical doctrines of word classes. An account of the distribution of the words of a language in different word classes is a basic prerequisite of any descriptive grammar, and it is well known that such grammars always imply a compromise in every step of the descriptions and also inconsistencies in the theoretical apparatus. It is, therefore, a theoretically commendable attempt to try to establish precise criteria for the identification of word classes elaborated from a certain point of view, in this case, the semantic or logical aspect. Second, Brøndal attempts to integrate the traditional field of morphology in his theory of word classes (cf. 'genitive-particles' as mentioned above), an approach that may be a way of solving the classical problem of defining the notion of word. Third, he is able to argue reasonably for the existence of universal categories, word classes and words, and the major reason for rejecting his theory today is not its theoretical flaws but the fact that it does not quite fit the prevailing image of the world of our time. Finally, Brøndal's theory is relevant because it demonstrates that it is possible to propose a theory of the semantics of words that does not include the problematic implications of universal generalizations from what I would suggest calling the 'local ontological semantics' of normal language-specific descriptive grammars, i.e. semantic explanations based on the perceptions of the world which are characteristic of the people speaking a specific language or dialect.[9] Brøndal had the courage to suggest universal explanations to word semantics as a basic part of his theory, and did not assume a simple word–entity relation as the solution to the problem of semantics.

The less flattering bias in Brøndal's theory is illustrated by its anthropological implications: it is fairly evident that it is not that easy to judge the cultural level of a population (because there is no consensus concerning the notions of 'culture' and 'cultural level'), and it is not that easy to estimate the potential for abstraction of a single language entirely based on the occurrence of certain word classes; the risk of conceptual bias is a real threat. But it is not enough to say that Brøndal was merely wrong. What was wrong with his theory was the vagueness of the theoretical status of his basic categories. Apart from their origin in the discourse of historical philosophy, then, on the face of it, they may only seem to be abstract inventions without any function apart from their defining role in establishing the word classes, so if Brøndal's system is to be used for further linguistic investigation, then the basic categories have to be clarified, the adequacy of his combinations have to be estimated, and this revised version has to be tested against empirical evidence. From this perspective some of his ideas and principles will be used in the theory of syntax outlined in Chapter 3.

As an epilogue to Brøndal, it can be mentioned that the most serious objection to Brøndal is that apparently he does not clearly separate words from concepts and things, and thus it is not obvious whether his classification of words is based on the assumption that the categories are properties of words or whether they are properties of things, but this is a common problem in linguistic theory. It may also be mentioned that regarding the background of Brøndal's attempt to shed light on the problem of which languages are possible and which languages are probable, it is a little puzzling to read Newmeyer's *Possible and Probable Languages* (2005) because the theoretical framework (its subtitle is: *A Generative Perspective on Linguistic Typology*) in a similar way puts certain limits on what can be considered comparable phenomena. In retrospect, it is, by all means, hard to decide which approach is the most justified.

Hjelmslev's theory of Glossematics

It is a well-known fact about the history of twentieth-century Danish linguistics that there were very close personal (but no family) relations between Viggo Brøndal, Louis Hjelmslev and Paul Diderichsen, and that the relationship between Brøndal and Hjelmslev developed into one of personal and professional animosity. Since Hjelmslev elaborated his theories mainly in the 1930s, it may be assumed that his opposition to Brøndal has influenced the often quite radical formulation of his theoretical views. It is a credible interpretation, but, as mentioned above, in this account I confine myself to the conceptual, theoretical and methodological substance of Hjelmslev's approach.[10] The modern extensive Danish exegesis of Hjelmslev's Glossematics is made by Rasmussen (1992) and the international perception of Hjelmslev is in general based on the translation by Whitfield (1953) of *Omkring Sprogteoriens Grundlæggelse* or the English posthumously (1975) published translation *Résumé of a Theory of Language* of the manuscript of 1943 *Sprogteori*,[11] but the following is a review of my own interpretation of, and opinions about, the theory to the extent that I can use it in my theoretical model in Chapter 3. I do not go into its finer details, nor do I follow the perspectives of its wider implications in science and philosophy.

Hjelmslev's own views on the substance of Glossematics are mainly found in his programmatic book of 1943 (1966) *Omkring Sprogteoriens Grundlæggelse*

[On the Foundation of the Theory of Language]. Similar to Brøndal, his point of departure is the theoretical framework of 'semiological structuralism':[12]

> *en lingvistik maa ... søge at fatte sproget ... som en i sig selv hvilende helhedsdannelse, en struktur* sui generis.

> a [science of] linguistics has to attempt to conceive of language as an in itself resting unitary formation, a structure *sui generis*.

(Hjelmslev [1943] 1966: 7)

This theoretical legacy is explicitly expressed by mentioning de Saussure as a 'predecessor' (p. 9) in the field of theoretical linguistics. No other historical individuals and no theoretical contributions before de Saussure are referred to in the same explicit way, and the unfolding of the theory can be seen both as Hjelmslev's own interpretation of de Saussure and as a demarcation of his own position and the part he himself played in the development of theoretical linguistics. He considered himself the founder of the only true theory of language, which, from his point of view, is opposed to:

> *den klassiske lingvistiks hovedindhold: sproghistorien og den genetiske sprogsammenligning*

> the main content of classical linguistics: the history of language and genetic comparative linguistics.

(Hjelmslev [1943] 1966: 7)

This tradition he also calls 'filologi' 'philology' (ibid.). Through his contribution to linguistics, it will become a 'science' ('videnskab', p. 10) and the concepts, theories and methods of the natural sciences are the ideals for his approach. Hjelmslev does not ignore the fact that his scientific subject has a history or that he has a number of very important predecessors – such an interpretation of his work is discredited by Hjelmslev himself, for instance, in his 1937 inaugural lecture (Hjelmslev 1959) – but he claims that his theoretical concepts are absolutely original and have no precursors. This may be true, but it can reasonably be assumed that his ideas were shaped by his insights into what other prominent linguists had proposed. Thus, he may have read Otto Jespersen's *Sprogets logik* '*The Logic of Language*', when he was at school (cf. Rasmussen 1992: 2), he had personal contact with Roman Jakobson,[13] who can be considered, more or less, as the one who inspired the foundation of the Copenhagen School of Linguistics, and the glossematic theory can be seen as being set up as an alternative to the Prague phonology (*ibid.*: 14, 24). In spite of these facts, he considers himself to be the first to design genuine scientific theories about his academic subject and thus establishes linguistics as a real science like the twentieth-century natural sciences. From this frame of reference in the philosophy of science he establishes a theory of language and, hence, his methodology in finding appropriate basic theoretical concepts is quite different from that of Brøndal: instead of a historical search for suitable philosophical concepts, it is a survey of the current accepted paradigms of scientific notions.

This implies a number of assumptions about what kind of requirements can be made of a linguistic theory and of a reasonable description of the object of investigation. First of all, he formulates the leading principle of scientific description: 'empiriprincippet' 'the principle of empirical description' (p. 12), which implies that the investigation will be non-contradictory, exhaustive and as simple as possible. It does not imply the use of a method that starts with some simple facts and then makes generalizations on still higher levels; on the contrary, Hjelmslev rejects this method that he calls 'inductive' and 'synthetic' (*ibid.*). For him, the scientific method of description is the 'deductive' and 'analytic' one, in which the empirical requirements are met by the initial recognition of the object of investigation, the 'text' (p. 13) and in which the method is the analysis of the text brought about by the implementation of a deductive theory. Consequently, it is Hjelmslev's aim to create such a satisfactory theory, a 'purely deductive system' ('et rent deduktivt system', p. 14) and he explicitly tries to reconcile the traditional discrepancy between, on the one hand, developing more or less formally expressed theories and, on the other, their application to empirical facts. This implicit question of the tradition may be put in another way: how is it possible that a formal theory (sometimes) matches reality so well when its origin is an invention without any association with reality? Hjelmslev's answer is that a prerequisite for the theoretical framework is 'the arbitrariness of the theory' ('teoriens vilkaarlighed' p. 14), which implies exactly the feature that all its parts are established by deduction, and, furthermore, that another prerequisite is the 'appropriateness of the theory' ('teoriens hensigtsmæssighed' *ibid.*). By this, he means that:

> *Teorien indfører visse forudsætninger, om hvilke teoretikeren véd at de opfylder betingelserne for anvendelse paa visse erfaringsdata.*

The theory appeals to certain presuppositions about which the theorist knows that they fulfil the conditions for application to certain empirical data.

(Hjelmslev [1943] 1966: 14)

Or put another way:

> *han udfinder visse egenskaber der er til stede ved alle ... emner ... for dærefter at generalisere disse egenskaber og fastsætte dem definitorisk.*

> He [the theorist] extracts certain properties which are present in all subjects [of investigation] and thereafter [he] generalizes [over] these properties and determines their definitions.

(ibid.: 17)

By this conceptual arrangement Hjelmslev avoids the straitjacket of an historical tradition, but then, consequently, he is obliged to account explicitly for his basic assumptions concerning the epistemological problems, concerning the nature of the deductive system and concerning the nature of the investigatory subject of language. From a reading of the preliminary formulations above, it is pretty obvious that the core theme of his concern is the question of the methodology of linguistics, which he wants to make as accurate as possible, and this also implies a clarification of his epistemological assumptions, i.e. the claims about the status of the knowledge one gains when applying a specific scientific method.

Hjelmslev is not entirely explicit on this point. If we, for the sake of the argument, resume the quotations above taken from p. 14 and juxtapose them, then the requirements on the theory are presented in this way:

> *Teorien fremtræder i sig selv som uafhængig af enhver erfaring.*

> The theory presents itself as independent of any [kind of]experience.

> *(teoriens vilkaarlighed)*

> (the arbitrariness of the theory)
> and:

> *Teorien indfører visse forudsætninger, om hvilke teoretikeren véd at de opfylder betingelserne for anvendelse paa visse erfaringsdata.*

> The theory adduces certain presuppositions about which the theorist knows that they fulfil the conditions for application to certain empirical data.

> *(teoriens hensigtsmæssighed)*

> (the appropriateness of the theory); as quoted above

If these two claims are taken, not as an recipe for setting up a theoretical system, but as epistemological propositions, then they either contradict each other or they presuppose (presumably based on some kind of epistemological rationalism) that one can have *a priori* knowledge, which one can use to create a deductive system, and that one can generalize over a number of experiences and invoke some presuppositions as constraints on the deductive system. What, then, one has knowledge of is the theory, i.e. the theoretical system and the constraints on the system, and experience cannot confirm or invalidate the theory (p. 14), only the applicability of the theory. What can be evaluated by experience are hypotheses:

> *Paa grundlag af teorien og dens teoremer lader der sig opstille hypoteser ..., hvis skæbne i modsætning til teorien selv udelukkende er afhængig af verifikation.*

> on the basis of the theory and its theorems it is possible to establish hypotheses ... the destiny of which, as contrasted with the theory, is entirely depending on verification.

> > (*ibid.*: 15)

Therefore there are two kinds of knowledge involved in this theory: the more or less *a priori* knowledge of the deductive system, and the knowledge of the object of investigation that is achieved through verification of hypotheses formulated by the theoretical system. Since it cannot be reasonably assumed that Hjelmslev wishes to contradict himself, then, in my view, this interpretation is the most plausible, but apart from the paragraphs mentioned, Hjelmslev has only scattered remarks on the topic or general references to the philosophical discipline of epistemology. Within his theoretical framework the issue seems to him more or less uncontroversial.

The deductive system that he wants to create has certain characteristics. He clearly says (p. 15) that the system itself does not contain any axioms or postulates, a claim which may be disputed, but that it is based on a number of 'strictly formal and explicit definitions', 'the deepest level of which [the system of definitions] has to deal with the principle of the analysis, establish the nature of the analysis and of the concepts that are applied in this analysis' (p. 20). Since the object of investigation is the text as an undivided unity and since the scientific method is the analysis (see above), then consequently the procedure of investigation is the division of the subject into its parts, and if one wants to say anything of interest about the object of investigation and its parts, then one must have a theory about the relations between the parts. On these grounds the basic notion in Hjelmslev's theory is that of 'dependence' ('afhængighed', p. 22 *et passim*), and he defines a number of different dependences according to the assumed kinds of relation between the parts (pp. 23–4). Thus he calls the two-way (bilateral) dependences *'interdependenser'* 'interdependences', one-way (unilateral) dependences *'determinationer'* 'determinations' and independences *'konstellationer'* 'constellations', and according to the assumed occurrence of the dependences in a '[linguistic] system' ('system',[14] p. 23) or in a '[linguistic] process' ('forløb', *ibid.*) he is able to bring about a network of definitions. This is part of the 'principle of the analysis' ('Analysens princip', pp. 21-6), and the definitions are claimed to be, what he calls, strictly 'operational' (p. 23), meaning an analogy to scientific laboratory experiments where some things are defined by what you do when you carry out an experiment. The other part of the preliminary work is the 'form of the analysis' ('Analysens form', p. 26), and in this part it is assumed that the dependences are characterized by a state of 'uniformity' ('ensartethed', p. 27), both between the different parts and between the parts and their sub-parts, and this assumption is used as a criterion in the justification of a definition of 'division' ('*Inddeling*', *ibid.*) or 'analysis' ('*analyse*', *ibid.*):

> Inddeling *eller* analyse *kan vi da i en formaldefinition bestemme som beskrivelse af et emne ved andre emners ensartede afhængighed af det og af hinanden.*
>
> Division or analysis can, in a formal definition formulated by us, be determined as a description of an entity by means of the uniform dependences of other entities in relation to it and to each other.
>
> (*ibid.*: 27)

Armed with these prerequisites, Hjelmslev is prepared for the definition of the elementary term of his deductive system, namely, a 'function': 'En afhængighed der opfylder betingelserne for en inddeling vil vi benævne en funktion' 'a dependence which fulfils the conditions for a division we will call a function' (*ibid.*: 31), and what he calls the 'terms of a function' are called 'functives' ('*funktiver*', *ibid.*). To elaborate the theoretical system, he introduces the terms *'tilstedeværelse, nødvendighed, betingelse'* 'occurrence, necessity, condition' respectively (*ibid.*) as 'not specified indefinables'. They have been used in the previous context, but not until now are they used as intuitive technical terms, and in the procedure of definition he is now able to define e.g. 'konstant ... et funktiv hvis tilstedeværelse er en nødvendig forudsætning for tilstedeværelsen af det funktiv som det har funktion til' 'a constant [as] a functive the occurrence of which is a necessary condition for the occurrence of the functive that it has a function to' (*ibid.*: 32) and a 'variable' as 'a functive, the occurrence of which is no necessary condition [etc.]' (*ibid.*). The inauguration of this limited apparatus of dependence relations seems to be what is needed for the diligent elaboration of the extensive theoretical system (the central terms are introduced, pp. 32–7) that is supposed to cover the description of all parts of language.

The general consistency criterion, i.e. that the theoretical system really is a self-contained one, is demonstrated by the fact that it is possible within the system to define e.g. the notion of 'definition' (p. 65) and the notion of 'language' (p. 94), and the explanatory power criterion, that the theoretical system appears to be, in some sense, relevant to academic fields outside linguistics, seems to be demonstrated by the fact that Hjelmslev is able to make reasonable definitions of the notions of a 'game' (p. 96), of 'symbols' (p. 100) and of 'scientific meta-languages' (p. 106). If this is taken seriously, then it implies a large-scale conceptual diffusion from one scientific field (linguistics) to other fields, e.g. logic and mathematics, and while in the past logic has sometimes been taken as the model for grammar and in the late twentieth century the icon of linguistics has been mathematics, then Hjelmslev's proposals turn the tables by suggesting that linguistics should be the model for all the symbol-manipulating sciences. Because part of the justification of this status is the demonstration that the theoretical system is really a formal system with its standard characteristics, it is interesting that Hjelmslev's system has been transformed into a kind of 'glossematic algebra' by Uldall (1957). Hjelmslev's own term for his theory is 'glossematics' (*'glossematik'*, p. 72); accordingly he calls the 'smallest formations' ('mindsteformer', *ibid.*) that the theory works with 'glossemes' ('glossemer', *ibid.*), and he views the glossematic system as a kind of 'linguistic algebra' ('sproglig algebra', p. 86). A symbolic and more systematic account of this glossematics was elaborated by Uldall (1957).

In general, Uldall gives an extensive and clear-cut account of what he understands as the philosophical and theoretical background of the theory (1957: 1–35). To a certain extent it differs from the viewpoints of Hjelmslev (in fact, it is partly inconsistent with Hjelmslev's claims), and it is not evident whether the account was approved by him (cf. Rasmussen 1992: 42–4), but Uldall's important contribution to the theoretical development of Hjelmslev's ideas is that Uldall built a formal and a symbolic system (an algebra) expressing the 'deductive definitions' of Hjelmslev. Thus, in the shape given by Uldall, the theory is a stepwise presentation of a number of propositions presenting and defining the concepts, their expressions and the corresponding symbols.

According to the Hjelmslevian presuppositions, the point of departure is the notion of 'function', which is initially defined: '(1) By a *function* is understood any dependence. Symbol: j'. Uldall points to the fact that this is no definition since 'the concepts used in it have not been previously either defined or accepted as axioms' (1957: 36), and it is taken to be intuitively understood. The same goes for the second proposition: '(2) Anything that enters a function is called a *functive*. Symbol: F' (p. 37), because the term 'anything' appears for the first time here (and the semantics of the term 'enters' is presupposed), but from now on it is possible to formulate most of the propositions without introducing *ad hoc* terms. Thus proposition number 3 says: '(3) The functives bound together by a given function are called the *terminals* of that function' (*ibid.*), and the functional relation between functives can then be expressed by the formula: 'F1 j F2' (p. 38). Since this linguistic theory is expected to cover all the structures of language, the traditional notions of both syntactic (i.e. syntagmatic) relations and paradigmatic relations are used, but they are introduced in a way that is (almost) purely formal, and their denotations have no significance outside the theory. Thus, '6. By a *connexion*, or *syntagmatic function*, is understood the function 'both-and'. If *a* and *b* are two functives, their connexion is symbolized by *a.b* or *ab*' (p. 42), and in this way the theory is capable of handling what Hjelmslev calls the linguistic 'process' ('forløb', see above) as opposed to the linguistic elements 'substituting' for each other: '15. A unit that has been registered as not occurring as a terminal of a given connexion, is said to be *negated* in respect of that connexion. Symbol: – : *(–a).(+b)*. Assertion [defined earlier] and negation are called *paradigmatic functions*' (p. 50). These terms have not been picked up to solve just the problems of traditional syntax, word class theory or phonology but are elaborated to describe major areas of the entity of language, including semantics. They are, at that point, not completely formally defined, which is illustrated by no. 6 in which the term 'both-and' is introduced as a 'primitive idea', but in this respect the theory does not differ from e.g. traditional logic that uses the same trick of using so-called analytical sentences to introduce operators.

The algebra quickly becomes rather complicated, a fact which can be illustrated by a quotation from p. 63:

A simplex category has $2^1 = 2$ members, namely, the paradigms <+*a*> and <–*a*>. Its category of the second power has $2^{2^1} = 4$ members, namely, the categories

$\{+<+a>+<-a>\}$
$\{+<+a>-<-a>\}$
$\{-<+a>+<-a>\}$
$\{-<+a>-<-a>\}$

in which the table resembles the truth tables of traditional logic and has an equivalent function, namely, the mechanical checking of the combinatorial interrelations of a set of symbols. Like most symbolic systems the glossematic system is not that hard to understand when one becomes acquainted with it, but as to whether it is worth the effort of learning depends crucially on whether it can be applied empirically in analyses. Such applications are made in the examples, e.g.:

> Our example above, of the English consonants p and l is a case in point: in the category generated by the connexion with ei (*'play'*, *'pay'*, *'lay'*, *'A'*) all the members are asserted:[15]
>
> {+pl+p¬l+¬pl+¬p¬l}.ei
>
> (Uldall 1957: 62)[16]

but the question is whether one is able to apply the theory to the object of investigation as a whole or to major parts of it, in this case, a language or selected levels or sets of data. If one wants to test the theory by attempting to make such an implementation, it is important to realize that this theory takes for granted a number of basic assumptions about the nature of its object of investigation, and that the acceptance of these assumptions is a prerequisite if the application is to be successful.

What one is looking for when analysing language is, according to Hjelmslev ([1943] 1966), the 'system' of language, which he distinguishes from the 'process' (*'forløb'*, p. 36). It should be observed here that the term 'system' is used as denoting only the vertical or paradigmatic dimension of language as its object of investigation, and that 'process', then, is the term for the horizontal or syntagmatic dimension of language. Thus, the 'system is the constant' ('systemet er konstanten', *ibid.*) and 'existensen af et system er en nødvendig forudsætning for existensen af et forløb' 'the existence of a system is a necessary precondition for the existence of a process' (Hjelmslev [1943] 1966: 36).

What is interesting, then, is the system behind the phenomena and this is, of course, in accordance with the normal scientific search for regularities in the world. The notion of a 'general constant' is also, by Hjelmslev, opposed to the notion of a 'variable' (*ibid.*: 94; cf. above) and under certain circumstances, viz. when the system is 'manifested' in a process, the 'constant' of this manifestation is called the 'form' of a language and the 'variable' is called the 'substance' (*ibid.*). One may notice the evident parallel between these external relations of the system and the internal ones described above.

It is a well-known fact that the interconnections between these theoretical notions go back to de Saussure, cf. e.g.:

La substance phonique n'est pas plus fixe ni plus rigide; ce ne pas un moule donc la pensée doive nécessairement épouser les formes, mais une matière plastique qui se divise à son tour en parties distinctes pour fournir les signifiants dont la pensèe a besoin.

(de Saussure 1916: 155)

This concerns the phonology/phonetics relation, a passage which is also quoted more extensively by Hjelmslev ([1943] 1966: 46). One should note the distinction between 'la langue' and 'la parole' (de Saussure 1916: 37), which corresponds with the Hjelmslevian distinction between the 'system' and the 'process' of language (the major concept of which Saussure called 'le langage'), and one might finally notice the key word of 'system': 'la langue est un système qui ne connaît que son ordre propre' (*ibid.*: 43). It is also a well-known fact that de Saussure did not write the book of 1916 (cf. Harris 2003), but that it was a compilation of lecture notes made by some of those who had attended his lectures, but the quotation from p. 43, and abundant amounts of quotations from other parts of the work, are in the tradition of de Saussure's interpreters normally attributed the implication that language can be investigated as an isolated system building an immanent structure (cf. the quotation above from Hjelmslev [1943] 1966: 7).

By Hjelmslev, this notion of language is being associated with the Saussurian concept of the linguistic sign (de Saussure 1916: 97–103) so that language is considered a 'system of signs' (*'tegnsystem'* (Hjelmslev [1943] 1966: 39)), where the term 'system' denotes the overall semiological function of language, i.e. the linguistic system is applied to de Saussure's binary division of the linguistic sign into *'udtryk'* 'expression' and *'indhold'* 'content' (*ibid.*: 44). The reason for this is that the theory was conceived as a theory of the totality of language, and Hjelmslev would never, I suppose, think of language as expressions separated from meaning. As a consequence of the previous division between 'form' and 'substance', the two parts, 'expression' and 'content', of the (narrow) systemic dimension as well as the process-dimension of language and sign are both assigned these properties:

Vi konstaterer altså i det sproglige indhold, i dettes forløb, en specifik form, indholdsformen, der er uafhængig af og staar i et et arbitrært forhold til meningen, og former denne til en indholdssubstans ... dette gentager sig for indholdets system.

Thus we realize in the linguistic content, in its process, a specific form, the form of content, which is independent of and has an arbitrary relation to meaning and forms this to a substance of content … this is repeated with the system of the content.

… *udtryksmening* … formes … og … dærved tilordnes … udtryksform som udtryks*substans*. Vi har konstateret dette for udtrykkets *system*; … kan vi ogsaa paavise det samme forhold for *forløbet*.

'expressional meaning … is shaped … and … thereby is assigned … expressional form as expressional substance. We have realized this about the system of expression; … the fact can also be pointed to by us concerning the process'

(Hjelmslev 1943 p.51)

What is meant here is, in my reading, more than just a little opaque and enigmatic, and formulations like these by Hjelmslev have given rise to many and deep contemplative thoughts and quite a few papers over time; and not all of them consistent with each other. I am not totally convinced that one will gain much insight into linguistic theory or the philosophy of language by trying to understand it, and in the end it is not relevant for the linguistic ontology that I have developed.

But whatever kind of reading one makes of some of the details of Hjelmslev's ontology of language does not affect its general image of language as a logocentric and immanent structure that can be totally unravelled by means of a process of deductive analysis. This idea has to be accepted if one wants to use the theory as it is, and if one does not accept this world-view, then either one will find nothing when actually using the theory, or one will be unable to make the theory match or explain what one actually finds. This seemingly complementary relation between the theory and its object of description is the background for much of the criticism directed at Glossematics as an approach and a tradition in linguistics.

A number of objections can thus be made to Hjelmslev's theory, and, as is often the case with all-embracing theories, it has provoked much debate. I will not take up the controversies about, or the interpretations of, Hjelmslev in the literature, but two of the more noticeable problems in the theory will be dealt with briefly. The first is the question whether the 'glossematic algebra' really is a formal system in the modern sense. One might claim that Hjelmslev is building his theory on a notion of dependence relations, and one might question whether dependence relations can be found in formal systems, because all relations are established by convention. I do not subscribe to this view. The way I see it, there is nothing that *a priori* prevents one from stipulating dependence relations within a formal system; one may put any kind of relations into the system as long as one keeps the rules and as long as the basic properties of the system are in accordance with prevalent conventions concerning formal systems.

The second serious objection that may be made to Hjelmslev's theory is that it confuses the theory with the description and the description with the internal structure of the object of investigation, and the several kinds of semantics of the term 'system' may indicate that this may be the basis of a reasonable argument.

The glossematic confusion of theory, description and object of investigation respectively is, in all likelihood, due to its structuralistic methodological principle: the object of investigation is the linguistic 'text', and the structure of the text is found by means of an analysis, the principle of which is the testing of hypotheses regarding which units are parts of which unities. This is done by the operations of commutation and permutation respectively, and if one's intuitions are verified, one's description looks strikingly like a theory. The technical status of such a theory is that of a combinatorial system estab-lished through generalizations, but if one does not realize this status, one is not able to evaluate the theoretical adequacy of one's analysis because one does not conceptually separate the theory from one's perception of the object of investigation. Not to mention the question: which actual text will meet the requirements of empirical justification; or is there a universal text that may serve as a universal exemplar?

Or put in another way: there is a risk (namely, that all later generations of linguists would be out of work) implying that what Hjelmslev has created is actually an exhaustive description of all the more important features of the entity of language, and this is one of the theoretical problems of Glossematics. On the one hand, Hjelmslev claims that he has direct, *a priori*, knowledge about the 'system of language', but on the other hand, he has to formulate his theory, and that he does in a 'deductive system'. The question is, then, whether these 'systems' are, actually, only one 'system', or whether the 'systems', at some point in the line of reasoning (or in the real world?), merge, to the effect that the theory is identical to the description and the description is identical to the linguistic system. To Hjelmslev, this question is apparently uncontroversial. The way I see it, the conceptual structure of his account implies that the theoretical 'deductive system' is conceived as a direct description (reflection, simulation or imitation) of the 'system of language'; it is a kind of hyper-descriptivism. Consequently, one might say that, from a traditional point of view, Hjelmslev has in fact no theory at all. According to his own account, he only carries out a stepwise, consistent and intuitively true registration of the general structures of all languages, and since he seems to be extremely successful in doing so, then he claims that he has created and formulated the ultimate 'theory' of language.

This is a serious objection to Hjelmslev's Glossematics, and it should be kept in mind that he was not successful in spreading the ideas inherent in his theory as a whole. No one has ever made a total or major partial analysis of a language or a dialect (not to mention all the languages of the world) by means of Glossematics; a goal which ought to be the natural and ultimate ideal for Hjelmslev's theory. One can mention two investigations using the glossematic basis, one of a Danish dialect and one of a Central American language, while Rasmussen (1992: 34) enumerates a number of Scandinavian investigations. A Swedish dialect study has been carried out on glossematic grounds by Eriksson (1971), and it is characteristic that what dominates glossematic investigations are analyses of the (mostly phonematic) expression systems of (primarily Danish) dialects. Of those referred to in standard accounts I am acquainted with Andersen (1958), and furthermore, in my view, Ejskjær (1954, 1970) and A. Bjerrum (1944), who are mentioned in neither of these accounts, are clearly glossematic attempts. The theoretical account of Ejskjær (1970) displays some of the central problems of Glossematics, and so, because of the lack of exhaustive glossematic analyses and because of the theoretical problems of limited investigations, the concepts and the methods of Glossematics cannot justifiably be said to be descriptive, and consequently the 'theory' is not a startlingly successful descriptive generalization.

Summarizing this evaluation of Glossematics. it is my view that the conceptual network that was indeed developed by Hjelmslev and Uldall – whatever they thought they did – was a complete linguistic theory including a formal system for formal (but not structural) description – an unconventional formal system but nevertheless a genuine one. So, an alternative construal of the glossematic system may be that it is: (1) a uniform formal system covering both 'syntax' and 'semantics' like a kind of Montague 'grammar' (cf. McCawley 1981: 406–24) but with identical formal functions in expressions and content and assuming no truth-functional semantics; (2) indicating no distinction between the descriptive *formal* system and the object of investigation; and (3) offering no satisfactory clarification of the notions of form and substance. But, at this point, interpreters of Hjelmslev's thoughts sometimes admit that they are never quite sure that they do understand Hjelmslev, and in my view the theory can be said to be essentially inadequate in two respects; first, the entity of language cannot justifiably be assumed to be a singular, isolated and immanent structure, a kind of organism, and it cannot be reasonably described in this way; second, it seems that no single uniform formal system can cover the whole of language as an object of scientific enquiry, and hence the ambitions of Glossematics as a total theory of language will presumably not be satisfied.

In a more limited sense, however, I think that Hjelmslev has made important contributions to linguistic theory. The unconventional formal system he developed resembles what I shall call 'occurrence logic', i.e. the basis of a formal system with the potential to describe how the occurrence of certain linguistic units is related to the occurrence of other units. In accordance with my remarks above I do not believe that such a system (neither the glossematic nor other formal systems) can be applied to all aspects of all languages, but different analogue systems may, in my view, be adequately applied to the different structures of linguistic expressions and their meanings. Thus, there is, for the moment, no system that has the status of a 'general theory of occurrence' – the apparently implicit ambition of Glossematics – but different systems may work as special theories of 'occurrence' (see Chapter 3).

A theory covering the expression structures of language may take the form of an occurrence logic using the tools of modern logic, and one might ask why Hjelmslev did not see the potentials of Boolean algebra and instruments of that kind. The way I see it, the reason is that either Hjelmslev did not understand formal, symbolic logic, which is not very likely, or he actually wanted to create a formal system that would be able to include all other formal systems, an objective that would, today, be seen as a kind of hubris by many scientists. A more worldly explanation may be that his basis in linguistics was phonology, which in its various theoretical shapes is just descriptions of mutual dependences between manifestations of sounds of speech.

Modern symbolic logic – or derivations thereof – is not the only way of describing the world in formal systems, and it may not be the best or the ultimate, but it is the heritage of the tradition, and apparently Hjelmslev wanted to develop his own accurate way of understanding the totality of language from a perspective which he did understand, namely, the field of phonology. Here the glossematic apparatus may work strikingly well, if one is not too dogmatic, while other fields of linguistics are apparently outside its domain. Applications here are not always theoretically convincing,[17] sometimes they lead to bewildering results, and implementations outside linguistics to literature and media studies are often hard to reject because of interpretative opacity. Consequently, glosse-matic theory has been most widely accepted by phoneticians, in Denmark, such as Eli Fischer-Jørgensen and, in Sweden, Bertil Malmberg (Rasmussen 1992: 55; Malmberg 1969), and one way of demystifying Glossematics may be to claim that its proper status, in the conceptual and terminological form it has, is that of a reasonably acceptable theory of phonemes.

Diderichsen's theory of sentence topology

Paul Diderichsen (1905–64) was a little younger than Hjelmslev (1899–1965) and quite a lot younger than Brøndal (1887–1942), and it was his destiny to play the role of a younger generation member of the Copenhagen School of Linguistics and to lead the path into the future. While Brøndal is nowadays almost unknown and Hjelmslev is well known by most theoretical linguists (and some people in literature and media studies) and virtually nobody else, Diderichsen and his descriptive methods are well known by people outside the sphere of theoretical linguistics, modern languages and traditional philology. This is due to the pedagogical advantages of his descriptive sentence model. Almost any modern school and higher education textbook on grammar in Scandinavia takes up his theory of sentence formation and uses it to describe the sentence structures of the Scandinavian languages. It is also the background to the account of sentence structure in the descriptive grammar of the Swedish language, published by the Swedish Academy (*Svenska Akademiens Grammatik*, SAG), where the basic topical description of Swedish sentences is illustrated by Diderichsen's model – with the addition of a presumably formal-grammar-inspired underlining of the verb phrase (including object and predicative) as having its own topology.[18]

Since Diderichsen had experienced both the personal and the theoretical influence of the principal individuals of the Copenhagen School of Linguistics, they played a major part in the explicit and implicit background to his sentence theory. Brøndal is invoked in the definition of word classes, which is the basis of the notion of sentence constituents, and the Hjelmslevian formalism is the theoretical framework on which basis the sentence theory is developed. As mentioned above, Hjelmslev did not think that syntax was essential or especially relevant to linguistics, but with his academic background in Scandinavian philology, Diderichsen had noticed the historical development of fixed (or rigid) sentence structures in Danish as related to a declined morphology, and it seemed to him so essential and of such interest that it ought to be accounted for theoretically. Glossematics was unable to account for it – it did not fall under the domain of that theory – but it can be reasonably assumed that Diderichsen's scrutinizing elaboration of his theory and its relatively high level of consistency were inspired by the glossematic machinery.

The main theorists who create Diderichsen's direct theoretical frame of reference are explicitly referred to in his introductory paper of 1936 ('Prolegomena til en metodisk dansk Syntax' 'Prolegomena of a Methodical Danish Syntax', 1936 (republished 1966)), which has the subtitle: 'Med udgangspunkt i Ries's Sætningsdefinition; se J. Ries: Was ist ein Satz? Prag 1931' 'With Ries' sentence definition as the point of departure; What is a sentence? Prague 1931', referring to the German grammarian John Ries. The point where Diderichsen's and Ries' interests coincide is the notion of the sentence as the 'smallest unity in the use of language': 'den mindste Enhed, der har den realiserede Tales Funktion' (1966: 22), and the traditional view that sentences are combinations of words is replaced by a methodological approach saying that sentences are unities used by somebody to say something. Except for mentioning the Danish grammarians H. G. Wivel, Kr. Mikkelsen and Aage Hansen (Høysgaard is also mentioned and Aage Hansen's sentence theories are referred to by Diderichsen in other contexts), the only general reference is made to de Saussure and his distinction between 'language as system and language as realization' ('Sproget som System og Sproget som Realisation', *ibid.*: 21), and this is made an argument in proposing the notion of sentences quoted above, namely, 'syntax as the theory of the realization of language' ('Syntaxen som Læren om Sprogets Realisation', p. 22). Whether this is in accordance with de Saussure's own project is hard to evaluate, but it has no influence on the specific form of the theory.

A more implicit function as an ancestor of his theoretical framework can be ascribed to the above-mentioned Danish grammarian Jens Pedersen Høysgaard, a relation which is pointed out by several of the authors of the articles in *NyS 16-17* (the 50th anniversary publication celebrating the 'birth' of Diderichsen's 'sentence scheme'), and in fact Høysgaard had in his account of Danish word order ([1747] 1979: 430–42) outlined some of the insights of the Diderichsen topology. As is also mentioned by some Danish linguistic scholars, it does not mean that Diderichsen tried to avoid quoting Høysgaard – he was in a position where he did not have to conceal anything – and in later considerations about the status of his theory (Diderichsen [1964] 1966) he directly refers (p. 367) to Høysgaard's 12 constituent types mentioned in § 390 (Høysgaard [1747] 1979:

431–2), but it may be seen as a kind of subconscious transformation effected by Diderichsen's extensive knowledge of Danish and other languages.

This empirical knowledge was partly available in the, by then, current descriptive grammars, and it may be claimed that most of the material on which Diderichsen's sentence topology is based can be found as descriptions of Danish grammatical constructions in, for instance, Mikkelsen ([1911] 1975), but, as is well known, Diderichsen made his own investigations, especially in the text corpus of Danish Philology. Hence, his major contribution to the tradition was his doctoral thesis: *Sætningsbygningen i skaanske Lov* 'The Sentence Structure in the Law of Scania' (Diderichsen 1941), but the subtitle of the thesis points to his theoretical ambition: *Fremstillet som Grundlag for en rationel dansk Syntaks* 'Accounted for as the Basis of a Rational Danish Syntax'. It also indicates the theoretical allusions of his work, namely, that of Høysgaard (1747) and that of the seventeenth-century 'rational' French grammarians (known as Port-Royal) and Cartesian philosophy (cf. Kristeva 1989: 158–71; Arens 1969: 88–93), and this is, in my view, the closest he comes to the later Chomskyan theoretical paradigm (cf. Chomsky 1966). Since his linguistic inclinations were that of a combination of a traditional philologist and a linguistic structuralist in the Saussurian spirit, his primary ambition was to make satisfactory descriptions by means of a satisfactory theory, and thereby bridge the scientific discrepancies between philology, modern languages and theoretical linguistics.

The theory itself is compiled in Diderichsen ([1946] 1966), which was, until the publication of Hansen and Heltoft (2011), the modern standard account of Danish grammar, and it is also the one primarily referred to by grammarians writing textbooks on Scandinavian grammar and syntax, or proposing their own versions of the model. As a standard account it has been widely used as a textbook in higher education courses on grammar in Denmark and throughout Scandinavia, and generations of Danish and Scandinavian students have felt the ruthless commitment to understand 'Diderichsen', but it is not only its standard account status that has made it so successful; it is also the general pedagogical perspective of most of Diderichsen's activities in his lifetime. This perspective is expressed, for instance, in his posthumous book of 1968 entitled *Sprogsyn og sproglig opdragelse* 'Linguistic Attitude and Linguistic Education'. Accordingly it is hardly surprising that the Introduction in Diderichsen ([1946] 1966: 1–11) offers a number of pedagogical considerations about the meaning of grammar as a subject in science and education, and that pedagogical remarks are scattered throughout, but what is in fact surprising – and what is the major obstacle to an easy understanding of the theoretical descriptions at an elementary level of higher education – is the fact that he contradicts his intentions in the 'Prolegomena'. Instead of starting with the sentence as a basic unity in linguistic investigation, and consequently in a systematic account, he starts out accounting for Danish words, their classes, derivations and inflections. There seems to be two non-theoretical reasons for this: first, during most of the period when he was creating and elaborating the theory, he was influenced and supported by Brøndal, who had then become interested in syntax, and it was Brøndal's word definitions that were used in the account of word classes; second, words were the traditional subject of linguistics and philology and hence the basic unit of descriptive grammars and grammatical textbooks (Diderichsen [1946] 1966: 7), and starting with words ought to make it easier to follow the train of thought. But, in the textbook, it is not quite like that, mainly because of the implementation of Brøndal's abstract categories (p. 24 seqq.) in the account of the word classes, which makes it a hard read for students. There are no more surprises in the first part of the book; it is a traditional account of the morphological system of Danish, but what may be considered unusual is the fact that things are actually discussed, and that it is explicitly admitted that some things cannot be determined yet. An example of this is his reflections on the 'boundary between inflection and derivation' ('Grænsen mellem Bøjning og Afledning', pp. 20–1), where Hjelmslev is referred to:

> *I nyere Tid har man (Hjelmslev) lagt Vægten paa, at Bøjningsformerne staar i et vist Afhængighedsforhold til andre Størrelser i eller uden for samme Sætning: Genus og Numerus fx. kan i Adjektiver og Pronominer fremkaldes ('styres') af et Substantiv osv.; i saa Tilfælde bliver fx. Tempus og Modus paa Dansk 'Afledninger', fordi der ikke (som fx. i Latin) er Verber, der 'styrer' Konjunktiv, eller Konjunktioner, der 'styrer' Præsens. Dette radikale Princip har vi ikke fundet det opportunt at indføre i nærværende Fremstilling.*

> Recently it has been emphasized (by Hjelmslev) that the inflectional forms have a dependence relationship with other entities inside or outside the same sentence: gender and number of adjectives and pronouns may be manifested (governed) by a substantive etc.; in that case e.g. tense and mood in Danish become derivatives because there are (as opposed to Latin) no verbs governing the subjunctive, or conjunctions governing the present tense. We have not found it expedient to introduce this radical principle in the present account.
>
> (Diderichsen [1946] 1966: 21)

This decision is quite fortunate since it is difficult to follow this line of reasoning without being familiar with Hjelmslev.

Diderichsen's topological model is famous in Scandinavia under the label 'sentence scheme',[19] and most of the straightforward examples are easily filled in:[20]

k	S/A	v	s	a	V	S	A
og	saa	kunde	han	ikke	faa sagt	det	nu
'and	then	could	he	not	get said	it	now'

In the conventional terminology of Scandinavian syntax, this is taken to mean that there are a number of positions marked by symbols, that the last sequence of the six symbols ('v s a V S A') indicates a reduplication of its preceding three positions ('v s a'), in which the difference is marked by using letters in the lower and the upper case respectively, and that this can be the basis of a division of the sentence into 'fields':

| k | S/A | vsa | VSA |,

In this version they form four fields (here between the vertical bars ' | '). The symbols can be said to be derived from the class of words that typically fill the corresponding position; thus 'k' means: 'Konjunktion' 'conjunction', 'v': 'Verbum' 'verb', 's': 'Substantiv' 'substantive (i.e. noun)', and 'a': 'Adverbium' 'adverb'. This is not quite the way Diderichsen does it but it will do for the moment. Conceived in this way, the sentence is supposed to have a fixed linear word order, except for the second field in which (normally) either a substantive or an adverb may be placed, or which may be empty. On the same page in the book there is a table and a formula for the subordinate clause, and the difference between the two sentence types is that the last clause type has no facultative second field and that the linear word order deviates a little.

If we accept the idea that some positions are allowed to be empty, and the sentences that we try to analyse are well-formed, then we will have convenient solutions for most of the sentences in the Scandinavian languages that we could think of, and this raises some basic theoretical questions: (1) what is the nature of the word-types put into the positions of the table, if they are not to be characterized by the stipulations of traditional grammar?; (2) what is the nature of the sentence conceived of as a series of word-types?; and (3) what is the nature of this specific order of words as positions in a sentence, and is it a matter of a fixed linear order (of units) or of fixed positions (for units)?

It should be noted that there is so far no circularity in the kind of reasoning, the result of which is displayed as the sentence table above. If words are marked[21] (because they have some properties, which they have because they belong to specific word classes), and words marked in the same way according to their word class match perfectly with some specific slots in a chain, then this must be registered as a matter of fact and the necessary generalizations have to be made. Nothing has to be explained, because what has been achieved is just an empirical description, or a hypothesis, the verification of which could be tested by letting a fairly large number of sentences run through the table and, as mentioned above, for quite a lot of Danish and Scandinavian sentences this actually works, provided one is able to identify the (set of) marks of the word classes and the marks of the actual words, and in the end find the right slot for each word. This is the standard procedure for making empirical generalizations, but the problem is that one is not always able to find the right slot for each word, and furthermore it can be said to be theoretically unsatisfactory that nothing is explained by the model.

Diderichsen tries to solve the problems by ruminating on the notion of syntax. In the first lines of the second part of the book he defines syntax:

> *Syntaks (egl.: 'Sammenstilling') er Læren om Bygningen af de Helheder ('Syntagmer'), hvori Ordene optræder som Led (§ 2).*

> Syntax (orig. juxtaposition) is the study of the construction of unities (syntagms) in which words function as units.

> (Diderichsen [1946] 1966: 139)

The definition deals with the relations between words functioning as constituents, not only as loose combinations or juxtapositions but also as building unities, the structural composition of which can be supposed to be quite solid. There may be unities consisting of only one unit, but:

> *De andre Helhedstyper adskilles dels ved Leddenes logiske Forhold til hinanden (§ 53), dels ved den Tæthed, hvormed Leddene er sammenknyttet (§ 54). Inden for de enkelte Helheder kan Leddenes Forhold angives alene ved Brugen af Ordklasser (§ 56), dels ved særlige Bøjningsformer (§ 57) eller konjunktionale Led (§ 58), dels ved Leddenes Stilling (§ 55) og Tryk (§ 54).*

> The other unity-types are divided partly on the basis of the logical relationship between the units ..., partly by the closeness between the units ... Inside the individual unities the relations between the units can be indicated partly by the use of word classes [only]..., partly by special inflectional forms ... or conjunctional units ..., partly by the position of the units ... and [the]accent [of the units].

> (*ibid.*: 140)

Thus there are different types of unities, and what differentiates between the types is, on the one hand, the internal 'logical relations' and, on the other, how closely the units are connected. Diderichsen implements three kinds of 'logical relations': 'Sideordning' 'coordination', 'Underordning' 'subordination', and 'Neksus' 'nexus' (*ibid.*), the last one of which is characterized as being neither of the two other relations. The theoretical concepts and the term nexus have been borrowed from Otto Jespersen (cf. Jespersen 1924: 96, 97, 114 *et passim*; Jespersen 1937): 'Et saadant forhold kalder vi (efter Jespersen) Neksus' 'such a relationship we call (according to Jespersen) nexus' (Diderichsen [1946] 1966: 142).

'Coordinate' constructions are labelled with the term 'Paratagme' 'paratagm' (p. 141) and 'subordinate' constructions with the term 'hypotagme' 'hypotagm', and the corresponding relations inside the unities so named are called 'Parataks' 'parataxis' and 'Hypotaks' 'hypotaxis' respectively, while 'nexus' is used as the term for both the relation and the unity. Now Diderichsen is prepared to define the kind of unity he will identify as a sentence, namely, as a special kind of 'nexus'. In the 'nexus' relation the units are called 'Subjekt' 'subject' and 'Prædikat' 'predicate' (p. 142), which is in accordance with the use in traditional grammar as based on propositional logic. It is also in accordance with the sentence theory of Aage Hansen (Hansen 1933: 22 seqq.), who proposes a definition of a sentence as a 'linguistic communication' consisting of 'two constituents: the entity which one wants to say something about and a statement of what one wants to say about it'. But, as part of his own definition, Diderichsen has to add an extra criterion:

> *Som Regel indgaar der i en Neksus et finit Verbum ... [derfor]er det mest praktisk at opstille en Helhedsform, der bestaar af et finit Verbum med eventuelt Neksussubjekt og underordnede Bestemmelser. En saadan Helhed kalder vi for en Sætning.*

> Usually a nexus involves a finite verb ... [therefore] it is more practical to establish a unitary form consisting of a finite verb, possibly with a nexus-subject, and subordinate specifications. Such a unity we will call a sentence.
>
> (Diderichsen [1946] 1966: 142)

While it is an achievable objective for Diderichsen to propose a definition of the sentence that is almost totally based on 'logical relations', and thus is in accordance with his original project, namely, to see the sentence as the 'smallest unity in the use of language' (see above) – a project which would be in the spirit of modern pragmatics – in the end, he has to appeal to word classes and inflections to define what a sentence is. Since there are other nexus relations than those involving a finite verb, it seems to be impossible to locate a clear dividing line between the set of sentences and the set of other unities without the criterion concerning the occurrence of a finite verb, and this is apparently the theoretical reason why the account of word classes and morphology had to precede Diderichsen's account of syntax. Furthermore, Brøndal's abstract word class categories had to be the basis of the word class definitions because the traditional concepts were not theoretically satisfactory for Diderichsen. Consequently, so far, Diderichsen's theory of topological syntax is based partly on descriptive recordings of linear word order, partly on Brøndalian categories and partly on a notion of hierarchical structures of 'logical relations'.

The so-called 'logical relations' are the glue that binds together the semantic categories of Brøndal and the topological or morphological properties of words, and it may be appropriate to make the notion a little more substantial. This is why Hjelmslev is indirectly referred to in characterizing the syntactic relationships when Diderichsen makes 'Forudsættelse' 'precondition' a technical term:

> Hypotakse skulde saaledes kunne defineres som ensidig Forudsættelse, Neksus som gensidig Forudsættelse, medens Sideordning slet ikke har noget Forudsættelsesforhold mellem Leddene.

> Thus hypotaxis might be defined as one-sided precondition, nexus as reciprocal precondition, while coordination has no relationship of precondition at all.

> (*ibid.*: 142)

This idea of preconditioned interrelations is fairly close to the Hjelmslevian dependence relations, where the existence of some units is determined more or less by the existence of other units. Why this is so in syntax is not made especially explicit, and only in connection with the actual analyses of linguistic examples it is taken for granted, and in that case intuitively, that some elements, words and word classes are more important than others.

In accordance with these ideas it is assumed that the 'logical relationships' are indicated by expressional means such as unit position, word class and morphology, and there are a number of principles that govern the use of these tools. First, it is assumed that 'Ord, der hører sammen, følger umiddelbart efter hinanden og ikke kan adskilles af uvedkommende Led' 'words belonging together follow each other directly and cannot be separated by irrelevant units' (*ibid.*: 146).

And if more than two units belong together, the unity can be analysed according to a principle of a nest of Chinese boxes where words or word groups cover other words or word groups in a hierarchy, more or less in parallel with the notion of the scope of operators in formal logic or bracketing analyses in generative linguistics. Another principle is that 'hver Ordklasse ifølge sin særlige Klassebetydning har en forkærlighed for visse syntaktiske Funktioner' 'each word class has, according to its special class semantics, a preference for certain syntactic functions' (*ibid.*: 148).

And a third principle is the distinction between, on the one hand, units as parts of the unity and, on the other hand, units which are units as parts of other units (*ibid.*: 150). One last, but important, principle is the procedure for discovering the 'common formula of a syntactic unity-type' (*ibid.*), and on this point Diderichsen differs substantially from traditional principles of analysis. Instead of assuming a primitive structure of basic units that is successively extended by being applied to still more complicated constructions, Diderichsen makes the fully elaborated construction the point of departure in modelling the formula: 'gaa ud fra et Eksempel, der indeholder det størst mulige Antal af forskellige Led' 'begin with an example which contains the largest possible number of different units' (*ibid.*: 150).

Less complicated constructions are, consequently, analysed by stipulating the necessary number of empty positions in the table that depict the formula of a unity. The positions are not just numbered but 'Erfaringen har vist ... at der er visse faste Led i Helheden, som ... markerer ... Afsnit inden for den større Helhed, som vi vil kalde "Felter"' 'experience has shown ... that there are certain fixed units in the unity which ... mark ... sections within the greater unity, which [sections]we shall call "fields"' (*ibid.*: 151).

By means of the tripartite theory accounted for above and by means of these principles, Diderichsen has developed and elaborated the apparatus for analysing, describing and explaining the unities of Danish syntax, i.e. sentences, sentence-like unities, phrases and subordinate clauses.

In this way the traditional problem of sentence syntax has been solved by defining a sentence as quoted above, or as expressed by Diderichsen (p. 161): 'a sentence is a syntactic unit containing a finite verb', and subsequently a theory of sentence topology, in which the linear distribution functions as an indication of 'logical relations', is elaborated as a kind of formula presented as a SENTENCE TABLE. It is brought about by placing units belonging to the same basic word classes beneath each other in a table and calling the columns 'positions' (ibid.), and Diderichsen displays such a table with a number of examples filled in (p. 162). The units of the special syntactic unity of a sentence are then characterized and defined by the term 'Sætningsled' 'sentence constituent' (p. 163), and in doing so all the elements of the general theory of syntax are used. First, the constituents are found by means of the procedure using the sentence table, which is the element of descriptive generalization, and then the constituents are defined by means of the 'logical relation' of nexus

> *Ved et Sætningsled forstaar vi dels Subjekt og Prædikat i den sætningsdannede Neksus, dels de denne eller Verbalet underordnede Led.*

> By a constituent we understand, on the one hand, the subject and the predicate in the sentence building nexus, on the other hand the units which are subordinated to this [the nexus] or the verbal [constituent].

> (*ibid.*: 163)

Finally, this is furnished with a test-based definition:

> *Et sætningsled kan som Regel kendes paa, at det uden at deles kan stilles paa Førstepladsen i Sætningen.*

> A sentence constituent can usually be recognized on the basis of the fact that it can, without being divided, be placed in the first position in the sentence.

> (*ibid.*: 163)

Now this is combined with the theoretical concept of word classes as a matter of affiliation: 'De tre Hovedtyper af Led har et nært forhold til visse Typer af Ordklasser' 'the three main types of constituents have a close relation [i.e. affiliation] to certain types of word classes' (*ibid.*: 164).

This means that the columns of the sentence table are most frequently filled with words satisfying the criteria of belonging to certain word classes, and in this way the basic constituents are labelled 'Verbal' 'verbal (constituent)', 'Substantial' 'substantial (constituent)' and 'Adverbial' 'adverbial (constituent)' (pp. 161, 164 seqq.), and furthermore they are the names of the positions in the sentence table depicted above.

From a theoretical point of view, this is obviously not quite satisfactory because of the use of non-consistent notions in characterizing the constituents and because of the invocation of test-based definitions, and this is admitted by Diderichsen in a general discussion of the problems in defining the constituents of sentences (pp. 167–8). Thus he ends up with the traditional combination of characteristics as the criterion of identifying a constituent: case, position, 'logical relations' and semantics, and he mentions the theoretical background of the notion of sentence constituents in Danish grammar, namely, the need in education for a bridging idea in translation between, on the one hand,

Danish and, on the other hand, Latin and German – a kind of mediator which could explain the relation between the case forms in foreign languages and the meaning of Danish sentences. In the traditions of grammatical descriptions the distinctions between word, word class and sentence constituent are not always made clear, and one of Diderichsen's achievements is that he has contributed to bringing about a more accurate notion of sentence constituent as an analytical concept in linguistics, namely, as an intermediary between the parts of traditional propositional logic: subject and predicate, and the way these parts are expressed linguistically in the units of sentences, traditionally conceived of as words. Provided one accepts that the notions of the constituents are not formally satisfactory Diderichsen proposes relatively clear and intuitively understandable definitions of the main constituents in a typical Danish sentence:

> *Verbal ... angiver, hvordan de ved Substantialerne betegnede Genstande forholder sig.*
>
> [the] verbal [constituents] ... indicate how the objects denoted by the substantials are related.
>
> *Substantialer ... betegner de Genstande, hvortil Verbalindholdet umiddelbart angives at være knyttet.*
>
> Substantials [i.e. substantive (nominal) constituents] ... denote the objects to which the content of the verbal is bound.
>
> (*ibid.*: 169)

and:

> *Adverbialer er kun negativt definerede, ... ikke er hverken Verbaler, Substantialer eller Prædikativer.*
>
> Adverbials [i.e. adverbial constituents] are only negatively defined. .. [they are] not verbals, substantials or predicatives.
>
> (*ibid.*: 179)

Consequently, the main constituents are verbal constituents, substantials (substantive (nominal) constituents) and adverbial (constituents) – predicatives are not defined in a consistent way and they are not important because they do not have their own position – and the reduplication of these three constituents builds the two basic fields of the sentence table preceded by the open position and the position of the conjunctional constituent. This partly descriptive and partly formalistic theoretical construct of a sentence model made by Diderichsen brings us to the point where we are able to answer the questions asked above about the nature of constituents, sentences and topology in the model.

Despite the initial ambition of making the sentence the point of departure in syntax, the general impression of Diderichsen's theory is that words still form the central entity in description and explanation. Words, then, are used in two ways in this theory: first, they are the concrete entities making up the sentences that we actually construct in linguistic communication, and, second, they are the abstract entities that are created by word classes, assuming that words belonging to particular sets have certain properties in common. It is word classes that have the ability to establish syntactic functions, meaning that in some way they mark, label or signify a syntactic relationship, and because Diderichsen's theory is a topological theory of syntax, then this marking, etc. is done in the linear distribution – the topical properties in the sequence – of the word classes of the language under investigation. In primitive or simple sentences there is a correspondence (words belonging to certain word classes) between the actual words and the word classes, marking a special slot in the abstract word order, and more complex examples, where, for instance, so-called 'prepositional phrases' occupy the slot for adverbs, can be solved by assuming that phrases can be analysed according to the same principles as sentences, i.e. they can be conceived of as units consisting of units (cf. Diderichsen's sentence definition above), and that the correspondence is not an absolute one but only an affiliation (see above). The correspondence may be established by means of the 'logical' or morphological properties of words and word classes, or by their semantics, and in Diderichsen's syntactic theory, semantics is the property that is drawn most heavily upon in using Brøndal's formal analysis of word meaning. In his framework sentence constituents are neither those of traditional propositional logic, nor are they words having certain semantic functions in denoting things, states or events; Diderichsen's constituents are word classes having certain syntactic functions, in this case, topological functions, in sentences, and this should answer the question first asked above.

The second question concerned the sentence, and it is a consequence of the line of reasoning offered by the theory that sentences are (in this case linear) constructions of constituents. Thus a sentence is a unity of a number of units, in the sentence the units are of different kinds of nature (according to a word class theory) thereby creating sentence constituents, and what differs between sentences and other unities is that one of the constituents of a sentence belongs to the class of verbs and that the verb has a finite inflectional form. When one produces a sentence in linguistic communication, then one creates a series of words and (in topological languages) the sequence has to correspond or affiliate to the abstract word order, thereby also being a series of word classes. Explained in this way it should be evident that Diderichsen's syntactic theory, also at this level, is inextricably conflated with word class theory, and that neither constituents nor sentences can, within the scope of the theory, be accounted for without appealing to a notion of words in classes.

The last question concerned the nature of the order of words as positions and, as can be seen from the quotation above from Diderichsen ([1946] 1966: 140), he thinks that the job of the linear order of the constituents is to indicate the 'logical relations' between them, when it is not done in some other way, e.g. by the use of word classes or by inflectional forms. What the nature of these 'logical relations' is and what general linguistic functions they have are not explained by the theory, and evidently there is an appeal both to undefined meta-theoretical concepts and to common sense. This does not *per se* disqualify a scientific theory – in fact, this state is more common in science than the opposite – and Diderichsen's theory is indisputably more than uninitiated descriptive analyses.

It should be observed, however, that there are some uncertain points in the theoretical status of the field (or position) SENTENCE TABLE on Danish syntax, and they are mentioned in question (3) above: is it a matter of fixed linear order or of fixed positions? The difference is that fixed linear order implies that preceding units determine the occurrence of a specific unit, as in a combinatorial system, and that fixed positions imply only a specific spatial relationship between whatever occurs. In the first case a specific unit will not be found if one or more preceding units are not found, or one or more special conditions are not satisfied, while in the other case anything may occur without being related to the occurrence of other units, provided they are found on certain coordinates in an imagined network. The way Diderichsen's syntax theory is accounted for, it appears most likely to be the latter option.[22] It cannot be used in deciding whether a sentence is well-formed in the sense that there are a sufficient number of constituents; only when one has determined whether it is well-formed can it yield the topical constraints on the actual constituents. This is not contradicted by the dependence functions of the 'logical relations'. The topical formation of the sentence table is an expression of the 'logical relations' (it marks, labels or signifies them), but the existence of an instance of a 'logical relation' is no condition for the existence of a certain linear construction. This theoretical status is also what is displayed in the columns of the sentence table, where (1) one is allowed to fill in whatever one likes, provided the units one posits satisfy the demands of just that position; (2) one is allowed to replace units by other units with the same function to test one's solutions; and (3) one is allowed to leave some of the positions open. There is an analogy between this framework and traditional morphology and phonology. Thus it is obvious that empty positions resemble zero-morphemes in inflection and that replacement of units resembles the commutation test in ascertaining phonemes, and if one bears in mind the prominent status in traditional Modern Languages grammars of non-manifested case endings and in structuralist phonology of the substitutional methods of the commutation test, then this may be the most salient example of the merging of the two traditions in Diderichsen's sentence theory.

Ever since Diderichsen published his sentence model it has been a challenge to Scandinavian grammarians; it has been commented upon, elaborated, revised and expanded, and almost any Scandinavian scholar in the field of syntactic analysis has felt an urge to make his own version of the sentence table. Some more memorable examples of contributions in syntax are Diderichsen's ([1964] 1966) own comments on the theory on its 30th anniversary and the above-mentioned *NyS* Vol. 16–17 celebration of its 50th anniversary. Diderichsen himself did not change his principles of analysis, and apart from terminological changes the most interesting proposal is an elaborated analysis of adverbials of Danish sentences (1966: 379). *NyS* Vol. 16–17 is a compilation of a number of evaluations of the sentence table from a late twentieth-century point of view, not all of them technical discussions but also including historical investigations and accounts from the perspective of the philosophy of science, and the most striking feature in the volume is the fact that the sentence table, conceived as a theoretical model, is taken at face value. In some theoretical summaries the agreement of the topological approach with other syntactic theories is explained, in an historical account it is the origin of the topological approach that is the topic, and some technical revisions propose extensions with new fields and positions that are not always coherent with the original theoretical framework; but there are not many attempts to question and investigate the theoretical foundations of the model, and in this way the publication is, for the most part, a retrospective historical celebration.

Summarizing the account of Diderichsen's theory of sentence topology I will express my personal view that it reflects a combination of the traditions of descriptive grammars and theoretical linguistics. Thus I see it as a descriptive theory of syntax based on empirical generalizations and illustrated by a lucid model. Since Diderichsen always attempted to adjust the theoretical concepts to the empirical facts, the theory is endowed with the advantages of the best descriptive grammars, and since he always pursued the goals of rational thinking, the theory also has the benefits of a clear-cut conceptual framework within theoretical linguistics, but the unacknowledged risk is that the theory itself is confused with the illustrating model, in analyses as well as in theoretical development.

Summary

The theories of what I have called Grammatical Analysis in the Classical Danish Tradition, the works accounting for them and the people behind them, did not have the same objectives. The purpose of Brøndal's word semantics was to claim the existence of universal conceptual and expressional classes and to use them to account for different languages and cultures, the aim of Hjelmslev's formal algebra was to create an all-embracing theory of the scientific object of investigation that language is conceived of in the modern western culture, and the idealistic ends of Diderichsen's sentence syntax were to understand rationally and to expound pedagogically the intrinsic structure of his mother tongue. But their common trait is that, once they had focused on the specific part of reality in which they were interested – and which they thought could answer their questions – they pursued their goals quite far, and the concepts, theories and methods that they proposed and demonstrated, created the background for later generations of Danish scholars in linguistics.

The natural question here is: what can these theories be used for? In my view a formalistic word class semantics is not the most urgent task of modern linguistics. The very concept of word as a theoretical term can reasonably be questioned within the framework of contemporary linguistics (see Chapter 3), and assuming transcendent Aristotelian or Kantian categories in epistemology is not quite in accord with contemporary western philosophy, but the Brøndalian scheme points to the fact that we use different kinds of linguistic expressions for different specific linguistic purposes, and that the meaning of the expressions, whatever it is, may have something to do with the purposes, whatever they are, and this may be conceived of in universal notions.[23]

The Hjelmslevian Glossematics has been accused of being too ambitious, i.e. Glossematics claims to cover the whole object of language in a single theory (but language is too complex for such a scheme to succeed), and it has been accused of being too abstract, i.e. it assumes that language is a single unitary system having its own existence (but language is an aspect of human behaviour).

I think that both accusations miss the point. First, there is by itself nothing wrong with uniformly formulated theories about large entities – such theories are produced by theoretical physicists all the time – and explaining complex structures, for instance, by iterated principles (recursive procedures) does not deprive the structures of their complexity. A theory should be judged on the basis of whether its explanations are good or bad, and a formal universal theory may yield better explanations. The question about language is whether one single uniform system is able to explain everything, whether a number of more or less connected formal systems will do, or if there will always be something left over that cannot be explained in this way. As for the second accusation, to my knowledge Hjelmslev has never denied that language is something human. What his claims do imply is that we must assume that language has functions and systems that are beyond direct individual human control if one wants to participate in linguistic communication. But that does not dehumanise language, and it does not prevent human beings from thinking about and – more or less consciously – changing these functions and systems. For Hjelmslev, the presupposition that language has systematic properties was a prerequisite for a scientific study. I agree with him, and in my version it takes the form of what I call an 'occurrence logic of linguistic expressions'.

Finally, the Diderichsenian sentence topology has more or less proved its own legitimacy as a syntactic theory. Its basic descriptive achievements in Scandinavian syntax have never been questioned, it has never been rejected as a scientific approach by competing theories, and while it shares both advantages and deficiencies with other descriptive theories – i.e. a descriptivist always knows when he has found something but he does not always know what it is – it also shares both advantages and deficiencies with other more or less formalistic theories – i.e. a formalist always knows what he is looking for but he does not always know when he has found it.

The Chomskyan Approach

A turn in linguistics

Generative (Transformational) Grammar: what is it?

The following is not another narrative on Chomsky,[1] his life and his contributions to theoretical linguistics, notably to syntax and the architecture of the mental systems handling linguistic processes. That has been done extensively by other scholars. The following is a very short summation of what I see as some salient – and in this context the most relevant – features of, on the one hand, Chomsky's basic assumptions about language and, on the other hand, the kind of grammar that he proposed and that he and quite many linguists have elaborated on and further developed since then.[2]

It all started – so the story goes – with the publication of the books *Syntactic Structures* in 1957 and *Aspects of the Theory of Syntax* in 1965. The breaking news was the idea that the way to uncover the structure of sentences was to assume a number of categories expressed as symbols and a number of rewrite rules handling the symbols. When, by means of lexical rules, the symbols representing categories were assigned natural language expressions, then the complex of the symbolism represented a structural analysis of the sentence in which the natural language expressions were units, and the achievement of the system was the accuracy with which sentences could be described. A necessary precondition was, however, that the rules would produce (generate) all and only the (structural analyses of) sentences of the language studied – in which case the set of categories and the rules were called a generative grammar; in the following labelled Generative Grammar when referred to as a school of thought. If attested sentences would not quite fit the rules but anyhow had to be accepted as sentences in a language, then the basic rules were furnished with a set of transformational (movement) rules yielding derived sentences from basic sentences. Since the derived sentences were the ones in the end produced by a speaker, then the basic sentences had to be assumed to be underlying, so-called deep structure, sentences, while the sentences which were generated by transformations were perceived as surface structure sentences. The question is how this was envisaged in the first place.

Chomskyan linguistics: some basic assumptions

From the background sketched above, Generative Grammar – in its historically different shapes – has become a widely accepted framework in theoretical linguistics, and no doubt the Chomskyan line of reasoning is the most influential approach in syntax in current linguistics. I shall not go into the details of Chomskyanism here – and I am aware of the fact that the Chomskyan era in the form of his personal contributions to linguistics may belong to the past – but I will mention that, in my view, the overall impression of what may be called the broad Generative Grammar tradition followed by many contemporary linguists is that it has developed into a descriptive grammar based on sometimes rather disparate data and utilizing an abstract, formalistic theory, of which the analytical concepts are sometimes a little opaque; and, one may feel inclined to add, the apparatus producing the structural descriptions has become quite complicated. Furthermore, Generative Grammar seems to run into some of the same problems as Hjelmslev's Glossematics: is a structural analysis in Generative Grammar an application of a formal system to a series of expressions (typically words) or is it a direct reflection (an image) of the mental mechanism handling linguistic processes? In the latter, it follows that it is an extremely successful descriptive model with direct access to the mental machinery, and as far as I know regarding generative accounts, I have not come across any formulations that make a clear distinction between (1) the theory, (2) the formal system intrinsic to the theory, (3) the application of the theory (the formal system) in the form of analyses, and (4) the data that the application is an analysis of. But, as opposed to these critical remarks, I would like to make clear the fact that apart from my foundation in the Danish grammatical tradition, Chomsky's personal attempts to solve the mysteries of syntax are one of the main sources of the ideas offered in Chapters 3 and 4.

In this brief account I will make no comments on other – more or less generative – modern theories in syntactic theories, such as (cf. Newmeyer 1998:

11–13; Brown, and Miller 1996: 54–80; Ludlov 2011: 162–3) LFG (lexical-functional grammar), GPSG (generalized phrase-structure grammar), HPSG (head-driven phrase-structure grammar), IA (item-and-arrangement model of description in morphology), IP (item-and-process model of description in morphology), etc. but will limit myself to comments only on the Chomskyan (i.e. Chomsky's) principles and theories.

For an unbiased appraisal of the contemporary state of Chomskyan linguistics I will mention the review article by Blevins in *Journal of Linguistics* (44 (3), 2008, 723–42), but, for the sake of clarity, I shall emphasize that the following is not an attempt to make a totally unbiased presentation of Chomskyan thoughts; it is a personal reading of a few parts of what he and others have written.

One of the basic assumptions in the Chomskyan approach seems to be the 'mentalistic'[3] principle. So it was in 1965: 'Hence, in the technical sense, linguistic theory is mentalistic, since it is concerned with discovering a mental reality underlying actual behavior' (Chomsky 1965: 4), and so it seemed to be in 1995: 'The current situation is that we have good and improving theories of some aspects of language and mind, but only rudimentary ideas about the relation of any of this to the brain' (Chomsky 1995a: 11), and so it was in 2000:

> I will understand the term 'mental' in much the same way, with something like its traditional coverage, but without metaphysical import and with no suggestion that it would make any sense to try to identify the true criterion or mark of the mental. By 'mind' I mean the mental aspects of the world, with no concern for defining the notion more closely and no expectations that we will find some interesting kind of unity or boundaries, any more than elsewhere; no one cares to sharpen the boundaries of 'the chemical.'
>
> (Chomsky 2000: 75)

It is, accordingly, mentalism, not in the tradition of philosophy, but as a point of departure in 'a naturalistic inquiry' (Chomsky 1995a: 12) searching for 'some elements of Jones's brain', 'the language faculty' (*ibid.*), and 'There is good evidence that the language faculty has at least two components: a "cognitive system" that stores information in some manner, and performance systems that make use of this information for articulation, perception' (Chomsky 1995a: 12).

I now fully subscribe to this scientific approach and mentalism in linguistics, and I see my own EFA(X) theory as an alternative model based on the same principles and ideas, namely, that language (and in a broad sense: grammar) is an entity only found in the minds of human beings. However, I prefer the way this principle is phrased by Kenny (1981):

> I think that Chomsky employs in his writing a confused notion of the mental. I should perhaps begin by explaining what I think a non-confused notion of the mental looks like.
>
> The mind is the capacity to acquire intellectual skills. The chief and most important intellectual skill is the mastering of language.
>
> Someone who has acquired a language knows that language. Knowledge of a language is an ability.
>
> (Kenny 1981: 245–6)

Accordingly, in Chapters 3 and 4, I shall not take up the question of how to describe and explain the mind's general capacity to acquire linguistic skills; I shall only take up the problem of how speakers' knowledge of Danish and Swedish may be described in an alternative way.

As opposed to my (rephrased) general agreement with Chomsky on 'mentalism', I do not subscribe to what Chomsky calls 'internalism' or an 'internalist approach' (Chomsky 2000: 134 seqq. *et passim*). In my reading this is about methodology and what kind of empirical evidence we can have for saying something about linguistic phenomena, namely, that we can only check the linguistic knowledge in our own heads; and indirectly in the heads of others. Chomsky does not disregard the fact that environment has played a role in the end result (so far) of the evolution of the human language faculty:

> To the extent that the answer to question (2) is positive, language is something like a 'perfect system', meeting external constraints as well as can be done, in one of the reasonable ways. The Minimalist Program for linguistic theory seeks to explore these possibilities.
>
> (Chomsky 1995b: 1)

Then, the difference between Chomsky and my theory at the epistemological level is only whether knowledge about external factors is relevant when we want to describe and explain the functions of the 'language faculty'; or to put it another way: how the alleged opposition between 'internalism' and 'externalism' may be dissolved. I deal with this in brief in Chapter 3.

Another basic feature of the Chomskyan theoretical models seems to be that grammars are 'generative'. As is well known, this term has been misunderstood by many, and, as pointed out by the notably critical assessment by Botha (1989), the concept 'generative' in the Chomskyan generative grammar (only) means that a grammar is 'explicit' (cf. Botha 1989: 1–3) and has no other connotations. Concerning the Chomskyan model it follows that:

> For a grammar to meet the requirement of explicitness, Chomsky initially proposed, it should take the form of a system of formalized rules and other related devices which mechanically enumerate all and only the grammatical sentences of the language, assigning to each of these sentences an appropriate structural description.
>
> *(ibid.:* 2)

Whether these criteria are satisfied in the different versions of Chomskyan linguistic theory, I am not in a position to judge, but if the meaning of the term 'generative' accounted for here is appropriate, my own EFA(X) theory might, hypothetically, be considered a kind of generative syntactic model. Accordingly, I will also subscribe to this basic Chomskyan principle of explicitness, but so do all formalistic approaches, and my use of the word may differ a little: when I say that syntax is about how linguistic expressions are generated and interpreted, I am actually referring to the mental processes by which these events take place, not to the formal system used to describe them.

One of the latest developments in the Chomskyan line of thoughts is apparently that Chomsky approves of a theoretical narrowing down of the idea of the mind as a bearer of linguistic functions (including what he called 'the language faculty'[4] as an 'innate organ') to specific biological functions of the brain. Thus we are told in Chomsky's Foreword to Andrea Moro's (2008) English translation of *Confini di Babele* that:

> The modern study of language within a biological context began to take place in the 1950s. In 1967, a now classic work—Eric Lenneberg's *Biological Foundations of Language*—laid a substantial basis for the emerging discipline … Nevertheless, until fairly recently the 'biolinguistic perspective', … remained to a large extent an ideal.
>
> (Foreword by Chomsky, in Moro 2008)

Whether 'biolinguistics' is a recent development or goes back to the dawn of Generative Grammar may be a matter of debate (in an Appendix, James McGilvray mentions (in Chomsky 2012: 246) that the term was introduced in 1974). Chomsky thinks that: 'Ever since this business began in the fifties … the topic we were interested in, how could you work this into biology?' (Chomsky 2012: 21); whereas Jackendoff's perception is: 'In recognition of the goal of interfacing linguistic theory with biology, practitioners of the minimalist program have begun calling the enterprise "biolinguistics'" (Jackendoff 2012: 589), referring to publications after 2000.[5]

However, the ideal mentioned above by Chomsky has, apparently, now been brought down to earth by Moro. To what extent this is the case may, also, be a matter of debate:

> [S]he worries that brain imaging is still a relatively crude tool. On its own, she says, it 'cannot inspire a theory of how the brain works. All it tells you is that if you do this or that, different bits of the brain light up on a scan—it doesn't tell you why or how or what that means.'

'She' is Susan Greenfield, former Director, The Royal Institution, London, and the quote is given (p. 151) by the interviewer Alison Goddard (Griffiths 1999). Susan Greenfield goes on to say:

> 'We know that brain cells work on the scale of thousandths of seconds,' says Greenfield. 'In terms of finding what in the brain matches up with different moments of consciousness, we are going to need brain imaging to be much more sophisticated.'

> > (*ibid.*)

And this may be put into perspective by Moro's own formulations: 'The illusion of "seeing thought" is still an illusion, ... It is unclear whether this illusion will ever dissolve, due to an explicit theory' (Moro 2008: 141). And '[N]obody yet knows how you go from the principles that allow us to form sentences to the neurons or the cortical areas that underlie this task' (*ibid.*: 129). So, maybe Chomsky's Foreword to Moro (2008) is an effect of a preserved lack of clarification of the basic notions, cf. 'In fact Chomsky's mental structures seem to belong at times to the world of software, at times to the world of hardware' (Kenny 1981: 247).

In sum, whereas I, like Chomsky and others, still believe that language is in the mind and that the mind is in the brain, I do not feel sure that we have come closer to being able to describe or explain linguistic processes in the brain.

Chomskyan grammar: theory and model

If our ability to 'see' such processes are, so far, limited then, what is left for enquiry is the set of what we call linguistic phenomena, in short: grammars. As for Chomsky's thoughts on language, grammar and syntax, no one will deny that they have been extremely influential. Another question is to what extent they were revolutionary, or whether evolutionary may be a better word.[6] The latter view is the one expressed by E. F. K. Koerner in his *Toward a History of American Linguistics*, reviewed by J. T. Andresen in *Language* 86 (1), of March 2010, whom I, for convenience, quote here:

> The way K [i.e. Koerner] sees it, by contrast, American linguistics during the 1940s and 1950s involved more evolution than revolution. His point, however, is not to chastise Chomsky—or anyone else—for distorting the historical record.
>
> (Andresen 2010: 227)

The topic concerning 'distortion' has to do with whether Chomsky is able to recall that he had read Bloomfield's 'Menomini morphophonemics' before he wrote his MA thesis 'Morphophonemics of Modern Hebrew' (Chomsky 1951), a claim that Chomsky rejects. In Koerner's view, Chomsky just has a bad memory, as we all have (cf. my remarks on Diderichsen in Chapter 1), but in the context of the development of science it may be interesting to note the following from Andresen's review:

> K identifies the 9th International Congress of Linguistics held in Cambridge, MA, in August 1962 as the decisive event, 'ably prepared and effectively run' by Morris Halle, where the strategy had become 'to sell Chomsky's ideas as having little to do with the linguistics of his American teachers and predecessors ... [such that] ... connections with the work of Chomsky's immediate predecessors had to be minimized, if not erased (234)'.
>
> (*ibid.*: 227)

Maybe the more radical shift of theoretical basis was not 'the Chomskyan revolution in linguistics' but instead the detrimental blow to the mind-set of traditional behaviourism delivered by Chomsky in his review of B. F. Skinner's *Verbal Behavior* (Chomsky 1959), a knockout meant to justify the mentalism to come.

As for syntactic modelling, it is a well-known fact that since the nineteenth century the art of diagramming sentences has been an exercise in American school textbooks on grammar, and, even though we cannot know to what extent this practice had inspired Chomsky, it is not a big jump from diagramming sentences according to one of the systems proposed by the textbooks to diagramming a sentence in a late Chomskyan tree structure. What makes the difference is only the theoretical underpinning of the later version. I shall not go into the potential significance of different ways of graphically visualizing the structure of sentences in the Chomskyan tradition, from rewrite rules in Chomsky (1957), to tree structures and movements in Chomsky (1965) and in Chomsky (1995b); I shall only acknowledge that any of these can be used to depict the formal or formalistic systems that make up the bulk of Chomskyan approaches to grammar. In such grammars a number of symbols are being manipulated in accordance with explicit rules, and in order to understand which symbols and which rules a grammar in the Chomskyan tradition has selected, it is convenient to realize what an undergraduate student textbook in Generative Grammar like Ouhalla (1994) takes as its basic assumptions when building a methodology that can be followed when analysing grammatical constructions.[7] He says, about the hierarchy visualized as a basic tree structure (called 'an abstract diagram') on p. 18, that the symbols represent 'constituents' (p. 19) and that these letter symbols are 'categorial labels' (*ibid.*). So, when we attach some lexical items to the branches of a tree we have to know that we are doing it right, and that knowledge about 'the correct structure ... is an empirical issue' (*ibid.*: 20). And we know what we are doing on the basis of a number of 'constituency tests/criteria' (*ibid.*), namely:[8]

i displacement
ii deletion
iii coordination and
iv replacement with a proforma.

On the face of it, this looks like a benchmark for a formal system: by manipulation symbols may change distribution ('displacement'), may be substituted ('replacement'), may be replaced with nothing ('deletion'), must follow the same rules in a corresponding context ('coordination') and may be replaced with function expressions, but on the other hand it also looks like what we all do when trying to figure out what belongs together in a sentence and what does not. But, following this strictly empirical principle, we do not need a theory – and may in fact not have one – about why certain items belong to one category and not to another category, and when arriving at a full analysis, as a result of parsing a sentence, Ouhalla (1994) breaks down the hierarchy, visualized as a tree structure, into a 'Verb Phrase (VP)' and a 'Noun Phrase' (pp. 21–2) with an 'aux' left with its own branch in the tree. The naïve question is, of course, how do we know that verb phrases are verb phrases and that noun phrases are noun phrases? But, as Ray Jackendoff said to me on one occasion: 'You don't argue with gravity.' By this move, Ouhalla (1994) relocates grammar from the question about how sentences are built to the question about how phrases are built and, in accordance with the Generative Grammar tradition, how sentences are conceived of as no more than special kinds of phrase structures. And real sentences produced by people (as so-called 'Surface Structures', p. 12) are considered the results of a number of transformations, which are operations performed on more basic phrases called 'Deep Structures' (*ibid.*). Exactly how these transformations work has kept generativists busy for years, but one striking feature is worth mentioning: the criteria for identifying constituents in an empirical analysis (1–4 above) are identical to the outcome of transformational rules, i.e. things are moved, removed, adjusted and represented in the mind of the language user in the same way as the linguist goes about it when ascertaining constituents. Which rules the mind follows is a more complicated question, and in Chomsky (1995b) it was narrowed down to one specific rule:

> Exactly how these principles of interaction among levels of should be understood is not entirely clear. I will adopt the general assumption that S-structure is related to LF by iterated application of the principle Move α (substitution and adjunction), deletion, and insertion—that is, by the principle Affect α in the sense of Lasnik and Saito (1984)—and to PF by this principle and the rules of the phonological component.
>
> (Chomsky 1995b: 132)

As is obvious from Chomsky (1995b), tree structures (in parallel with labelled bracketing) and movements are still the favourite devices for describing output constructions in natural languages, and a critical assessment of Generative Grammar may take this as a starting point.

Chomskyan grammar: some shortcomings

Chomsky's paper 'Three Models for the Description of Language' (Chomsky 1956) by definition (following from the words in the headline) deals with grammars of natural languages and with the question 'whether or not they [the grammars considered in the paper] can provide simple and "revealing" grammars that can generate all of the sentences of English and only these'. However, Lars Svenonius in his review of Chomsky (1956), talks about 'A more natural way to produce sentences in English or in a logical language' (Svenonius 1958: 71), which means that no distinction is made here between natural and artificial (formal) languages. And the question is which languages Chomsky's

(1956) paper – the three models of which are now broadly known as a 'Chomsky hierarchy' – aimed at: natural languages or formal (artificial, and specifically computational programming) languages, or all of them? As may be inferred from Svenonius's review, the distinction may not have been made then, and the underlying assumption may be that there were no perceived essential differences between natural and artificial languages, even though Chomsky may not be fully unambiguous on that point: 'Similarly, the set of "sentences" of some formalised system of mathematics can be considered a language.' (Chomsky 1957: 13) if one feels inclined to focus on the reservation 'can be considered'. Anyhow, it looks as if Chomsky's grammar ended up looking the way it does, because of this lack of distinction, and that makes it vulnerable to certain kinds of criticism.

One may, as alluded to above, ask how we know that, e.g. a noun is a noun, and the answer seems to be that it is because it can be a head of a noun phrase. Which, in turn, may lead to the question how we know what a noun phrase is, and the answer seems to be that it is because the head of a noun phrase is a noun. If we, for the moment, ignore Jackendoff's suggestion that questioning word class categorization is like questioning gravity, the only way out seems to be a detailed theory of word classes, like Brøndal's, but this does not seem to be an option for Generative Grammar. Neither is it an option to conceive of structural descriptions of natural language sentences as non-derivational (non-transformational) events. On the contrary, it looks as if most such sentences have had to pass through a number of transformational steps before they are, so to speak, spat out. But what is the mental counterpart of such a transformational process? It cannot be ascertained by introspection, and, provided the mind is considered a computational system run by the brain, what would be the benefits of a system that transforms a number of times the alignment of a number of lexical items in order to make the end product look like the sentences we actually experience, if all this is seen from the point of view of process efficiency? Such complications are not problems for artificial languages because everything is established by convention, and tautologies like 'an NP is an NP because it is an NP' are just stipulations. And some scholars actually think that the structure of artificial languages has no bearing on the structure of natural languages:

> [D]esigning an artificial language allows no empirical conclusions on human language design. Its design will depend on the designer's purposes … The design of human natural language is simply what it is. The artificial language

may be specifically designed to enable communication, but this would not necessarily tell us anything about natural language design.

(Hinzen 2006: 25)

Another question has to do with one of Chomsky's basic ideas about where language comes from in the minds of humans, the so-called 'innateness hypothesis'. Apart from the fact that Chomsky says that there is no such hypothesis:

> Another form of dualism that has arisen in the discussion of language acquisition is illustrated by the curious debate on 'innatism' or 'the innateness hypothesis.' The debate is one-sided: no one defends the hypothesis, including those to whom it is attributed (me, in particular). The reason is that there is no such hypothesis.
>
> (Chomsky 2000: 100)

he maintains that there exist 'problems of "poverty of stimulus" so extreme that knowledge in these regards too can only be assumed to be in substantial measure innately determined' (*ibid.*: 126).

So, it seems as if the question of the 'Innateness of Language' (the so-called input/output paradox referred to by the notion 'poverty of stimulus') stays with us, and I shall claim that the Formative Grammar (FoG) approach advanced in this book puts the problem in a different perspective. To discuss it on 'neutral ground', I relate to the account of the paradox offered in the *The MIT Encyclopedia of the Cognitive Sciences* (1999: 408), namely, that the argument goes as follows:

1 Human language has the following complex form: G (for Grammar).
2 The nature of the information about G available to the learner is the following: I (for Input/Information, called Primary Linguistic Data in Chomsky 1965).
3 No learner could take the information in I and transform it into G.

This argument is illustrated by the following examples:

(4) (a) Mary is eager to please
    (b) Mary is easy to please

It is argued that '(4a, b) seem to have identical surface structures, yet in (4a) *Mary* is the subject of *please* (she will do the pleasing) and in (4b) *Mary* is the object of *please* (she will be pleased).' In my view this argument is simply invalid. First, we do not know exactly what 'transform' in proposition (3) means, a fact that weakens the argument, but, second, the crucial problem is the vague use of the notions of 'subject' and 'object'. In the traditions of the language sciences, it is not unusual to find confusions of, on the one hand, subjects and objects (as in scenarios of action, where a subject performs an act of which some entity is the object) and, on the other hand, grammatical subjects and objects. In the case of (4a, b) Mary may be the acting subject (the agent) or the passive object (the patient) of the act of pleasing in (4a) and (4b) respectively, but this is not reflected in the 'surface' (i.e. syntactic) structures of the sentences. A Formative Grammar analysis will bring this to light:

```
(4) a.
    Mary is eager to please
    subj v(phr)----- obj
    b.
    Mary is easy to please
    subj v subjpred------
```

In this analysis the superficial similarity of the words and the minor phono-logical and phonetic distinctions are deceptive features, and they do not reflect the constituent structures of the sentences, which, furthermore, are not identical. In (4a), the verb phrase *is eager to* is considered a collocation with a combinatorial semantics and the following infinitive is considered the (grammatical, i.e. syntactical) object according to the FoG definitions in Chapters 3 and 4. Some reasons for the analysis can be offered, namely, that *please* can be replaced by other infinitives, e.g. *run, eat ice cream* or *bake*, and that the verb phrase without the particle *to* in *is eager to* has a semantics close to *want*, which accordingly can replace *is eager*. In (4b), the adjective *easy* is evidently used as a (logical) predicate specified by the following infinitive, including the infinitive marker *to*, and therefore the phrase *easy to please* is considered a (grammatical, i.e. syntactical) subject predicative according to the FoG definitions offered in Chapters 3 and 4. In the theoretical context of FoG 'displacement' (cf. above) – in the special sense that one may move linguistic expressions around in order to test the cohesiveness of clusters of expressions specifically as a reason for their constituent status – is not accepted as a valid argument. Of course one may move *to please* in (4b) to make the construction *to please Mary is easy*, while this is not possible in (4a) **to please Mary is eager*, but such operations may indicate that (4a, b) do not even 'seem to have identical surface structures' as claimed above. But the main reason for rejecting the 'movement operation' is that, in my view, the result of such a procedure is simply another sentence: *to please Mary is easy* has another subject (namely, the infinitive phrase *to please Mary*) than (4a), and in Formative Grammar there are no movements (cf. Chapters 3 and 4). Then, the outcome of this analysis is (1) that there seems to be no reason to assume that learners of English have not been introduced to syntactic structures that differ between (4a and 4b),[9] and that (2) the argument from empirical evidence is highly dependent on the theories used to describe data. Even a philosopher of Generative Linguistics points to the problem that

> Some linguists have argued that the traditional descriptive method in linguistics is more scientific because it begins with the data and only then proceeds to theory construction. ... [but] It is widely viewed [in the philosophy of science] ... that there is no such thing as raw data or raw sense perception. ... This point exposes the pernicious aspect of these calls against theory. Those who advance such calls have theoretical assumptions of their own and they are asking us, in effect, not to examine those theoretical assumptions.
>
> (Ludlov 2011: 84)

Furthermore, and ironically, Chomsky had, twenty years earlier, presented readings that repudiate the analyses above. In Chomsky (1979, in Chomsky 2007), he mentions on pp. 44–5 the constructions *John expected (Bill to leave)* vs. *John (persuaded Bill) (to leave)*, using the round brackets to illustrate the sentence structures, and the sentences can be seen in parallel with (4a, b) above and likewise demonstrating different 'surface structures' because of the semantics of the verbs.

A good question is, of course, if it matters whether there is a dispute about, in a broad sense, the 'innateness of language'. There is no obvious answer to that, but, first, it is a striking feature of this theoretical apparatus that, in order to explain a number of phenomena, one has to assume an unknown factor (in this case 'innateness'), whereas the lacking ability of the theory to explain things depends heavily on the design of that theory. Second, it may be a reasonable idea to adjourn the debate until more light has been cast on the relationship between genetic inheritance, the detailed architecture of the brain and the mind, including linguistic processes, and, so far, I find the idea of 'innateness' irrelevant to syntactic analysis.

No doubt, the Chomskyan approach has, in the past, raised essential questions about how to create, develop and elaborate a theory on syntactic, grammatical and linguistic analysis, but so did Brøndal and Hjelmslev. All three of them proposed formal, or formalised, systems as conceptual frameworks, and maybe one of the reasons why Chomsky and not Hjelmslev became so influential had to do with timing. Hjelmslev was late when the train of electronic computational machines left the station, while Chomsky and his thoughts appeared to be relevant to the way we interact with the electronic systems in such machines by means of formal, or (I would rather say) technical, systems. Whether Chomsky's grammar in the form of Generative Grammar will survive the technological, cultural and intellectual turmoil of the twenty-first century is yet to be seen. John Searle is not optimistic:

> Though Chomsky did indeed revolutionize the subject of linguistics, it is not at all clear, at the end of the century, what the solid results of this revolution are. As far as I can tell there is not a single rule of syntax that all, or even most, competent linguists are prepared to agree is a rule.
>
> (Searle 1999: 2071)

In the context of this retrospective, the present-day situation is interesting in three ways: (1) the status of the notions of grammar and syntax in basic presentations of linguistics; (2) attempts to underpin Generative Grammar with philosophical reasoning; and (3) attempts to underpin Generative Grammar by evidence from experimental linguistics.

As for the first, it is a striking feature that English language basic textbooks on linguistic matters often take it as an unchallenged truth that the Generative Grammar approach is the basis of our standard knowledge of grammar and syntax. One of the best introductory textbooks that I know of is Yule (2010), and in his book he actually explains in detail how linguists have arrived at the theories and models presented, but what we find on grammar and syntax is the line of reasoning in American Structuralism, from 'structural analysis' (*ibid.*, p. 87), 'constituent analysis' (p. 88), bracketing (p. 89), 'deep and surface structures' (p. 97), 'tree diagrams' (p. 99) to 'lexical rules' (p. 102) and 'movement rules' (p. 103), and finally 'complements' (p. 105). Each step is well argued, but not much is questioned and no alternatives are offered. In Fromkin et al. (2011),[10] the steps are not even well argued; the syntax chapter is one long series of presuppositions and leaves the student with the impression that all this is common standard knowledge.

As for philosophical concerns about Generative Grammar, Peter Ludlov has (in Ludlov 2011) offered an overview of a philosopher's perception of Generative Grammar and some philosophical matters associated with it:

> This work is an attempt to explore some of the many interesting philosophical issues that arise in the conduct of generative linguistics ... that branch of linguistics that attempts to explain and understand language-related

phenomena by constructing a theory of the underlying mechanisms that give rise to those phenomena.

(Ludlov 2011: xv)

Ludlov presents a summary of the history and current state of Generative Grammar followed by an account of its ontological implications, and then sets the scene for a discussion of basic problems in the domain, in particular the concepts of data, rules, representations, derivations and criteria for the assessment of theories, and he succeeds in portraying the philosophical foundations of Generative Grammar, but the outcome is, in my view, not a philosophical justification of that theory (a result that may not have been intended either). Actually, his reasoning could be appealed to as some of the basic philosophical assumptions of other more or less formalised theories of syntax like the one proposed in Chapters 3 and 4.

As opposed to this, Moro (2008) is an explicit defence of Generative Grammar, both by theoretical reasoning and by an attempt to provide us with empirical evidence that this is the one and only kind of syntactic analysis. On the one hand, he claims that:

> A fundamental discovery stemming from the structuralist theories and successively refined in generative grammar is that there are not only noun phrases but also other kinds of phrases and, crucially, that all these phrases have the very same asymmetric structure.

(*ibid.*: 70)

And 'A very important discovery in syntactic theory that goes back at least to Chomsky (1986b) is that the whole sentence has a phrase structure of the same kind as the phrases it is made of' (*ibid.*: 72).

Well, as recounted in Chapter 1 on Danish grammarians, at least Diderichsen (in his 1946 grammar but also in other publications) had proposed the same insights, but in Diderichsen's usual manner, tentatively. One may also question whether this idea of identical hierarchical structures is true, or even that phrase structures are neuronally hard-wired as suggested by Moro: 'it is worth observing that if a child is born with this architecture, then the possible number of word combinations for forming phrases is drastically reduced' (Moro 2008: 78). One may wonder if the fact that observable phenomena representing objects in the world cause all objects to be perceived as entities with properties, makes it, sort of, natural to use hierarchically organized phrases to talk about them: in the phrase *the little brown dog* the entity 'dog' is referred to as the head of the phrase and the properties 'brown' and 'little' are referred to as hierarchical attributes; all of this based on the fact that we actually see an object, a dog, having some properties, namely, the dog being brown and little; a line of reasoning that, as is well known (cf. Gianto 2005), goes back to Classical Greek philosophers. Moreover, one may wonder if it is, indeed, a fact that a sentence is just a peculiar kind of phrase structure, and I will come back to that in Chapter 3.

In the second part of his book, Moro presents a number of tests in experimental linguistics in which he claims to have demonstrated that phrase structures (in the Generative Grammar version) are in the brain. No doubt, his experiments are, in principle, ingeniously set up, but some of the premises expose some basic flaws. In short, the experiments consist of a number of tests carried out with learners who are not acquainted with the language used but are presented with a number of pseudo-words and 'impossible rules' (according to Generative Grammar assumptions) in order to see how the test-subjects handle counterfactual linguistic structures and to see what kind of brain processing goes along with the linguistic operations. Moro's conclusion is, not surprisingly, that the experiments confirm his ideas:

> The class of possible human languages is dramatically constrained by complex general principles such as structure dependence [i.e. the hierarchical phrase structure], which does not have an intermediate counterpart in other cognitive domains. We also verified that these boundaries are not just generalisations of accidental, that is, historical, conventional linguistic regularities, but that they correlate with specific neuronal activities.
>
> (Moro 2008: 189)

But if this conclusion is based upon certain kinds of analyses that do not sufficiently clarify which syntactic structures are dealt with, one may reflect on the adequacy of the experiments and the justification of the conclusions. I will illustrate this with just one example: on page 164, Moro mentions the 'famous rule of German syntax, the "verb second" or "V2"' rule, about which he says:

> A more accurate formulation of the rule, and in fact the only correct one, would be to say that the inflected verb in main clauses is always moved to the head of the first phrase of the clause (CP, ...). In fact, the inflected verb can be the second, third, or fourth word, depending on how many words are in the specifier of the first phrase.
>
> (*ibid.*: 164–5)

It is not quite clear what Moro is aiming at: is the V2 rule mistaken or is it just incorrectly formulated; on both counts, because the finite verb may not be the second word in the sentence? I know of no scholars in Germanic languages who hold that the V2 rule says that the verb should be the second word, so when Moro states as a 'principle of structure dependence, simplified version': 'No syntactic rule can make reference to the linear order of words' (*ibid.,* p. 168), not many would disagree. But syntacticians may have different reasons for not disagreeing. Moro maintains throughout his book that linear order is not an adequate notion in syntax – everything is about hierarchical order – while I would say that word order as such is of no interest in syntax. What matters is sentence constituent order (i.e. the order, linear or otherwise, of subject, verbal constituent, object etc., cf. Chapters 3 and 4), and the V2 'rule' points to the fact that the verbal constituent in main clauses in V2 Germanic languages is always the second sentence constituent; when we ignore conjunctions, which we usually do. In *Constituent Order in the Languages of Europe: EALT / EUROTYP 20-1* (Siewierska 1998), the V2 phenomenon is described as 'All the Germanic languages except English are V2, that is to say, in declarative main clauses the finite verb, main or auxiliary, typically appears in the second position of the clause' (*ibid.:* 78). And this may not be sufficiently accurate if we do not know what a position is, but an alternative formulation is: 'All the Germanic languages except English are V2 languages, that is to say, in declarative main clauses the finite verb is the second constituent of the clause ...' (*ibid.:* 77).

This seems to be the closest we can come to a kind of 'standard formulation' of how the V2 phenomenon works, and it is in accordance with my formulations above. The FoG is, actually, able to offer an explanation of the phenomenon, namely that the finite verb is the topological 'pivot' or the 'ground zero' in relation to which other constituents may be placed (cf. Chapters 3 and 4), while we may not know why 'the inflected verb in main clauses is always moved to the head of the first phrase of the clause'. It follows, then, that a certain vagueness emerges from Moro's account of the V2 case: the principle says that syntax is not a matter of linear order, whereas, anyhow, 'the ... verb ... is moved to ... the first phrase of the clause', and, by entailment, some other (nonlinear) kind of order directs the path of the verb to the position as head of the first phrase, and finally, by presupposition, this kind of order includes ordering of words, namely, in a hierarchy. But how can words, which always line up one after another, be known to be in hierarchical order, and how can we know that one of them, the verb, is found where it is but that this place is not where it came from, and how can we know that where it is found is the 'first' of something that we cannot see and that this 'first' is not a matter of linearity? How can we know that, especially when we do not know, if we, in each case, are talking about the word or its phrase, and when we do not understand how a word can move to another phrase and leave its 'own' phrase behind as an empty label? In this context, we only know because words are supposed to hang on the branches of stipulated two-dimensional 'trees', and, consequently if we are not too much in favour of that, we may not be too confident about the locution 'A more accurate formulation of the rule, and in fact the only correct one'. And, consequently, we may also query whether the pseudo-data used as input in the experimental linguistics tests have been put together in a way that justifies the conclusions.

This predicament seems to be an effect of the Generative Grammar habit of not offering a clear distinction between words, word categories and phrases, which, accordingly, sometimes look as if they are on the same (parallel) levels in tree diagrams and, furthermore, accepting phrases containing only one lexical item as phrases. When, finally, lexical items and phrases start to move around, more or less on their own, it is easy to confuse syntax and word order.[11]

In the larger context of contemporary linguistics it is a little strange to read (Ludlov 2011) and Moro (2008) since both may give one a feeling of being premature obituaries of Generative Grammar. Neither of them is, in my view, able to justify the idea that Generative Grammar is the supreme theory of syntax, and this opens the door to other approaches.

Epi-Formal Analysis

A theory on syntax

*Die grammatische Aufgabe der Sprache ist, theils die Art und Weise zu
bezeichnen, wie die einzelnen Vorstellungen in die Totalvorstellung von
einer Handlung oder einem Zustande, welche im Satze ausgesagt werden,
zusammengefaßt sind, theils das ganze Verhältniß und die ganze Stellung
des Satzes vor der Anshauung des Redenden als selbstständig oder als
untergeordnetes Glied einer mehr umfassenden Verbindung, als Ausdruck von
etwas Wirklischem oder bloß Gedachtem oder Gewolltem, des Gegenwärtigen
oder des Entfernten in der Zeit deutlich zu machen. Die Syntaxe der
einzelnen Sprache soll zeigen, wie diese Aufgabe in derselben gelös't ist.*
*(J. N. Madvig, 'Bemerkungen über verschiedene Puncte des Systems der
Lateinischen Sprachlehre und einige Einzelheiten derselben', in J. N. Madvig,*
Sprachteoretische Abhandlungen *[1843] 1971: 334)*

Introduction

The following preliminaries are not to be perceived as a claim that I have solved
some basic problems in philosophy, science, general research methodology – or
linguistics, for that matter. But since I am presenting some alternative ideas I
find it reasonably justified that I offer a brief account of what I think I am doing
when I set up these lines of reasoning. This will include basic assumptions about
my conception of what theoretical linguistics is and how the language sciences
work, about basic philosophical assumptions about how we understand the
world, and about how I think we should conceive of linguistic phenomena and
different kinds of languages as systems of expressions.

Syntactic theories are part of the general theories of language that are
normally dealt with in the scientific field of Theoretical Linguistics. According to
the choices made by a linguist in this field, he may emphasize one or more areas
as being prior to the understanding of language: phonetics/phonology, syntax

(grammar), semantics, pragmatics, socio-linguistics etc., and the primacy is normally more or less explicitly in line with the basic assumptions he has, more or less consciously, chosen from the fields of philosophy and the philosophy of science. Which assumptions are possible candidates is normally limited by what is considered plausible by the conceptual networks in the general tradition of linguistics and by the different schools or special traditions within the field.

The basics of a linguistic theory is in general conceived of as a number of propositions about the nature of the entity under investigation and about the procedures by means of which the linguist is able to ascertain the parts and wholes of the entity. As a scientist, one may emphasize the status of either part of the theory on the basis of one's assumptions: roughly speaking, a positivist may claim that theories are only conceptual models that we use in interacting with something we call the world, and a materialist may claim that he reveals how things really are, but no one seems to deny that, on the one hand, when one offers a theory, one always says something, and, on the other hand, when one offers a theory, one always says something about something, i.e. about (a part of) the world.

In the framework of this syntactic theory it is assumed that a scientific theory actually says something about the internal nature of the object of investigation: (1) the syntax of a language and of languages; which means that the theory is physicalistic (in a limited sense), assuming that the parts and wholes of the object are physical structures; which (2) entails that the theory is structuralistic (in a limited sense); and (3) that it is appropriate to call the procedure of investigation an analysis. Accordingly, when I call my theory a theory of syntactic analysis, I assume that the results of the analyses – provided they can be reasonably justified – are insights into the structures of the sentences of human languages.

The tradition of linguistic and syntactic analysis that forms the background of the theory proposed in the following is that of what I, in Chapter 1, call the Classical Danish Tradition in Grammatical Analysis, and the major twentieth-century contributors to the conceptual framework of this special scientific notion of language were Jespersen, Brøndal, Hjelmslev and Diderichsen. From this tradition I extract some ideas and principles while abandoning some others. Those which I accept I formulate as a number of theoretical concepts, a syntactic theory and a theoretical model. When doing so, I make use of some basic concepts – as mentioned above – and, while in the scientific fields of theoretical linguistics and Scandinavian languages (of which Danish and Swedish will provide me with the data used to exemplify my analyses) it is neither a necessary nor an appropriate common practice to offer extensive and detailed analyses of philosophical notions, in this context, it has some implications for the formulation of the theory that some basic concepts are briefly clarified and this will be done in the following. The fundamental issues can be taken to be answers to two questions:[1]

- What is a Language?
- What are Things in the World?

First, one basic problem in the language sciences is the fact there is no satisfactory definition of what a language is (as is the state of affairs with a number of other terms in theoretical linguistics). This is at odds with the frequency with which the generic term 'language' is used in order to explain other human phenomena. The problem is not easily solved but some unorthodox considerations may cast light on how it might be handled in a more transparent way.

To a certain extent I am, as mentioned in Chapter 2, in favour of the basic Chomskyan assumption that linguistic phenomena are 'internal affairs', i.e. mental structures processed by the neuronal systems of the brain and the rest of the neuronal systems of human beings (cf. Chapter 5, Conclusions and Perspectives). For some, this has led to the view that this is the whole story, more or less explicitly suggesting a Cartesian dualism in the solipsistic version where all you can know of is your own self and your language, i.e. extreme internalism. My view is that there is a difference between what is in the mind,[2] namely, internal processes that can interpret the sounds and glyphs outside the mind as linguistic phenomena, and, on the other hand, the fact that humans interact externally – but intimately – with each other and with the non-human part of the world, and do so extensively using internal linguistic tools.

So, I would like to (1) reject the (Kant-inspired) notion of 'language as such' (on 'Dinge an sich' see Kant [1781] 1925: 925–6), and (2) propose a more amalgamating idea, saying that languages are inherently in the heads of people but that these languages are fairly much alike (since otherwise no communication would take place), and furthermore that languages are essential in every kind of human activity, much in the vein of the biocognitive view put forward by, among others, Alexander Kravchenko (cf. Kravchenko 2010). I do not aim at reconciling viewpoints that do not conform to each other; rather I would like to see my theoretical efforts as unification by modification of basic notions.

So, second, what are Things in the World? I shall not question the nature of our daily experiences as human beings living in a physical world, but it is a common experience that if one contemplates too seriously what physical things really are, then there seem to be no good answers. So, as a point of departure, I shall suggest a number of basic notions that can be used when talking about these things.

The so-called physical world is, in my view, basically energy, and what is called matter is just a kind of especially inhomogeneous energy (in the form of more or less identified particles). Accordingly my foundational theoretical notion is a version of PHILOSOPHICAL PHYSICALISM[3] and it implies that everything can, in principle, be described in the scientific field of physics, or at least that all sciences could, in the end, conceivably be unified under the epithet 'physics' in some way or other.[4] In this context I assume a philosophical position that may be called epistemological physicalism, which claims that everything that is within the domain of possible knowledge is physical, and possibly can be described by a physical theory of some kind. What is beyond possible knowledge (what is ultimately transcendent; for the notions *transzendent* 'transcendent' and *transzendental* 'transcendental', see Kant [1781] 1925: 979–81), for instance, the traditional questions about the existence of God and of human souls (questions which, by no means, are easy to answer), is, according to this kind of philosophy, not relevant for physicalistic theories. It is obvious that the boundary between possible and impossible knowledge is, to a certain extent, not fixed but flexible – in that possible knowledge may be actual knowledge or potential knowledge – and that minor parts from the realm of current impossible knowledge may, step by step, be integrated into the realm of possible knowledge[5] – and it is, furthermore, obvious that this philosophical point of view is dualistic in that it makes a distinction between the different kinds of entities that may be known or not known to exist. But it is an epistemological[6] – and not an ontological (Cartesian) – dualism, i.e. the distinction is not established on the basis of assumptions about different forms of existence but rather on the basis of what we may assume we can know. Consequently the universe is conceived of as being the physics that lies within the scope of possible knowledge.[7]

Since I conceive of parts of the physical world as somehow ordered (even though it can be said to be inhomogeneous energy), I would like to use the term STRUCTURE denoting both solid matter and the more fluid and gas-like substances, and accordingly STRUCTURALISM is understood as an ontological doctrine, and, furthermore, as a specific philosophical taxonomy (or *TAXIOLOGY[8] since it is a conceptual structure) accounting for the more detailed construction of the parts of the universe. In linguistics, it may take the specific form of modern Linguistic Structuralism, the initiators of which were, according to the tradition, Ferdinand de Saussure (European Structuralism) and Leonard Bloomfield (American Structuralism), cf. Götzsche (2009: 'Structuralism'). When used in the first sense, the term structuralism can be combined with physicalism thereby laying the basis for the overall notion of PHYSICAL STRUCTURALISM, and as such it can be elaborated on, and then be the basis of the assumption, that the universe is to be conceived of by means of four METAPHYSICAL concepts:[9] ENTITIES with PROPERTIES in DIVERSITY and PLURALITY; and an ontological taxiology, saying that in the universe the entities are ELEMENTS, RELATIONS and PROCESSES. Elements, relations and processes build STRUCTURES (the properties of which are QUALITIES) appearing in certain MAGNITUDES (IN which the plurality of entities is QUANTITIES) and MULTITUDES (OF which the plurality of entities is QUANTITIES), and structures may consist of infra-structures and may create supra-structures, and in this way form a kind of Aristotelian level-ontology. In certain contexts, where more mechanical processes are mentioned, it may be convenient to use the term 'system' as a synonym for structure, and I will do that in the following.

This fairly straightforward and consistent (but brief) clarification of the basic notion of physicalistic structuralism has essential consequences for the elaboration of the theory on languages in what follows.

So, in my view, syntax is not an inherent property of linguistic expressions (and, for that matter, nor is semantics or pragmatics) but a general way of uttering (GENERATING) and understanding (INTERPRETING) them. Accordingly, the linguistic study of syntactic structures and their semantic and pragmatic functions is the study of how human beings utter and understand the linguistic expressions in a systematic way and a study of which intrinsic properties of the expressions are used for which purposes. The parts of these linguistic functions can be studied in general or in special cases, for instance, as phonetic features or the phonematic systems of specific languages, or as lists of words, either according to what they normally refer to or as grammatical recordings of morphology and word order, or in connection with the meaning we may attach to the words and sentences we interpret. But to me it seems quite difficult to establish a basis for assessment in these areas without testing the features in syntactic functions, and thus I wish to claim that syntax is central to a scientific understanding of languages and consequently to linguistics.[10] It is assumed, then, that the term 'syntax' denotes both the syntactic structures of natural languages and the concepts, theories and methods that describe and explain them. The boundaries of syntax in both senses are set up by what can be accounted for as a systematic use, i.e. usage, of a natural language. One may perceive of a language as being a huge amount of conventional or possible meanings conveyed by a number of more or less fixed expressions, but it is not until commodities from this box of potential tools are organized, by a language user, in a singular systematic statement (which may be connected with other statements), that a language can be said to function as an effect of the way it is used and understood, and thereby utilizing, re-establishing and recreating the language itself as a mental structure. A statement (by some called a proposition, cf. below) is expressed in what we normally call a sentence in a language, and, as is generally taken for granted, it is not quite easy to define and identify this entity, which is the object of investigation in syntax, but provided one accepts the theoretical outlines so far, it is unavoidable, and a definition will be offered below.

The syntactic theory presented in this book deals with the syntax of natural languages, and there is, as mentioned in Chapter 2, a problem in distinguishing NATURAL LANGUAGES from other languages. If we assume that the term 'language' denotes only what is communicated by verbal expressions and does not include other kinds of semiotic communication, then, to me, it seems plausible to make a clear distinction between the natural verbal (oral and written) languages and the artificial languages that are created by means of natural languages. In late twentieth century there were many such artificial languages on the market – for different purposes – and there still are, so the distinction is essential when isolating data, but it is evident that it is hard to determine exactly where the dividing line between the two types of language can be found. Many artificial languages are formal languages, and, for instance, the abstract and symbolic language of mathematics is clearly an artificial language, but, in all likelihood, it has, somehow, emerged out of the systems of numerals of different languages, and since numeral systems are in certain respects formal systems – and have presumably been created from the expressions of natural languages according to certain procedures and insights (cf. Hurford 1987; Chrisomalis 2010) – they could be claimed to be artificial languages. But on the other hand they form an integral part of natural languages and are used to solve everyday problems, so it would be inadequate to classify them as genuinely artificial. Therefore, I would like to extend this definition and furnish it with an additional number of criteria: an ARTIFICIAL LANGUAGE is a language which (1) is created out of a natural language; which (2) serves a specific purpose according to the demands of a specific group of people; and which (3) is systematic and discrete in such a way that one is able to clearly identify and demarcate its expressions and their combinations. Since, at the outset, I wanted to propose that the term 'structure' should be used about natural structures and the term 'system' about artificial structures, then I would prefer to use the term 'language-systems' about artificial languages, but I have, for practical reasons, now abandoned this distinction, and I shall henceforth use both of the terms NATURAL SYSTEMS and ARTIFICIAL SYSTEMS. However, the distinction between language-structures and language-systems is theoretically essential when specifying the demands on a syntactic theory (cf. the quote from Hinzen 2006 in Chapter 2), and the problem will be further reflected on below in connection with the relation between natural and formal sentences.

If syntax is the structures formed by the use and understanding of linguistic expressions, then the task of syntactic analysis is the description and explanation of these syntactic structures. In the modern tradition, for instance, in the Danish tradition of linguistics, two principles in linguistic analysis are opposed to each other, and either one of them can be chosen depending on which purpose has the highest priority in the investigation: the descriptive approach and the formal approach; or DESCRIPTIVISM VS. FORMALISM (cf. Stuurman 1996). If we emphasize the finding and recording of all relevant data, then it is fairly hard to avoid using *ad hoc* descriptions, which may be hard to adjust to the overall theoretical framework or even may be inconsistent with it; if, on the other hand, our main purpose is to explain the linguistic structures found, we may feel a strong urge to formalise our theoretical language and concepts to avoid inconsistencies. It is therefore hardly surprising that historical and national-language (mother tongue) linguistics (in the traditions of Philology) has mostly followed the descriptive path, nor that general and theoretical linguistics has developed ever more sophisticated formal models.

It follows, then, that, in my view, the linguist's primary concern should be the THEORETICAL (i.e. formal vs. descriptive), positions of certain conceptual models in linguistics, and I shall not comment here on what seems to be TRADITIONS (like the 'formalist orientation' or the 'functionalist orientation', cf. Newmeyer 1998, p. 7, or like Functional Grammar, Transformational Grammar and Generative Semantics, cf. Koerner and Asher 1995: 290–5, 326–48) in linguistics. These I shall hand over to the history of science.

The epi-formal theory and method: a parsimonious approach

In the previous account, the notion of formal systems has been briefly discussed. But for the sake of clarification and consistency – and because I will use a formal system for the specific purpose of describing and explaining certain linguistic phenomena – I will now offer a few basic assumptions concerning that issue. According to Bostock (1979), the general use of a formalism can be said to be the following practice, especially elegantly expressed by him:

> According to the usual formalism, we begin with a set of uninterpreted axioms and rules, and we find that the resulting set of derivable uninterpreted formulae can be given some useful applications. The only reason that can be advanced for beginning with one set of axioms and rules rather than another is that the resulting system is aesthetically satisfying and proves to have more useful applications than its rivals.
>
> (Bostock 1979: 296)

In that case, there are not many impediments to the construction of a formal system, and only the demonstration of adequacy in a number of empirical applications will justify the claim that a system is an adequate description of an object. But what is meant by 'aesthetically satisfying' is presumably that the formal system (formalism or calculus) has to satisfy a number of requirements to the extent they are attainable: (1) the system is consistent, i.e. it contains no contradictions; (2) the axioms are mutually independent; (3) the system is complete; and (4) the system is effective, i.e. it can be determined whether a formula belongs to the system or not.[11]

I will, in the following, try to live up to these requirements, and the reason is, of course, that the aim of such an enterprise is to underpin the relevancy and the adequacy of my formal approach, but the question arises to what extent it is necessary to produce a formal system. The topic 'Formal Rigor' is discussed by Ludlov (2011: 162–70), and his general view is that 'The moral is that one often has a theory that is rigorous enough to allow use of the theory for problem solving' (p. 268), and that the ambition of making the formal rigour live up to mathematical standards may not be appropriate:

> In the first place, mathematical frameworks, if available, need not be paradigms of formal integrity and do not guarantee clarity of exposition. Second, developing sciences will often expand too fast for the development of a mathematical framework to be possible.
>
> (*ibid.*: 167)

And he also says that 'In point of fact, there has never been a science in which all the consequences of a theory could be effectively determined' (*ibid.*: 164).[12] Consequently, the ambition of implementing my formal system in a software system, thereby requiring mathematical proof, in order to demonstrate its formal consistency will belong to the future.

As for the requirements mentioned above, I am not the one to dispute whether such demands can (or should) be applied to specific formalisms, and I will not comment on the questions raised by – and the discussions on substance and nomenclature between – specialists in the field, but for the sake of coherence between the different parts of the theory offered in the following I will present some definitions clarifying the use of the notion of a formal system in this specific context.

The general kinds of use of the notion 'formal systems' (of which in this context the expression 'formalism' will be used as a synonym) are, by all means, not always in harmony. If you check some standard reference books, for instance, *Chambers Dictionary of Science and Technology* and, in a more technical context, *Dictionary of Computing* (DoC), you find that the expression *system* is, in general, used as a synonym for *structure*, that the expression *language* in the entry 'language' is referred to in this way (DoC 1996: 268): '*See* programming languages, specification language, formal language', i.e. only, so to speak, electronic 'languages' are taken into account and the notion 'formal' is used only in specific contexts in a rather broad meaning. A standard work of reference in philosophy like *The Oxford Companion to Philosophy* opens the door to natural languages in that a 'formal language' is assumed to have at least two features: 'symbols' and 'rules', but then we are left with the tricky problem that we may not know what 'symbols' and 'rules' are, and in a typical philosophical fashion we are offered wide-ranging discussions about the different views on these theoretical concepts. In *The MIT Encyclopedia of the Cognitive Sciences* we are told that a 'formal system' must live up to 'sharper criteria' (1999: 322) than the prerequisites of 'the axiomatic-deductive method' (*ibid.*), namely the requirement of 'proof' (*ibid.*) – a concept that is not explained in that context. If one wonders why I have to seek recourse to dictionaries and reference works the answer may be another question:

> What does it mean to say that logic is formal? The short answer is: it means (or can mean) several different things. Given the crucial importance of the notion of the formal in current discussions in logic, philosophy and mathematics (among other fields), it is surprising to note that the literature specifically on this concept is very scarce, if not to say virtually non-existent.
>
> (Novaes 2011: 303)

So, it looks as if we only know for certain what these mental instruments are when we are asked to handle them in specific contexts and situations, in general in order to solve contingent, more or less technical, problems; which are usually taken up in scientific articles and monographs. Since I want to present a new formal system in the following – and since I do not want to fall victim to the methodological fallacy of Hjelmslev in not distinguishing clearly between the theory and the object of investigation – I feel an obligation to clarify what a formal system is in this context.

The basic premise is the assumption stated above that there is a difference between natural and artificial languages. According to this assumption I will make a distinction between, on the one hand, LOGIC as a natural language feature, i.e. a natural language semantics accounting for relations between concepts and statements (cf. below on sentences, statements and propositions), and, on the other hand, FORMAL LOGIC as a formal (artificial) language feature, i.e. a formal language semantics accounting for relations between formal concepts and propositions (cf. below on propositions, terms, formulae and algorithms). A FORMAL LANGUAGE belongs to one subset of (artificial) FORMAL SYSTEMS (a set of characters and rules for their combinations) in that the other subset is what I would rather call TECHNICAL SYSTEMS specifically operating (handling and controlling) the OPERATIONS of mechanisms and machines. So-called 'programming languages' belong to the latter set because – to the extent I understand something of what goes on in an electronic computational system – these kinds of 'languages' are sets of 'instructions' (also a kind of figurative speech) to machine code out of which can be made sequences of such 'instructions' making electrons behave in certain ways in the circuits; in the end, either causing things to happen in mechanical systems (machines) or turning on and off dots on screens, which can, in due course, be interpreted by humans as media of information. As is well known, expressions from grammar and linguistics have diffused into the jargon of programmers and some also talk about programming languages as 'descriptions' of the electronic systems and of the 'grammars' of programming languages. Such expressions are useful metaphors but the habit may lead to the (maybe unfortunate) idea that formal languages used for describing natural languages are of the same nature, and furthermore that the mental ability of humans to use language may be a computational system run by the brain. Whether this is so, we do not know so far.

A formalised language may be formal to a certain degree (it may be partly formal like technical nomenclatures and terminologies), and a special kind of formalised language is, then, a FORMAL LANGUAGE, which can be defined as: a formal system, developed and elaborated for a specific descriptive and explanatory purpose, i.e. there are expressions – made of (combinations of) characters – that can be used to refer to something. In terms of formal logic, it is composed as a set of axioms, a set of deductive rules, and a set of theorems. The use of a formal language for making theorems for empirical applications (whether these are mathematical models or syntactic constructions) is often called a CALCULUS, and I shall use that term in the following.

Of course, one may ask what justifies the use of formal systems in the investigation of syntax, and, if languages are different all over the world, is it then possible, necessary or even plausible to apply formal theories to languages? The answer may be that it is a basic theoretical assumption in the present context that syntax is a global entity (a property of all human languages, i.e. as mental systems) with global features, that universal claims can be made about it, and that local syntactic phenomena are generated by a fairly limited number of variational factors. If this is true, then different syntactic structures are simple systems that can be described and explained by means of simple theories. Such simple systems are different from complex systems, i.e. systems built of structures incorporating a large number of qualities and large-scale quantities. Complex systems (such as historical events or climatic states and events) require broad explanations involving concepts about tendencies, influences, probabilities, mathematical calculations, etc. A theory about simple systems offers the best kind of explanation if it is formal – because of the characteristics of a formal system – and accordingly it is at least plausible to apply formal systems to syntactic structures and constructions.[13]

Since I want a close connection between the descriptions and the explanations, I do not want the formalism to be completely arbitrary, and therefore I also propose a special kind of formalism with a number of special constraints: (1) the formalism expressing a set of concepts has a limited extension; (2) it has, as a set of concepts, a limited intensional value; and (3) at least one of the expressions has a specified categorial semantics. A formalism of this kind I shall call an EPI-FORMAL SYSTEM (EFS). The first criterion implies that it can, so far, only refer to a limited number of objects in the world, in this case, the phenomena of a language or a number of languages. Criterion number two implies that it can only be applied to certain kinds of objects; in this case, the syntactic structures of a language or a number of languages. And the last criterion implies that one or more of the expressions of the formalism have no arbitrary categorial function but a specified one. The empirical application of an epi-formal system I shall call EPI-FORMAL ANALYSIS (EFA), and the general methodology of an EFA is the basic assumption that it may be convenient to delineate the general meaning of the formalism before deciding on its expressions and rules. The meaning of a formalism in scientific description and explanation can be said to be that of an accurate conceptual liaison between our basic assumptions about the part of the world that we investigate and our actual investigation of this part of the world. I assume that when we start an investigation we make clear what kinds of basic assumptions we make, clarified in a number of basic theoretical concepts, as well as formulating some empirical generalizations from basic and preliminary observations of the object. This procedure is carried out in a kind of dialectic process in which neither part can be ignored.[14] As for syntactic analysis I assume that some of the basic concepts have to be taken from the discipline of pragmatics and that they should reflect syntactic functional categories. I furthermore assume that if these concepts can be adequately specific and distinct, and thus made fairly accurate, they can serve as a formal vocabulary (an EPI-FORMAL one), and that they can provide me with the preliminary formulations about the potential for combinations of the expressions of the vocabulary. If this works fairly well, a set of symbols and a set of rules for their combination (implying development of derivational symbols and operator symbols) can be established, and these can be used to make general or even universal claims about the object. In this case, when we are dealing with syntax, the claims actually are universal or general propositions about syntax, but they do not, for the moment, assert that such structures exist, not even potentially as some kind of abstract entities; only that the concepts can be used in analysis. Nor do universal claims imply that some entity exists that may be called 'language as such', a claim that I reject. Whether it is reasonable to claim that global structures exist is, first, a matter of whether the language functions of most or many people can be said to be sufficiently much alike and, second, it is a matter of empirical applications to data from a large number of languages. The general or universal claims will function as the basis of theoretical instantiations in the form of special claims, which have to meet the empirical generalizations made on the basis of observations of data, and this is what may be called the procedure of analytic interpretation. The procedure includes the steps of (1) the theoretical application of the formal system to the empirical generalizations, and (2) the empirical application to structural descriptions of specific sentences (i.e. data), which, in turn, are the basis of empirical generalizations. If we make the applications to syntax, we may, for instance, demonstrate the nature of the specific syntactic structures of some of the Scandinavian languages, in this case, Danish and Swedish, or those of dialects of these languages, depending on what level of generalization we choose and provided our descriptive generalizations are adequate.

This epi-formal approach has been created, developed and elaborated as an attempt to eliminate the assumed contrast in the language sciences between, on the one hand, explanatory and formal methods and, on the other hand, descriptive methods. The principles are by themselves not peculiar – they probably form the background of much scientific work – and to the extent I deviate from the general pattern, I only do so in accepting the consequences of the principles and applying them to the formal system.

A pragmatically based theory of syntax: syntax in use

To use pragmatic notions in the construction of formal analytical terms in syntax is, indeed, no new idea, and in the social context of formalists when doing so I run the risk of becoming a theoretical dissident.[15] In order to escape this embarrassment I will follow another path than just claiming that languages are social constructs and then setting out doing fieldwork in socio-linguistic settings. Instead I will pick up the ideas proposed in the 1970s by Lorenzen and Schwemmer (1975),[16] which is an approach they call 'constructive' because of the overall aim to build a 'constructive ortho-language': 'Die konstruktiv aufgebaute Sprache soll "Orthosprache" heißen' (*ibid.*: 24).

The wider perspective of the Lorenzen and Schwemmer approach was not to propose analytical linguistic concepts but to create an artificial language that could be used in communication between scientists to the effect that their results might be more easily transferred and evaluated against each other; an ideal that Lorenzen and Schwemmer seemed to share with, among others, David Bohm (cf. Bohm 1996). Technically it is, of course, easier to check the truth-value and the empirical implications of scientific assertions if one knows what people are talking about. Thus the particularly interesting aspect of Lorenzen and Schwemmer's idea in a contemporary context is not whether or not it can be used in the investigation of natural languages but that it is based on a pragmatic notion about how dialogues can be used in situations: '[M]uß man ausgehen von Situationen, in denen lediglich empragmatisch geredet wird, d.h. in denen Reden mit nichtsprachlichen Handlungen "verbunden" werden' (Lorenzen and Schwemmer 1975: 29).

So, by connecting linguistic expressions and 'non-linguistic' interactions, two or more people can negotiate about the exact meaning of the expressions and by stipulations extend the linguistic apparatus in an accurate way. The result is a clearly discernible number of classes of expressions labelled with the traditional term 'word': 'Nennen wir nun alle sprachlichen Unterscheidungen Wörter' (p. 55), and the classes contain the three main classes: 'Eigennamen', 'Prädikatoren', 'Partikel' (*ibid.*), of which the class of predicates contains a number of sub-classes. The functions of the particles have been generalized so that they resemble the operators of formal logic, and when, next, the classes are represented by symbols, it becomes evident that what has been created is a formal language (and on the basis of how it is constructed I might call it an epi-formal system). The difference from standard developments of formal systems is that Lorenzen and Schwemmer explicitly acknowledge that there are people and situations involved, and that they do not assume an intuitive interpretation of the semantics of propositions as a point of departure, and that, furthermore, they avoid the intricacy following from, in the tradition, the fairly insoluble problem: which comes first, meaning or truth? What is relevant for a pragmatic approach in the 'constructive' framework is the fact that linguistic expressions are connected to human acts, but this basic insight is not sufficient to create a theory of how people use language for communication (and cognition) in a society. To do so, a philosophy of language will have to offer basic assumptions or knowledge about human societies (a social theory), about the general function of languages in societies (a pragmatic theory of the linguistic sign), and about the structure of linguistic entities (a theory of the structural linguistic functions of pragmatics and semantics and a theory of the structural linguistic functions of syntax). These far-reaching societal and social aspects of languages and language use will not be taken up here. Instead the account will focus on the technical details of human communicative interactions and cognitive actions with special emphasis on syntax.

The first issue to be taken up is the question of the linguistic sign as a pragmatic entity. The founder of the modern European version of semiology was Ferdinand de Saussure (cf. Harris 2003). I will not go into the details of his ideas, neither on the results of his research in linguistics. I only want to pick up the overall idea of languages and other media as 'systems of signs', implying that these systems can be studied by a science called 'sémiologie' (de Saussure 1916: 33), and the specific notion of 'le signe linguistique' (*ibid.*: 99).

Thus, I would like to suggest a special notion of the linguistic sign, and, since for the general science of the signs of human communication I prefer the term 'semiotics',[17] accordingly, the following is a rudimentary framework of a semiotics of languages. In de Saussure's conception the sign was a two-sided phenomenon, divided into '*Concept*' and '*Image acoustique*', and this entity is regarded as an entirely mental one: 'une entité psychique' (p. 99); its external relations are not directly considered. Instead I wish to propose a tripartite linguistic sign: expression, explication and content, where the expression resembles the Saussurian '*Image acoustique*' and the explication resembles de Saussure's '*Concept*'. The notion of the Saussurian linguistic sign is, of course, that of a single concept connected with a single acoustic (basically auditory) image, but since a theory of language developed from a social and pragmatic framework cannot identify concepts and single sound images before they have been externally defined, I only wish to make the following assumptions: that the linguistic sign has linguistic EXPRESSIONS; that it has some 'meaning' somehow attached to them; and that it has some implications about how the 'meaning' is organized (the EXPLICATION) and how it has been generated and should be interpreted (the CONTENT). If we extend this framework and say that a linguistic sign related to other linguistic signs establishes UTTERANCES in discourse utilizing the structures of a language, and furthermore say that the parts of a linguistic sign as an utterance correspond to structural parts in the actual language – and, since the theory claims to be universal, the parts of any language – then I am able to propose a primitive and preliminary model of our object of investigation.

The linguistic sign

Note: because this is a model all the letters of the words and terms are in the lower case.

linguistic material structures (media): sounds and writings

|

MEDIUM ASSIGNMENT: the mental and material processes of producing (creating or utilizing) articulation and writing

|

mental images from perception (representations) and cognition

(discourse:	structures:	constructions:	
utterance	language	sign	minimal sign)
expression(s)	form (gramma-*)	style	sentence (of
			constituents)

|**

explication(s)　　sense[18] (sema-*)　　　logic　　　statement (of
concepts)

|**

content(s)　　meaning (pragma-*)　　information　　stratification (of
configurations)

mental images from perception (representations) and cognition

|

OBJECT ASSIGNMENT: the processes of activating (creating or retrieving) one or more concepts (of mental objects or (as mental representations of) material objects) – so that they are part of the conscious mental universe – connected (as reference) with related interactions with the world

|

material structures: the world

Notes: ** mental structures of SIGNIFICATION
* structures.

It should be observed that this model distinguishes between MENTAL and MATERIAL entities and properties, and this is a distinction different from the one between, on the one hand, physical entities, properties, etc. (those within the limits of possible knowledge) and, on the other hand, metaphysical entities, properties, etc. (those beyond the limits of actual knowledge but within possible knowledge); accordingly both mental and material entities and properties are considered physical. The assumptions and the line of reasoning that this model is based on are as follows.

I totally agree with de Saussure (1916) that the linguistic sign is 'une entité psychique' (p. 99), but I prefer the modern notion of 'mental entity'. Since I also want to, moderately, adjust this notion to the Chomskyan theoretical concept of a language faculty, and to my basic claim that these mental functions have to be seen as part of the total anthropological functions (cf. Chapter 2 on Chomsky), I will propose a notion of the linguistic sign as a kind of road map of the mental linguistic functions used in discourse and thinking. This has no implications for imaginable theories on the origin of language – a topic on which I will make no comment – but I find it hard to deny that one of the essential functions of language is human communication and cognition, i.e. as a means in discourse and thinking. I consider it evident that a linguistic sign (or 'specimens' of it) produced in discourse or thinking is located in the mental universes of all the individuals taking part in the discourse, or of the thoughtful individual.

A linguistic sign produced on a certain location, at a certain time, and by a certain person can be called an UTTERANCE. Whether discourse includes 'mute' utterances, 'talking to oneself', or 'the language of thinking' (cf. Dummett 1993: 166–87) is not directly relevant to the notions in this model, but my remarks above indicate that I believe that thinking is a kind of talking to or with oneself. The difference between de Saussure's theory and my model is that my model of the linguistic sign is tripartite and not mono-expression (word) based: I assume that an utterance has more than one EXPRESSION,[19] has an EXPLICATION, and has a CONTENT, and that the structures of expression(s), explications(s), and content(s) are FORM, SENSE, and MEANING respectively. The structures of a linguistic sign are constructions established in accordance with the general structures of the language in which the utterance is produced, and the terms 'form', 'sense' and 'meaning' denote both universal structures of all languages, general structures of a specific language, and the constructions of linguistic signs. In order to narrow down this theoretical framework to focus on syntax I want to make a crucial distinction between the linguistic sign in general and the special minimal linguistic sign: the structures (i.e. constructions) of the expression(s), explication, and content of a linguistic sign are STYLE, LOGIC, and INFORMATION respectively; and the structures of expression(s), explication, and content of a MINIMAL LINGUISTIC SIGN are SENTENCE, STATEMENT, and STRATI-FICATION respectively.

The connection (or 'interface') between this mental entity and the material entities of the world is – presumably – established by what I will label ASSIGNMENT, handled, more or less, by what Chomsky calls performance systems. One kind of assignment, MEDIUM ASSIGNMENT, takes care of the materializations and perceptions of the expressions through articulation of sounds or writing of graphic representations and the processes of perceiving these expressions, and the other kind of assignment (OBJECT ASSIGNMENT) takes care of the, mainly manual, interaction with other people and natural objects.

A special kind of function in this, so far semi-theoretical model, is 'reference' (cf. Higginbotham 2001), and in general reference is characterized as the act of 'picking out' an object (or a number of related objects) by the use of one or more expressions. It is seldom spelled out what is meant by 'picking out', and within the framework of my theory I will propose that reference is seen as object assignment of a material object (a number of related objects), and the detailed specification of the notion is offered below. In addition, it may be plausible to make a distinction between REFERRING (the object assignment of material objects from common or shared experience), MENTIONING (the object assignment of mental objects), and INDICATING (the object assignment of material objects in the local perceivable environment in a situation (a setting)).

In the model introduced above, the third (the 'lowest') 'level' of (the actual and any) language, which is called meaning, functions as the link between the form and the sense of languages, on the one hand, and the non-linguistic objects of the world, on the other hand, but there is no indication of the way in which the parts are interrelated in the mental faculty. On the basis of the ontological contemplations above, I shall, for the moment, confine myself to claiming that there are structural relations between them and that each 'level' is also a more or less independent structure, and I shall confine myself to proposing the assumption that the 'lower levels' determine (i.e. establish the necessary but not sufficient conditions for) the 'upper levels'. The structural relation between these 'levels' of language and the linguistic sign I shall call SIGNIFICATION.[20]

In a more technical way we can say that (1) the EXPRESSIONS of a linguistic sign are constructed by means of the grammatical structure which is the FORM of the particular language; (2) the EXPLICATION is constructed by means of the semantic structure which is the SENSE of the that language; and (3) the CONTENT is constructed by means of the pragmatic structure which is the MEANING[21] of the language. REFERENCE, then, is the relation (mediated by interaction[22] with the world) between, on the one hand, the mental linguistic structures and, on the other, the non-linguistic objects of the world (normally called REFERENTS) referred to by linguistic signs. And ASSIGNMENT can be said to be, on the one hand, the act of material PRODUCTION of an organized linguistic medium (MEDIUM ASSIGNMENT), and, on the other, the human acts manipulating objects (OBJECT ASSIGNMENT) which give meaning to linguistic signs. The structuralistic principles do not imply that language structures are seen as autonomous, self-sustained entities, nor do they imply a kind of 'container view of meaning' (Moore and Carling 1982: 150) assuming that meaning is an inherent property of words or language. They only imply the assumption that we have to use these mental structures when we use and understand linguistic communication. Nor has anything been said about the definition of what a language is and which groups of people different languages belong to. This universal model only implies that it is possible to offer universal, particular, and singular claims about linguistic structures.

By saying that there exist pragmatic mental structures, by claiming that they constitute (by structural determination) the linguistic sign, and by identifying them with the meanings of languages, this theoretical model offers a special answer to the traditional problem in philosophy and linguistics, namely, the universal problem of linguistic meaning.[23] I do not wish to go into details about this. The only purpose of my remarks is to point to the fact that the semantic model has been extended with, on the one hand, a pragmatic link connecting mind, perception and cognition, and, on the other, with a dynamic, social dimension (interaction), emphasizing the purpose of the mental functions of meaning.

The crucial point here is the theoretical concept of the pragmatic 'level' in linguistic theory and as an object of investigation. As outlined above the (mental) pragmatic structure is, in my view, the foundation of the mental liaison between the material linguistic and non-linguistic phenomena, or we may say that the mental pragmatic structure creates, so to speak, the inter-section of the mental linguistic and non-linguistic structures.[24] The specific way this is established is the one described by Lorenzen and Schwemmer (1975) as quoted above, i.e. in settings by linking expressions and objects through human acts. The co-occurrence of saying something and doing something – and, of course, listening to other people – is presumably the way children learn to understand and use a language, but because human beings have the mental capacity of linguistic meaning to store (in memory) both images of acts (manipulating objects) and expressional images, then acts can still be the basis of meaning without being continuously iterated. I therefore want to define the MEANING (as pragma-structures) of a language as: the mental representation of the human acts (in the material environment) which give sense to the form of that language;[25] and accordingly the CONTENT of specific linguistic expres-sions can be defined as: the mental representation of the human acts (etc.) that makes an explication of the expressions. To illustrate the point of view we may consider the sentence (for the time being in a non-technical sense, as a series of concepts):

PETER HAS TRAINED THE DOG,

and, whoever Peter is and whichever the dog is, one refers to an act of some kind that is described by the sentence, whatever the ontological status of the act is. The only way some sense can be ascribed to the words of the sentence is through the meaning which is the mental representation of the act in which the entities mentioned by the words are involved. The actual co-existence of, or the direct relation between, sentence and act is, as is well known, not necessary; only that their interrelation is mentally established. The same thing can be said about sentences like 'the salami is on the table', 'the moon orbits the Earth', but it should be emphasized that according to my theory there always has to be some kind of act[26] that gives meaning to any kind of linguistic expression.[27] Thus, in the first sentence it is expressed that somebody puts the salami (a product manufactured by human beings and an object for eating) on the table (a human product), and if some people have never observed the moon and have never read or listened to an explanation of the motion of this celestial body they will confer no meaning (and very little sense) to the second sentence. The actual material existence of the act is not a necessary prerequisite because it may be fictional, but in that case it must be possible to have a conception of the act and its objects[28] based on real actions, which thereby indirectly function as the content or the meaning of some expression or a language. If we accept this theoretical framework, it may seem plausible to trace the mental structural relation from (the mental representation of) act as meaning, content and pragmatic structures to the founding elements of sentences.

So far Lorenzen and Schwemmer's idea works well, but there are two limitations to their principles in relation to natural languages: first, their aim was to construct a new artificial language, and it can hardly be assumed that this is what we do when we learn and use natural languages; and, second, they had no explicit notion of the structure of social situations (settings) but only an abstract idea about an uncontroversial dialogue between interlocutors with convergent interests.

In settings where people use natural linguistic communication (linguistic signs) it can be assumed: (1) that a specific and limited linguistic sign is produced by one of the interlocutors; (2) that the interlocutor has a linguistic and social background and experiences about the world which are represented in his mental universe (his pragmatic footing and basis); (3) that this is used when he expresses himself linguistically, thereby invoking a universe of discourse[29] (connected with the linguistic sign) that he wants to share with the interlocutors; and (4) that he presumes the same things about them. If, then, we furnish our theory about language use in settings with basic social notions from the fields of philosophical anthropology and sociology and then specify what can reasonably be assumed to be universal social relations concerning society, organizations, institutions and situations (settings), and, furthermore, we specify the social functions of a language as part of the overall social structures, then we have at least the basic prerequisites for a theoretical model of PRAGMATIC UNIVERSALS. If, according to this background, we want to say something about the linguistic structures of syntax or the linguistic structures of semantics and pragmatics, then we have to specify the relevant connections between the general pragmatic use of a language and the linguistic expressions.

This can be done on the basis of the generally accepted basic assumption, presupposed in the tradition of linguistics, that the expressions of a language, somehow, form ordered combinations of units, the purpose of which is also to tell the interlocutors how the information conveyed by the actual linguistic expressions is organized. One may suggest a stronger formulation of this insight: the way in which the syntactic structures of the sentences of a language are manifested in expressions is used (almost entirely) as different kinds of linguistic information in oral and written communication and cognition; and this implies that there is (and that it is possible to find) a structural relation between the pragmatic structures of linguistic communication and the specific form of sentences and expressions.[30]

The path between the pragmatic structures of linguistic communication and the specific form of sentences and expressions can be found on the basis of the idea presented above, namely, that there are certain limits to how small a linguistic sign can be, and that there are certain differences in the way the units of a small linguistic sign function. Accordingly we may define a SENTENCE as: the form of the smallest, most limited, linguistic sign;[31] and we may say that one of the units of any sentence functions as a kind of juncture[32] in the interpretation of it. It is furthermore supposed that the status of a unit as such a point of departure is conferred by the person who utters the sentence and that this is signified in some way, and if we assume that the person who utters the sentence expresses a number of concepts from his mental universe, one of which is appointed the most important, then we may say that this, kind of, anchoring concept is the subject[33] of his utterance, and that the subject together with the concepts connected with it make up a conceptual structure that can be called a statement.[34] In this view a sentence is not only the form of a minimal linguistic sign but also an expression of a statement functioning as a structure of concepts, and when specific concepts are expressed in certain linguistic expressions, they can be called (sentence) constituents. What establishes the constituents building the structure of a sentence is, then, neither the form or the properties of expressions, nor is it the combinatorial probabilities or the conventional meaning of the expressions, but it is the information – conveyed by features of the concepts and by the way their combinations work – that the interlocutor wants to express. There is, of course, a close connection between the constituents and the expressions that signify their meanings and relations, but that is a matter of convention, regularity and frequency and not an effect of which features the expressions have. Thus, if it is accepted that the subject of a sentence is the expression of the concept that is the subject of the statement, then a 'grammatical subject' is not the left-most word in a sentence, the noun in the nominative case or a semantic role, but the constituent that is, somehow, signified by linguistic means so that it should plausibly be interpreted as the one in relation to which the information of the sentence is organized, if the communication (or cognition) is to succeed. That a certain combination of expressions is an instantiation of a sentence and that there is a certain relation between the constituents are always signified, and the expressional means that are at our disposal can be labelled SYNTACTIC SIGNI-FICATION, as opposed to the SEMANTIC SIGNIFICATION of the expressions being used in sentences to distinguish the objects, states, or events, etc. of the universe of discourse.[35] This technical syntactic framework will be elaborated below in an epi-formal theoretical model but, in order to avoid misunderstanding, first, the theoretical notion of the term 'concept' will be reflected on briefly.

In the late twentieth-century field of cognitive science (cf. Branquinho 2001), concepts were often understood as being combinations of PERCEPTIONS, but I find it more plausible to distinguish between such combinations, which I shall call mental CONFIGURATIONS, and concepts, which I will define as follows: a CONCEPT is a mental connection between one specific linguistic expression and the configuration(s) of one or more (kinds of) objects, states, or events, etc. which are observable, assumed or fictive; or a connection between two or more linguistic expressions and the configuration of one (kind of) object, state, or event, etc. Some kind of notion of the ontological status of the entities of expression and object is presupposed here (cf. above on physicalistic structuralism and the model of the linguistic sign). The basic assumption is, then, that concepts are inviolably linked with language phenomena, and, following my line of reasoning, perception cannot by itself produce concepts but only mental images or perceptual figures or configurations (which do not always have the 'shape' of 'pictures' since not all perception is visual). These mental images are necessary links between the objects of the world and language, thus creating concepts, and they are in the same way, like concepts, accumulated in the minds of living creatures, but in my view not all mental configurations are connected with concepts: we may have mental images of things that we do not have an expression for. Accordingly a mental configuration is a necessary condition for a concept but the opposite is not the case. In this way concepts are, in my version, used to refer to (in the sense of the term reference proposed above) the objects of the world (or concepts are used to mention assumptions about these objects or fictive objects created by indirect references to real objects), and this referential function is made possible by the mental linking of images of the world with images of linguistic expressions (and in my view assumptions and fiction would not be possible without a language). On this background the relation between concepts and expressions does not imply circularity in the definitions: concepts are made (and accordingly defined) as the mental connections between linguistic expressions and the mental configurations of objects, states and events, etc., but this does not contradict the claim that the concepts of specific statements are expressed in the constituents of specific sentences.

In the previous account, combinations or structures of concepts in the minimal linguistic sign have been called statements, and in formal logic and linguistics this term is mostly used with the same meaning as the term proposition, i.e. an utterance which has a truth-value. In formal logic, propositions necessarily have truth-values, because formal logic by definition studies the truth-functional relations between propositions, but according to my preliminaries of a semantic theory, truth-value is not a necessary property of statements. In traditional linguistic theory it is in general assumed that 'Every statement that can be made by uttering a simple sentence expresses a proposition' (Lyons 1977: 503), or formulated in the modern technical language: [36]

> Let us assume that the semantic value of a sentence is a proposition (for instance as constructed in possible world semantics) and that the semantic value of a proper name is an element of a domain of individuals E.
>
> (Rooth 1992: 75)

This implies that truth is a necessary prerequisite for the meaning of natural and formal languages, but as a consequence of the account of language, meaning and the world given above, I do not agree with this, and I strongly advocate the view expressed by, for instance, Gärdenfors (1990): 'To put it tersely: Meaning comes before truth.' Thus, I want to make a distinction between statements and propositions so that statements belong to natural languages, and propositions belong to (artificial) formal languages. If we accept the notion of the minimal linguistic sign – the way it has been outlined above – we can say that the minimal signs of formal languages have to meet certain demands because they are used for special purposes, and the most salient feature of a formal language is that it can be used as an accurate mental instrument. Accordingly, the sentences of this kind of language have to be constructed by means of a number of discrete expressions (terms, taken from a finite set), and such a sentence is what is often termed a FORMULA. The statement expressed by the formula is accordingly constructed by means of a corresponding number of distinct, definite and unambiguous concepts, and a statement like that can be said to be a PROPOSITION. So far this is not opposed to the general idea of the sentences of formal systems, but since I claim that the meaning of a language and its expressions is established by human acts and interactions and the mental images of them, I also claim that formal sentences cannot have any sense or meaning attached to them unless they are embedded in procedures that ensure the accuracy of these concepts and terms, and therefore the pragmatics of a formal linguistic sign implies a mental representation of an exact material procedure, and this stratification of the configurations of a formal sentence and statement can be called an ALGORITHM.[37] Accordingly the 'levels' of a formal minimal linguistic sign then look like this: FORMULA (with TERMS), PROPOSITION (with concepts), and ALGORITHM (with configurations).

If this is plausible, then formal languages cannot have universal applications unless there exist universal social rules that demonstrate in what way the formulae are attached to meaning. Meaning in a formal language normally implies truth-value, and in my view it is a consequence of the precise way a formal language is constructed that it is possible to assign such values to propositions, and not the other way around. In my opinion truth-value is not a basic feature of (the semantics of) formal languages (or formal systems), but, on the contrary, we have to have a formal system at our disposal to assign truth-values and to make the language truth-functional. Nor can truth-value be a basic feature of (the semantics of) natural languages, so the term proposition in the technical sense should – in my view – not be used about the constructions of concepts in natural languages, and the term statement will in this context be used without any association with truth-value. A special question concerns the – more or less – ontological status of logical entities. In standard accounts and essays the problem is seldom touched upon but the implicit understanding behind much philosophical logic seems to be that concepts and propositions are, somehow, extracted from natural language as a kind of purified meanings. In the overview offered by, for instance, Blackwell's *A Companion to Philosophical Logic* (Jacquette 2002), there is a huge number of formalisms and analyses that apparently take it for granted that what people mean by saying something is easily identifiable by means of formal logical analysis and, thereby, sort of, made the object of conceptual surgery; as if meanings are properties of words and sentences, so that we just have to think deep enough to find them. As mentioned elsewhere, I think it is the other way around: logic in its philosophical and formal versions is constructs, which may be very useful. Which brings me to my own constructs.

EFA(X):[38] Epi-formal analysis in syntax: the system

If we accept the pragmatic theoretical model outlined above, then it should be a realistic objective to construct a syntactic theory using the basic theoretical concepts of the model, and it can be done as a combination of this model, of a reformulation of the ideas and principles of Hjelmslevian Glossematics and of Diderichsen's empirical insights into Danish syntax; and also inspired by Chomsky's ideas.

Diderichsen's sentence table has previously been used for formalizations, the purpose of which was to produce models that can generate the expressions in the right positions in the Scandinavian sentence topology. One such formalization is Ahrenberg's (1992) model based on rewrite rules and lexical tagging, and the idea is the same as Chomsky's early approaches: the information is stored in the lexicon and if the information attached to a specific expression fits the nodes of a field grammar sentence tree, then the expressions will find the correct positions. The 'fields' have a central function in this approach, and they may work well formally, but then they are, by Ahrenberg, attributed some theoretical implications which they did not have in Diderichsen's own account:

Afsnit inden for den større Helhed, som vi vil kalde 'Felter'; inden for Felterne [...] en række 'Pladser'.

[S]ections within the larger unity, which we shall call fields; within the fields ... a number of positions.

(Diderichsen [1946] 1966: 151)

In Diderichsen's account, the 'fields' had no basic theoretical significance; they were only labels of a number of positions (of which the ones in the 'nexus field' and the 'content field' displayed the same pattern (cf. *ibid.*: 140) and helped to sustain the idea of sentence topology as a coordinate system of fixed positions. Another, recent, try is the article in *Working Papers in Scandinavian Syntax 82* (December 2008) by Bjerre et al., in which the authors match a generative tree structure with the Diderichsen sentence table and argue, most notably, that they fit each other (a figure is displayed on p. 146). But maybe that hardly comes as a surprise because Diderichsen's table is based on Danish word order and you can always assign (or design) a tree structure that reflects that word order. What is not problematized is the question of what movements the tree structure is supposed to trace and how this is related to the rigid distribution of words in Danish sentences framed by the sentence table. Meaning: the graphic comparison tells us very little about the conceptual framework of the two kinds of theory, which in the article are accounted for separately.

Based on a pragmatic approach like the one delineated above I shall, instead, propose certain units, structures and mechanisms.

The basic assumptions in the previous section implied that CONSTITUENTS (CSTS) are expressions of CONCEPTS (CPTS), that a SENTENCE (STC) is an expression of a STATEMENT (STM), and furthermore implied that one of the CPTS, the SUBJECT, can be defined as: the CPT which is the mental object of the interlocutor uttering (creating) the STM – i.e. the CPT which the interlocutor, in a setting, makes the mental object of his act of linguistic communication or cognition, and accordingly makes his point of departure in producing every single minimal linguistic sign.[39] Accordingly the conceptual structure of the STM is the SENSE and the STC is the FORM of the minimal linguistic sign, and the subject is, then, the 'anchoring unit' (or juncture) by means of which the minimal sign, including the STM and the STC, is established (cf. my account above of a primitive, preliminary model of the linguistic sign). The next question is how the other CPTS are related to the subject and how the STC looks as an expression of this structure of CPTS. To account for this, I will propose the following assumptions (axioms and definitions (defs)):[40]

```
§Statement def:
a statement (STM) is the explication of the minimal linguistic sign
§ statements & concepts
the 'standard form' of a statement (stm) is a structure (forms as
functions) of concepts (cpt):

(1)SUBJECT(2)*VERBATE(3)*ADVERBATE(4)OBJECT/PREDICATE
   (5)CONJUNCTION

S, V, A, O/P, C (capitals are symbols for CPTs)
```

What these units are, and what their relations are, can be clarified by the definitions of the concepts:[41]

```
CPT-defs:
SUBJECT: the concept which is (in a situation (a setting)) the mental
object [conceptual entity] (i.e. a configuration) of the act of linguistic
communication (i.e. transfer of information) or cognition (i.e. transfor-
mation of information) of the interlocutor uttering the statement
*VERBATE: the concept which *subjects and/or *conjects the subject
*ADVERBATE: a concept which is either a specification or a predication
of the *verbate
```

```
OBJECT (or *SPECIFICATE): a concept which is an assertive specification
of the subject by *conjection
PREDICATE: a concept which is a predication of the subject by *conjection
CONJUNCTION: a concept which may connect different statements or, within a
statement, concepts of the same category, or concepts related by comparison
```

and by the definitions of the relations:

```
CPT-relations, defs:
*subjection: assertive (a-)specification, or predication
a-specification: a CPT subclassifies another CPT
[cf. stipulative (s-)specification: a subclassified CPT]
predication: a CPT (re-)classifies another CPT
*conjection: a relation between two CPTs specified by a third CPT
*verbation: the *subjection or *conjection which constitutes a STM
equation: predication by class identification
comparison: predication by class intersection
negation: a-specification or predication by complementary classification
```

Two of the CPTs are known from traditional grammar (object and predicate), and the so-called *VERBATE is supposed to be the CPT that connects them with the subject, or, without any support from other CPTs, specifies or predicates the subject, potentially specified by the *ADVERBATE, another artificial term proposed by my colleague Susanne Annikki Kristensen. The only CPT that is not directly connected with the subject is the CONJUNCTION, which has the function of connecting STMs with each other, connecting CPTs from the same category with each other or connecting CPTs that are compared. The function of saying, by means of a CPT, something about another CPT, either through specification or predication, I call *SUBJECTION, because of the basic relation between the subject and the other CPTs in establishing the STM. Both SPECIFICATION and PREDICATION should be defined and explained by a general semantic theory, and in my view it should be done as a general (or universal) semantics based on a kind of set theory where sets are regarded as mental entities (cf. Götzsche 1991), but for the moment I take it that these terms as intuitively understandable. This is also the case concerning the terms EQUATION (not in the mathematical sense) and COMPARISON, only offering the clarification that IDENTITY between CPTs is established if they have the same specifications (because identical entities have the same properties), and that SIMILARITY between CPTs is established if they have at least one but not all specifications in common (because similar entities have at least one but not all properties in common). The most important distinction is the one between subjection and *CONJECTION, in that the first option allows a connection between two CPTs and the other option between three CPTs, and it looks as if this is what constitutes a minimal STM and a minimal linguistic sign. Maybe this is hardly surprising, and can even be said to have a 'natural' basis, if we bear in mind that we have to connect at least two CPTs to express information – a fact which is acknowledged in classical logic and modern formal (predicate) logic – and that the most efficient (minimal) way of expressing information about relations between elements is to connect two CPTs by a third CPT – in my view, this is reflected in the way the syntax of many languages work. And sentences express the information of STMs:

```
§Sentence def:
a sentence (STC) is the form of the minimal linguistic sign

§ sentences & constituents (syntax (STX))
a sentence is (generated as) the form [cf. ling sign] of a statement,
i.e. the constituents are (generated as) the forms of the concepts.
```

The standard form of a sentence (STC) is a *structure* of constituents (CSTs); the structural functions of the constituents are *syntactic functions* establishing *CST-categories* as sets of *categorial units*:

```
(1)subject(2)verbal(3)object/predicative(4)adverbial
(5)conjunctional

s, v, o/p, a, c (symbols for CSTs)
```

If we assume that the major part of the CSTs can be defined quite mechanically as inferred from the previous definitions:[42]

```
CST defs:
subject: form of the subject of the statement
verbal: form of the *verbate of the STM
adverbial: form of an *ADVERBATE
object: form of an Object of the STM
predicative: form of a Predicate of the STM
conjunctional: form of a Conjunction of the STM
```

The *formation* of a STC is a *construction* of actual CSTs *expressed* as morphemes (MPHs) in *syntagms* (STGMs); *syntagmatic functions* establish *paradigms* (PDGMs), i.e. sets of MPHs

then we arrive at virtually the set of syntactic analytical terms found in traditional grammar, but based on a number of pragmatically defined and systematically formalised theoretical concepts. It follows from the definitions, then, that the 'levels' of traditional grammar are interrelated in a specific way: the acoustic continuum is, as in the tradition, seen as a chain of phonemes (of phones), these phonemes build a series of morphemes that is called a syntagm, and each morpheme is 'picked up' from the paradigm to which it belongs, and one or more morphemes can function as a constituent; which, as is suggested by the definition, is the form of a concept. This approach differs from the tradition concerning the use of the term 'syntagm' in that this is often used as a label of succession of phonemes or as a synonym of 'phrase'. In this context the term 'syntagm' is used only as labelling a series of morphemes, and it should be noted that the whole series of morphemes that builds a sentence is seen as a syntagm, not just what in the tradition is called 'phrases'. Then some of the morphemes may function as constituents in their own right and some may join efforts and build phrases, which are constituents expressed by more than one morpheme (cf. below on phrase analysis in EFA(X)3).

As for the structure of the STC, it is established by the relations between the CSTs, and these are supposed to be the same as those between the CPTs of the corresponding STM. By means of the definitions of the CPTs and their relations, and by seeing CSTs as expressions of CPTs, a set of general (or universal) syntactic units has been defined, and because specific expressions in actual STCs have to represent these units (for the listener to understand the CPTs and their inter-relations) we can say that the general units establish CST-CATEGORIES (that they are CATEGORIAL UNITS) and accordingly they have SYNTACTIC FUNCTIONS (which term henceforth shall be used as the common label on CSTs in STCs). In human communication and cognition, the syntactic function of a specific CST has to be signified somehow (or, as interlocutors or thinkers, we run the risk of confusing the categories), and this is done by means of the expressions that we otherwise use to refer to, to mention or to indicate objects in the world. Accordingly, (acoustical or graphic) properties of linguistic expressions can be used for two purposes: they signify objects, states or events, etc. in the actual universe of discourse or contemplation, a function I will (as mentioned above) call SEMANTIC SIGNIFICATION (which is not to say that this meaning is a property of the actual expressions); or they signify the syntactic category they belong to by convention (which is not to say that the category is a property of the actual expressions), and this function I will (as is also mentioned above) call SYNTACTIC SIGNIFICATION. It is the way in which (acoustical or graphic) properties of linguistic expressions are used to SIGNIFY, syntactically and semantically, that should be accounted for in theoretical syntax, and in tentative form one part of it – a formal theory on the occurrence conditions of CSTs – will be delineated in the following. I shall utilize the ideas and principles of Hjelmslev's Glossematics, but since I consider the techniques of classical and modern logic adequate for the purpose, I see no reason for designing a totally new system in the way Hjelmslev did it.

The system I intend to develop is a combinatorial system that I shall call an epi-formal system in accordance with the basic methodological assumptions accounted for above, and the principles governing the system can be characterized by the label OCCURRENCE LOGIC (cf. below). The other part of a syntactic theory about the signification of linguistic expressions is the one that deals with the relations between morphemes that do not function as constituents on their own – a theory much needed in phrase analysis – but this presupposes a preliminary (epi-formal) theory of morphemes, and it will be taken up below.

If the symbols representing units are to be manipulated in an efficient way according to the conventions of the occurrence logic, it is convenient to stipulate a number of additional symbols, thereby creating a special COMBINA-TORIAL SYSTEM:[43]

```
combinatorial symbols & rules for distribution (distr) & substitution
(subst), i.e. combinatorial system (CMB SYS)
```

In general, I conceive of a combinatorial system as a set of rules for distributing and substituting expressions, most conveniently in the form of symbols, and this is what is expressed here. The rules may be introduced like this; first substitution:

```
# combinatorial substitution rules
## combinatorial production (i.e. 1 symbol substb n symbols) rule:
>>    is produced as

## combinatorial occurrence derivation (i.e. 1/n symbol(s) substb 1/n
symbol(s)) rule:
=>    occurs as
=}    may occur as

## combinatorial linearization (linear vs non-linear occ) derivation
(i.e. 1/n symbol(s) substb 1/n symbol(s)) rule:
->    is linearized as
-}    may be linearized as
```

and then distribution:

combinatorial *distribution* rules: *occurrence*

occurrence *symbols* (combinatorial *vocabulary* [constituent symbols = 1 character symbols]):

s	[subject
v	verbal
o	object
p	predicative
a	adverbial
c	conjunctional
z,y,	
ä,ö,ü	any symbol (symbol variables)
zy	sub-category of y (subconstituent = 2 character symbol)
e	ellipsis]

occurrence *lists, sets & strings*

occurrence symbol lists & strings (non/vs occurrence relations):

(• any operator, ° any occurrence operator, cf. below)

z,y,ä, etc.	list (combinatorial)

(list, def: any collection of unrelated symbols)

z•y•ä	set (combinatorial)

(set, def: any collection of related symbols)

z°y°ä	string (combinatorial)

(string, def: any set of occurrence related symbols)

occurrence *markers*

occurrence symbol markers (of *absolute* occurrence *values*):

z	obligatory (OBL)
(z)	facultative (FAC)
{z}	labile (LAB)

(lability, def: occurrence value may be indefinable)

occurrence *operators*

occurrence symbol operators (*relative* occurrence *values* (indicates symbol co-occurrence (condition) relations)):

°	any occurrence operator
~	occurrence negation

connectives (binary occurrence operators):

°^	conjunction
°\	exclusive disjunction
°/	inclusive disjunction

```
°>                  strong implication; def: z °> y, y occ iff z occ

°}                  weak implication; def: z °} y, if z occ then y occ

consequential (relation of necessary co-occurrence in) strings:

°>z°y°zy°>          strong consequential implication

°}z°y°zy°}          weak consequential implication
```

This looks like heavy machinery, and admittedly it is. But the set of symbols chosen is found on a standard western keyboard, and the terms have been borrowed from contemporary formal logic. The basic idea is that we have to start out with something, i.e. production ('>>'), which in due course may appear as something else (derivation: '=>, =}'), and, due to the significance of linear order in syntax, there may be restrictions on the linear symbolic distribution ('->, -}'). All of this has to do with occurrence, meaning that these rules control the occurrence of the symbols in the formalisms and that the resultant calculuses should adequately be used to describe the occurrence (by syntactic signification determined) interdependences[44] of the units in natural language sentences. This is done by means of a number of symbols, forming strings (in which some occurrence relations are found, but we do not know which ones: notation '°'), by means of some markers defining whether a symbol must be found (obligatory) or may be found (facultative), and ending up with a number of occurrence operators. These have been extracted from the formal logic nomenclature and have undergone some modifications, but as far as they concern occurrence they have been furnished with a small '°' signifying this feature.

The next step is setting up a device that can handle a basic differentiation in the world's languages: some languages have their sentence constituents conform to a linear order – for instance, Danish and English – while other languages – for instance, Latin and Finnish – have their constituents spread out almost without restrictions; and some of them are combinations of these principles – for instance, German. The device should also handle a basic characteristic of all languages, namely, that they should be able to signify (in the technical meaning in this context) where a sentence has its beginning; and indirectly also where they end. First linear order:[45]

```
# combinatorial distribution rules: linearization

(def: linear vs non-linear occurrence, i.e. dimensionality)

## linearization symbols (combinatorial vocabulary [CST symbols])

s              [subject

v              verbal

o              object
```

```
p            predicative

a            adverbial

c            conjunctional

z,y,

ä,ö,ü        any symbol (symbol variables)

zy           sub-category of y

e            ellipsis]
```

```
## linearization strings linearization symbol strings (non/vs linear
occurrence relations):
(°  (º,  ª)   any operator (linear, non-linear), cf below)
...z°y°ä...   linearization string (linear vs non-linear)
...zºyºä...   linear string
...zªyªä...   non-linear string
```

This apparatus can distinguish between combinatorial lists (unordered collections of symbols), combinatorial sets (ordered collections of symbols) and strings, either undetermined as for linearization:

x°y

or linear:

zºy

vs. non-linear

$z^a y$

All of these are also undetermined as for starting points:

...z°y°ä...

so a number of markers are needed to signify this:

```
## linearization markers
linearization symbol markers (of absolute linearization values, i.e. sequen-
tiality (def: initial state definition (i.e. un/defined starting point)):
obligatory initial state definition:
zºyºzy   linear sequence (LSQ)
[topological signification (CST-coordination)]
zªyªzy   non-linear sequence (alignment by frequency) (NSQ)
[morphological signification]
(sequence, def: a linear or non-linear string with a defined initial state)
facultative initial state definition:
```

```
zºyºä…       linearization string (undefined initial state)
zᵒyᵒä…       linear string (undefined initial state)
zªyªä…       non-linear string (undefined initial state)
             labile initial state definition:
…zºyºä…       linearization string (no initial state)
```

These markers can handle some rather different kinds of constructions. In principle, we could imagine languages where there were no or only undefined initial syntactic states, and this is expressed by the facultative and labile-state notation at the bottom of the list of markers above, but we might also expect that communication by means of such languages would be fairly complicated. However, this is what is presupposed in some approaches in linguistics. Halliday with his 'systemic (functional) grammar, for instance, does not tell us where we should look for the beginnings and ending of sentences (cf. the summaries in de Beaugrande (1991: 223–64), Chapman and Routledge (2005: 116–22) and, for instance, Halliday (1985)), and since Hjelmslev's Glossematics conceives of ordered linguistic expressions as just texts as objects to be divided into their parts, we will never know whether sentences start or stop. Provided sentences are considered the basic unities in linguistic communication and cognition by conveying information, we need the devices to describe either non-linear sequences:

```
zªyªzy
```

or linear sequences:

```
zᵒyᵒzy
```

The first option will be applied to languages using morphological signification (indicated in square brackets above) while the second option will be applied to those using topological signification. Then, for the combinatorial systems to be applied to occurrence dependence relations in syntactic constructions, a number of linearization operators are needed, and they are picked up from the occurrence operators by taking away the '°' that indicates 'occurrence':

```
## linearization operators
linearization symbol operators (relative linearization values
(indicates symbol linearisation (condition) relations)):

º        any linearization operator
(cf °     any occ operator, ª    any non-linearization operator)

¬    negation
```

```
connectives:
^    conjunction
\    exclusive disjunction
/    inclusive disjunction
>    strong implication; def: z > y, y occ iff z occ
}    weak implication; def: z } y, if z occ then y occ

subsequential strings:
>zºyºzy>    strong subsequential implication
}zºyºzy}    weak subsequential implication
(subsequence, def: a linear sequence of implications)
```

By means of the operators we are also able to put together strings that indicate strictly ordered successions ('subsequences'), and these will be used below. There may be some constraints on the ordering:

```
## special linearization value constraints
linear sequence constraint:
[topological signification (TPL SFC)]
zºyºäº etc. {z}    alternative (labile) position

linear & non-linear sequence constraints:
[morphological signification (MPL SFC)]
z[µ]                symbol & morphemic expression (MPH XPR)
z[µ]                obligatory (OBL)
z[(µ)]              facultative (FAC)
z[{µ}]              labile (LAB)
```

And such constraints are meant to handle, first of all, the fact that some expressions sometimes may pop up where they are not expected to do so (topological variation), or they sometimes look different from what is expected (morphological variation). The apparatus will be implemented below.

Occurrence Logic: a formal language[46]

Not everyone is granted the liberty of proposing a new kind of logic, even though people in the business come up with new ideas all the time, and the number of contemporary logical systems is fairly high (again, cf. Jacquette 2002). A fundamental question associated with that theme is, as is mentioned above, whether logical systems are entities that are extracted from natural languages or whether they are entities that are designed on the basis of natural languages. In accordance with my deliberations above on artificial languages I am in favour of the last option. Thus, I consider my Occurrence Logic an artificial (formal) language, and I will make no comments on this issue in addition to my remarks above, but some comments on how this logical system has been designed seem to be appropriate.

In general, the vocabulary and the rules of the combinatorial system introduced above seem to correspond to, and to be in accordance with, the truth-functional relations established in traditional symbolic logic. But this is not quite so, and the line of reasoning advanced in the following will be illustrated by the problem connected with the term 'implication' used as the label of one of the operators.

In the tradition, one is allowed to infer the possible truth-values of a proposition q from the actual truth-value of another proposition p, for instance: $p \Rightarrow q$ 'if p is true, then q is true', i.e. the truth-values of conditional compound statements depend on the pattern of truth-values of their components (Material Implication). It means that only in case p is true and q is false the compound statement is false, and in all other cases with different patterns of truth-values, the compound statement is true; which, of course, is the way Material Implication is defined. These truth functions are the reason why Copi in his textbook (1982: 294) stresses the fact that: 'It should be noted that the material implication symbol is a truth-functional connective, just like the symbols for conjunction and disjunction.' And in the case mentioned, where p and the compound statement are true, we are allowed to claim that q also is true by necessity (Modus Ponens: $p \Rightarrow q$ 'if p is true, then q is true'). But, evidently, q may be true also when p is false, and therefore we cannot infer from the fact that q is true to the conclusion that p is true; only that if q is false, then p has to be false if the compound statement is true (Modus Tollens: $p \Rightarrow q$ 'if p is false, then q is false'). But, evidently, as is the case with the other connectives (conjunction and disjunction), we cannot infer the pattern of truth-values of the components on the basis of the truth-value of the compound statement of an implication.

When dealing with occurrences of entities, one may say that it follows from the rule of the formula $z > y$ (y occurs if and only if z occurs) in the combinatorial system that one is allowed to infer from the occurrence of y to the occurrence of z. And this is in accordance with the conventions of the occurrence logic. Thus, the formula does not mean that z and y are logically equivalent (Material Equivalence), because z and y are not propositions but symbols (representing entities in the system for syntactic analysis implemented below), which either occur or are absent according to the rule combining them. The formula can be translated into propositions of occurrence logic and, thus, it 'means' the same thing as Material Implication ($\Rightarrow$) in symbolic logic, but in a reversed notation:

combinatorial system rule:

z °> y, y occ iff z occ   (i.e. y occurs if and only if z occurs)

occurrence logic propositions:

p: 'y occurs'
q: 'z occurs'

symbolic logic inference (Modus Ponens):

p $\Rightarrow$ q   'if p then q'
p   'p is true'
∴ q   'therefore q is true'

occurrence logic inference:[47]

p 'y occ' $\Rightarrow$ q 'z occ'
        'if (it is true that) p 'y occurs', then (it is true that) q 'z occurs''
p   '(it is true that) p 'y occurs''
°∴ q   'therefore (it is true that) q 'z occurs''

That the formulae z > y and p $\Rightarrow$ q can, some way or other, be said to be reversed or inverted versions of each other should be evident when the symbolisms of symbolic logic and occurrence logic are compared by the following formulae (Material Equivalence: $\equiv$):

p $\Rightarrow$ q $\equiv$ p 'y occ' °$\Rightarrow$ q 'z occ'
p 'y occ' °$\Rightarrow$ q 'z occ' $\equiv$ z > y
p $\Rightarrow$ q $\equiv$ z > y

I call the occurrence rule mentioned (z > y) STRONG 'IMPLICATION' because of the relationship with the logical truth function of Material Implication and because of the relationship of necessity between the occurrence of the components. The so-called WEAK 'IMPLICATION' is the more direct translation of the logical function into the occurrence logic and the combinatorial system, and therefore p and q have to represent the opposite occurrence propositions as compared to strong implication:

combinatorial system rule:

z } y, if z occurs then y by necessity occurs

occurrence logic propositions:

> p: 'z occurs'
> q: 'y occurs'

symbolic logic inference (Modus Ponens):

> p ⇒ q   'if p then q'
> p   'p is true'
> ∴ q   'therefore q is true'

occurrence logic inference:

> p 'z occ' °⇒ q 'y occ'
>   'if (it is true that) p 'z occurs' then (it is true that) q 'y occurs''
> p   '(it is true that) p 'z occurs''
> °∴ q   'therefore (it is true that) q 'y occurs''

And, again, the symbolisms of traditional logic and Occurrence Logic can be compared by the following formulae (Material Equivalence: ≡):

> p ⇒ q ≡ p 'y occ' °⇒ q 'z occ'
> p 'z occ' °⇒ q 'y occ' ≡ z } y
> p ⇒ q ≡ z } y

Thus it will always be true that if z occurs, then y will also occur, but y may occur for other reasons (caused or effected by other conditions), and accordingly p may be false while q is true, and this is the reason why I call it a weak 'implication'.

The system

By means of the symbols accounted for above, the structural claims about STCS that they are generated by STMS can be formulated in a more formal way. Thus we can say, first, that a STC-construction is generated (as the structural process of GENERATION) by a STM as an EXPRESSION of that STM:

```
generation: STM generates STC (a statement generates a sentence)
```

and that the CSTS are expressed in the same way:

```
S,*V,*A,O/P,C generates s,v,a,o/p,c
```

which means that a CST of a certain category is an expression of a CPT from the corresponding category. Then, second, we can use the epi-formal system and apply a general combinatorial rule saying that:

```
## production (general formal system production rule):
∑ >> z°y°ä
(symbol ∑: sequence)
```

which means that a sequence is produced in the combinatorial system as a string of symbols with a defined initial state (a defined starting point). Some of the CSTs (represented by symbols) may occur the way they are, or they may occur sometimes (FACULTATIVELY, marked by parentheses) or in combinations as SUB-CATEGORIES (SUB-CSTS, labelled by two-character symbols), in both cases as DERIVATIONS:

```
## derivation (general occurrence rule):
z,y,ä => z,y,(ä),öy,(üy) etc.
```

Whether the CSTs occur in a STC depends on the occurrence of CPTs in the actual STM, but the basic CPTs are the ones introduced in the course of the presentation above: S, *V, *A, O/P, C. If we accept this as the choice an interlocutor has when he wants to express the information attached to a number of CPTs in a single linguistic sign, then he has to signify the categories of the CPTs and the categories of the corresponding CSTs, and to do so he has, as mentioned above, only two ways of using the linguistic expressions: either he can use special features of expressions for CSTs (their categories); or he can use the order of the linguistic forms expressing CSTs. By nature the expressions have to be distinct, either by means of special features or by features which in combination with other expressions (with certain features) can signify adequately what they are, or they have to be ordered in such a way that they can signify their category. Because speech is linear, as an effect of time, the only kind of possible ordering is a linear one: a linear topical system where the expressions are placed in a certain order to signal their different functions. These two ways of organizing the (acoustic and graphic) properties of the expressions are the instruments for signifying syntactic categories (syntactic functions of CSTs), and, as mentioned above, I call this mechanism syntactic signification. As is also mentioned above, this is opposed to semantic signification which is the use of (acoustic and graphic) properties of certain expressions to convey the meaning of CSTs and CPTs (by classification). The two options are two ways of expressing the syntactic signification of CSTs (which is here described by the concept of LINEARIZATION in the formal combinatorial system based on occurrence logic), and since expressions with a certain significance are in general called morphemes, the first option can be called MORPHOLOGICAL SIGNIFICATION, and the other can be called TOPOLOGICAL SIGNIFICATION. This is what can be described by means of the combinatorial notation offered above:

```
## derivation (general linearization rules)
[syntactic signification: structural deviations]:
either
linear sequence
[topological signification]:
z,y,(ä),öy etc -> zºyº{z}º(ä), etc.
or
non-linear sequence
[morphological signification]:
z,y,(ä),öy etc -> z[µ]ªy[(µ)]ª(ä[{µ}]), etc.

[syntactic functions generate syntactic signification, either morpho-
logical or topological]
```

According to the symbolisms stipulated above, the square brackets[48] denote morphemes, and the relation between the CSTs and their morphematic expressions can be stated as:

```
[morphematic expression: z is expressed as z[µ]]
```

An [m] denotes an unspecified morpheme paradigm, while a morphemic variable is represented by the symbol 'µ', and specific morphemes (as results of morphemic selections) are written in italics, e.g. [*sig*] ('-self', Danish and Swedish reflexive pronoun). In accordance with standard theories, morphemes are considered the minimal independent expressions of a language, and they are accumulated as sets (PARADIGMS) in the (mental) lexicon (cf. above) and they build constructions (SYNTAGMS) processed by some syntactic mechanism. They have mental properties that are representations of the properties of their material linguistic medium, and the morphematic structure is the 'level' at which the material properties of the linguistic medium, by generation or interpretation of morphemes, are connected with linguistic sense and meaning, and thereby (sense and) meaning 'meet' the medium of language as sounds or written symbols. I shall call this structural 'interface' established by expressions and syntactic functions: the FORM of language (cf. once more the model of the linguistic sign above), and, as mentioned, for the expressions in their

syntagmatic functions I find it convenient to give the common label FORMA-
TIVES.[49] Thus the application of CSTs in morphemes is the process where CSTs
generate language form by being assigned to a linguistic medium.

If, now, we go back to the assumed specific CST-categories, there are a
number of special conditions that hold for their occurrence in relation to each
other (described by the symbols of the occurrence rules), and this is based on
the definitions of the categories of CSTs and CPTs:

```
# special rules
## special occurrence rules:
[CST definitions & relations]
s°>v
s°^v°>o°/p
s°^v°>a
s°^v°>c
y =} zy
y°/zy
z°^z°^z etc. (notn: z^^)
z°^z =} z°^c°^z
```

This list only means that one will not find a verbal without a subject, and that
one will not find an object/predicative, an adverbial or a conjunctional without
a STC ('s°^v'). In addition, it is specified that sub-categories may occur instead
of or together with categories, and that all CSTs may be reduplicated and
connected by conjunctionals. When a number of CSTs actually occur in a STC,
they can be manifested in one of the two ways described above, i.e. either with
morphological signification of their syntactic functions, or with topological
signification, as described by the combinatorial formulae (for empirical reasons
the 'c' has been moved upfront):

```
## special linearization rules:
[syntactic signification: structural deviations]
either
### non-linear sequence:
[morphological signification]
cᵃsᵃvᵃo/pᵃa
or
### linear sequence
(sequential linear derivations):
either
cᵒsᵒvᵒo/pᵒa    (linear sequence)
```

```
[topological signification (CST-coordination)]
or
}cºsºvºo/pºa}   (weak subsequential implication)
[topological signification (CST-concatenation)]
or
>cºsºvºo/pºa>   (strong subsequential implication)
[topological signification (CST-consecution)]
```

The first (morphological) formula means that the CSTs are syntactically signified by morphemes, and they can, in principle, be distributed quite unordered. Inflecting languages like Finnish and Latin are to some extent characterized by such linear lack of order, while Icelandic, German and Turkish,[50] which are also quite heavily inflected, have strong restrictions on their topical order. Opposed to these languages the (Central) Scandinavian languages and English have quite fixed topical order with no significant inflectional systems, and this can be described by the two basic kinds of topological signification (CST-coordination and CST-concatenation/consecution respectively). In my view, there is a difference between these two options in that the first implies the possibility of a pure (sequential) coordinate system in which the CSTs are placed to show their syntactic significance, and that the other implies that the CSTs are linked in a sequence by some degree of necessity (either weak subsequential implication or strong subsequential implication). At this stage of general syntax, the formulae entail that all the CSTs are necessary, and that in the second formula there is a linear necessity too.

By using the technical apparatus of this formal system the linguistic analyst is, in principle, able to carry out formal descriptions of the syntax of any natural language and the relevant question is, of course, how this is done. The question will be answered in the following, but first there is a caveat. It is tempting to be enthusiastic and, in the spirit of Brøndal, to claim that the system can predict language types, for instance, in the form of the special linearization rules just displayed. This is not so. More in the Hjelmslevian vein, the system can be said to have hypotheses deduced in the form of theorems, and, on the one hand, these are to conform to the special linearization rules while, on the other, they will be applied to real syntactic constructions in a specific natural language. This may lead to modifications of the patterns of the special linearization rules and each modification may represent a specific language type, and this will be dealt with in the next chapter. But there is one striking aspect of these patterns: they seem to be able to characterize some of the major approaches in syntax. First of all, Diderichsen's sentence table tries to describe Danish syntax by what I call a 'CST-coordination' model, which is only capable of interpreting a sentence as a 'linear sequence' (cf. also Chapter 2). The Chomskyan model is a little more advanced in that it complies with the 'weak subsequential implication'. Basically, a tree model says that if some syntactic item is found in place, then some other syntactic item may be found in some other slot if this is not restricted by some *ad hoc* rules, which, in due course, tell us how the next step in the procedure is performed. So at least one advantage of the Epi-Formal System seems to be that it can characterize, fairly accurately, other theoretical approaches in syntax.

An implementation of the system in syntactic descriptions requires some relevant data and an empirically oriented elaboration of a hypothesis concerning the general syntactic structure of the language in focus. How this is done in accordance with some principles in the philosophy of science has been taken up above. In practice, a prerequisite is a specific Epi-Formal Calculus for each language, which has been brought about through empirical generalizations, and subsequently the calculus is to be applied to specific sentences as data from that language. Take Danish, for instance. A sentence might be:[51]

```
og derfor har Peter ikke trænet hunden i dag
'and therefore has P not trained the dog today'
```

The first step will be to find the syntactic categories used in this sentence, i.e. to annotate the chain of words with the relevant CST-symbols taken from the list of symbols above and augmented by some subcategories ('qa, na, pa'; all relevant subcategories will be listed in Chapter 4) and a morphematic symbol ('aux' for auxiliary):

og	derfor	har	Peter	ikke	trænet	hunden	i dag
c	qa	aux	s	na	v	o	pa--

This is a structural description of the construction. Assume, now, that a Danish calculus may look like this:

```
Dan CST calculus [STC formation: construction]
## parameters (>Ωz etc. >: strong subseql impl):
∑>Ω(c)πcΩs\{x}πs\{x}Ωvπv\◊auxΩ{s}π{s}/{o[m*]}Ω(a)πpa/qa/nz
Ω(v)πv/◊{aux}/vrb/vvaΩ/{ra}Ω(o/p)π{p}/o/{vva}>{o}/p/{s}/kc^kp
Ω(a)πra/pa>∑
sequence constraints:
[*mig, dig, sig, ham, hende, den, det, os, jer, dem]
```

When accepting these calculus symbols:

∑   sequence [sentence]

Ω   node, def: a derivation in a string [position]

π   parameter, def: a derived symbol [constituent]

the calculus can be seen as a construal of in which way constituents can be allowed to occur in each slot in the chain of the construction as reflected by the formal sequence. First by aligning the structural description with the nodes (Ω) of the formalism:

```
og   derfor  har Peter ikke  trænet hunden  i dag

c    qa      aux s     na    v      o       pa--structural description

c    qa      aux s     na    v      o       pa--  ⎫
                                                  ⎬ formal description
c_   s_      v_  s₂_   a_    v₂_    o_p_    a₂_   ⎭
```

```
OBS: the nodes of the calculus
(c) s\{x} v {s} (a) (v) (o/p) (a)
will henceforth be labelled with a simplified corresponding notation:
c_ s_ v_ s₂_ a_ v₂_ o_p_ a₂_
below the structural description; in the calculus this simplified
notation looks like this:
```

```
simplified notn
∑>Ωc_πcΩs_πs\{x}Ωv_π{qa/na}^v>{qa}\◊aux[ha]◊Ωs₂_π{s}/{o[m*]}\
[sig]>{s}Ωa_πpa/qa/nzΩv₂_πv◊ʃcs\ucʃ>{aux\¬aux[ha]}/vrb/vva◊/ra
Ωo_π{p}/o/{vva}>{o}/p/{s}/kc^kpΩa₂_π{ra}/pa>∑
```

and then by letting the calculus check whether the structural analysis is accepted by the formalism:

```
when the structural description
c qa aux s na v o pa---
is processed by the calculus (checked by all parameters):
```

```
∑>Ωc_πcΩs_πs\{x}Ωv_π{qa/na}^v>{qa}\◊aux[ha]◊Ωs₂_π{s}/{o[m*]}\
[sig]>{s}Ωa_πpa/qa/nzΩv₂_πv◊ʃcs\ucʃ>{aux\¬aux[ha]}/vrb/vva◊/ra
Ωo_π{p}/o/{vva}>{o}/p/{s}/kc^kpΩa₂_π{ra}/pa>∑
```

```
then the result is the following parametric values:
(bold: positive value; regular: negative value)
```

```
∑>Ωc_πcΩs_πs\{x≈qa}Ωv_π{qa/na}^v>{qa}\◊aux[ha]◊Ωs₂_π{s}/{o[m*]}\
[sig]>{s}Ωa_πpa/qa/naΩv₂_πv◊ʃcs\ucʃ>{aux\¬aux[ha]}/vrb/vva◊/ra
Ωo_π{p}/o/{vva}>{o}/p/{s}/kc^kpΩa₂_π{ra}/pa>∑
```

which is a formal description

Some additional information is needed when reading the formalism. The asterisk in '{o[m*]}' means that there are some constraints on which morphemes may be instantiated as an 'o' (object) in that position in the sequence, namely, the list of morphemes (words) referred to by the asterisk and displayed below the 'Dan calculus'. How this works will be illustrated in Chapter 4. The expression '{x≈qa}' means that the x-variable is, in this construction, instantiated by the special constituent 'qa'.

What is, however, evident from the structural description is the fact that constituents may include more than one morpheme, for instance, in the Danish phrase *i dag* 'today'. As is obvious from the English word – and from the Swedish version *idag* – it may be a matter of debate whether this is one or two words or morphemes, but if we, for the moment, ignore this intricate problem and accept the Danish solution, then the Epi-Formal System has been introduced to the challenge of how to handle phrase analysis. A brief account of some preliminaries in this area will be offered in the following.

Phrase analysis in EFA(X)3

As mentioned earlier, if this formal theory is to be taken seriously, it must be able to handle more sophisticated constructions than the one used as an example above, and one of the leftovers from sentence analysis is the question of what to do with constituents containing more than one word:

```
i dag 'to day'
pa---
```

This analysis says that the two words form an adverbial of a certain sub-category ('pa': predicative adverbial; cf. Chapter 4) and the broken line indicates that both the preposition and the noun are expressions in one constituent. This problem is dealt with in the Phrase Theory of EFA(X), a field mainly developed by Susanne Annikki Kristensen (cf. Kristensen 2004). In brief, the phrase (defined as a constituent containing more than one morpheme;[52] in writing: more than one word) *i dag* is considered as built of two units, called COMPONENTS, and that each of these components, like any morpheme (or word), is accumulated (as lexical items, maybe incorporating morphological information) in one of a number of mental systems called paradigms.[53] Most morphemes can function on their own as constituents, or they can become the components of a constituent. In order to handle this two-'level' analysis, constituents will be

annotated by one- or two-character symbols, while components will be labelled
with three-character symbols:

```
i dag
pa---
prp nom
```

By this is indicated that phrases, components, functions and categories can be
conceived of according to this definition:

```
§Phrase def: a phrase (PHR) is a constituent expressed in two or more
morphemes

§ PHR-functions (categories): structure & components
the standard form of a phrase (PHR) — as a part of the syntagm (STGM)
making a sentence — is a morphematic structure of components (CPNs);
the structural functions of the components are phrasal functions
establishing phrase categories as sets of categorial units (compo-
nents); expressions functioning as categorial units are accumulated in
paradigms (PDGMs) in the lexicon in accordance with their categorial
features; a phrase may integrate sub-phrases (SUB_PHRs)
```

The example above is an adverbial phrase and, as is well known, adverbials
do not make an easy case, so in Kristensen (2004) a number of unorthodox
solutions to the traditional obscurity of adverbials are offered. The simpler case
will be, for instance, noun phrases:

```
den   store,   gule   hund   med   de   dårlige   tænder
j     j        j      h      j     j    j         hj
det   adj      adj    nom    prp   det  adj       ·nom
the big yellow dog with the bad teeth
```

This analysis tells us that there are a number of specific relationships between
the components. Components are different from constituents in that constituents in sentences may enter a number of different relations with each other
(cf. definitions of constituent relations above). Not so with components. The
only relation between the components in a phrase is specification: a phrase is
a construction of expressions for concepts specifying each other, and this is
most likely in accordance with how most grammars conceive of phrases.[54] If
we look at the 'dog' phrase above as an example, then the analysis will tell us
that there is one 'core' component: *hund* 'dog', annotated by an 'h', and the other
components are annotated by 'j'. Resuming the basic assumptions of the theory,

constituents are considered expressions of concepts, and complex constituents (phrases) express complex concepts: concepts in which a 'core' or 'nuclear' concept (such a concept is called a NOTION when instantiated in a phrase or sentence) is specified by one or more other concepts (SPECIFICATIONS; as opposed to the a(ssertive)-specifications in sentence syntax, the specifications in phrases are called s(tipulative)-specifications; cf. below). The theory here suggests that the 'core' concept is expressed in the constituent as the component called the HABITAT:[55] 'h' of the constituent, and that a specification is expressed as a component called an INDEX: 'j'. The index 'j' can, in principle, function as a so-called SUB-HABITAT. This is what happens in the 'hj' (INDEXICAL HABITAT) case above in that *tænder* 'teeth' is combined with a preposition in what is in the tradition called a prepositional phrase, and therefore it can be used as a postpositional specification in the form of a SUB-PHRASE: *med de dårlige tænder* 'with the bad teeth' of the habitat *hund* 'dog'. It should be observed that this kind of annotation ('h' and 'j') does not indicate which index is pointing to which habitat, or which indices should be considered subordinate to other indices. To clarify that, the notational apparatus will require additional characters of some kind (for instance, a number of brackets) or, alternatively, one has to establish a convention saying that indices are 'decoded' from left to right, in accordance with western script, and adding some markers to turn around if needed. Basically, the outcome will correspond to what is depicted by means of a classical tree structure in Generative Grammar. But, opposed to the alleged prominence of hierarchical phrase structures claimed by – for instance, Moro (2008), referred to in Chapter 2 – the EFA(X) approach rejects the hierarchical way of handling (sentence and) phrase analyses. In parallel with sentence analysis, phrase analysis is seen as a procedure (1) identifying the component categories in the phrase; (2) identifying whether there are any sub-phrases (and their categories); thereby (3) presenting a structural analysis; and (4) checking the structural analysis by having it run through the adequate phrase calculus and thereby presenting a formal analysis. If it is licensed by the calculus, then the analysis seems to be correct. And this procedure has nothing to do with the perceived hierarchical architecture of a phrase. In my view – and contrary to Moro (2008) – there is no reason to believe that the structure of a natural language phrase mirrors a hierarchical organization of the items. I think we experience a hierarchy primarily because of the lexical semantics (in EFA(X) the semantic signification) of the expressions in the phrase, the finer details of which may not be easy to ascertain. This is one of the things that have kept logicians busy for quite some time when they try to find clear-cut solutions to what the

hierarchical architecture of a group of ordered words is. Among other things
they agree that there is a need for the theoretical concept of 'scope'. Which, by an
irony of fate, then comes back to linguistics as an analytic concept. The EFA(X)
phrase analysis procedure presented above needs no analytic concept of 'scope',
and it makes this notion redundant. The only interest of a linguistic analysis
of a phrase is to find out which categories signify their syntagmatic functions
by which means, being topological or morphological. But if one feels more
comfortable with a hierarchical understanding of phrases then EFA(X) offers
the habitat/index (indexical habitat) notation displayed above, and it is possible
to suggest a number of other kinds of notation for such a purpose.

Assuming the adequacy of the phrase analytic procedure presumed above,
the components are annotated with three-character symbols in line with their
categorial functions:

```
# component categories
symbols & definitions (empirical generalizations)
[component categorization (structural categorization):
components (CPNs) & subcomponents= 3 character symbols]
nom [noun: notion]
det [determiner: specification of referential in/determination]
adq [adjective: specification by quantification]
adj [adjective: specification by qualification]
prn [pronoun: referential in/determiner]
prp [preposition: specification by special semantics]
psp [postposition: specification by special semantics]
vrb [verb: notion]
aux [auxiliary verb: specification by finiteness]
mod [modal auxs: specification by special semantics]
vqa [quasi adverb: specification by presupposition] cf. qa
vna [negational adverb: specification by negation]  cf. na
vra [relational adverb: specification by relation]  cf. ra
vva [variational adverb: specification by variation of verb lexcl semantics]
con [conjunction]
```

This is, of course, a categorization based on empirical generalizations and
so far it should be taken at face value, but it should be observed that it is
not quite coherent with the list of sentence constituents in Chapter 4. This
problem will be taken up in connection with the account of Scandinavian,
Danish and Swedish syntax in Chapter 4. However, the components seem to
come in strict order in a Danish phrase, and if phrases are to be subjected to

a formal analysis, then the structural description must be checked by a special formalism, a calculus, for phrases; i.e. in the 'dog' phrase case above a noun phrase calculus:

```
##N_PHR calc (Dan):
>◊det/adq/adj^^/nom^^√prp/det/adq/adj/nom√psp◊>
```

A phrase calculus is based on the same principles as a sentence calculus, but in order to avoid confusion some additional symbols for phrase analysis will be suggested, among them:

```
# symbols
additional calculus symbols
æ,ø,å; æøå            any CPN (component)
◊                    PHR_parentheses/boundaries
√                    SUB_PHR-parentheses/boundaries
◊æ◊                  allocated (ALC) CPN (vs ◊æ•ø•å◊
                     attributed (ATB) CPNs)
analytic notation:
æøå¯¯¯æøå¯¯¯æøå        SUB_CPN markers    (SUB_CPNs in SUB_PHRs)
æøå⁀æøå¯¯¯æøå         SUB_PHR marker     (postpositioned SUB_PHR)
æøå-⁀æøå¯¯¯æøå⁀¯¯æøå   SUB_PHR markers    (postpositioned SUB_PHRs)
æøå⁀æøå¯¯æøå¯¯æøå--æøå SUB_PHR markers    (prepositioned SUB_PHRs)
```

And when this is combined with the general occurrence logic notation, the calculus just displayed can be read like this: it is a 'strong subsequential implication' ('>æ,ø,å>'; cf. above); some of the components may be reduplicated (æ^^); it is a phrase calculus ('◊æ,ø,å◊'); and there is a sub-phrase inserted ('√æ,ø,å√'). If we pick up the 'dog'-phrase once more:

```
den     store,   gule    hund    med    de      dårlige    tænder
det     adj      adj     nom     prp    det     adj        nom
the big yellow dog with the bad teeth
```

and make a full structural phrase analysis including sub-phrase notation:

```
den store, gule hund med de dårlige tænder
det-adj----adj--nom-⁀prp¯det¯adj¯¯¯¯¯nom
the big yellow dog with the bad teeth in (its) mouth
```

then it may be formally described by being checked by the phrase calculus:[56]

```
>◊det/adq/adj^^/nom^^√prp/det/adq/adj/nom√psp◊>
```

This formal analysis produced by the calculus tells us that a determiner is found in front of a non-occurring quantifier, followed by an adjective and a noun, and in the sub-phrase there is a preposition, a determiner, an adjective and a noun, and since the occurrences do not violate the rules of the calculus, then the phrase is a licensed construction.

We are now in a position where we can clarify the difference between sentences (and clauses) and phrases, i.e. to explain why they are not identical although they have analogous features (cf. the definitions of concept relations above). A sentence (and a clause) are a way of putting together a number of concepts in order to assert something to other people, or to oneself while contemplating things, an assertion which in due time may be accepted or rejected by others or by oneself. If such a statement is not a predication (which in EFA(X) is only expressed by a predicative constituent), then it is an assertive specification (a-specification: the concept sub-classifies another concept), which is similar to a phrase:

```
P has trained the dog
… the dog trained by P
```

But a phrase is not an assertion, it is a stipulation, a state of affairs taken to be accepted as a fact, and therefore I suggest the idea that a phrase is a stipulative specification (s-specification: a sub-classified concept).

Since phrases are found in sentences, then, evidently, the two calculuses have to be integrated into one uniform calculus in order to make the system produce formal descriptions of complex constructions, i.e. sentences containing constituents that are either complex (i.e. are phrases) or are embedded sentences. This will be done in Chapter 4 on particular languages where the specific calculus for Danish will have an almost fully integrated sentence formalism and phrase formalism.

Summary

In this chapter I have offered the outlines of a syntactic theory that is based on a number of assumptions about how languages are used and understood by human beings, and this can be said to be a pragmatic approach to syntax (in the narrow sense of the word pragmatic in this context). The background is current and historical ideas and principles applied to empirical achievements in grammatical analysis, especially those of the Danish linguists Louis Hjelmslev and Paul Diderichsen, and from this point of departure I have specified what I consider the basic theoretical concepts, theories and methodologies in this approach in syntactic analysis. After having clarified some of the theoretical prerequisites from philosophy and the philosophy of science I have established what I call an epi-formal theory of syntactic analysis. The theory has been developed into a formal (combinatorial) system based on what I call occurrence logic, which can be used to describe and explain the basic general (universal) and particular syntactic structures of languages, and the formal description has been established as a calculus for formal description of sentence and phrase structures and constructions in an abstract language, here illustrated by examples from Danish.

It may also be mentioned that it looks as if the formal and logical capacities of the combinatorial system are able to produce derivations which are precise descriptions and classifications of other theories, e.g. Hjelmslev's Glossematics and Diderichsen's sentence table.

Deviational Syntactic Structures

De, som behøver at vide, i hvad orden en Dansk propositions ord skal følge
hverandre, ere vel fornemmelig de fremmede, som skøtter om at lære Dansk;
dog misbruges ordenen ej alene af dem, men ofte af indfødde Danske selv,
besønderlig i Vers, som derfor gemenlig ere sammenlappede af fordærved
Dansk. Det danske sprog holder en mere naturlig orden end det Latinske og
mange andre, og derpaa grundes en stor del af dets tydelighed.

Those who need to know in which order the words of a proposition in
Danish must follow each other are presumably first of all the foreigners who
undertake the task of learning Danish; however, the order is not only misused
by them, but also by Danes, especially in poetry, which, for that reason, is
usually patched up by corrupted Danish. Danish has a more natural order
than Latin and many other languages, and a large part of its clarity is based
on that.
(*Jens Pedersen Høysgaard:* Accentuered og Raisonered Grammatica,
1747, §§ 388–9)

The EFA(X)3 descriptions of Danish and Swedish syntax

The assumptions and suggestions offered in Chapter 3 can be theoretically applied to the Scandinavian languages, and in the following it will be stipulated that the Central Scandinavian languages (at least Danish and Swedish – I am not going to make comments on the details in the diversity of e.g. Norwegian dialects) – on a certain syntactic 'level', have identical structures, a claim which is based on descriptive generalizations. Thus, it looks as if certain constituents have facultative occurrence (in accordance with the notational conventions of EFA(X) marked by brackets; and, for convenience, the 'c' has been moved upfront):

```
FORMAL CALCULUS (THEORETICAL APPLICATION)
efc (epi-formal calculus)
```

```
EFAXSca (Scandinavian syntax)
# general rules
## production (general Sca production rule):
∑ >> c°s°v°o°/p°a
## derivation (general Sca occurrence rule):
c°s°v°o°/p°a => (c)°s°v°(o°/p)°(a)
```

And that there is a fairly high number of sub-constituents:[1]

```
# symbols
additional symbols:
[constituent categorization (structural categorization):
constituents (1 chart symbols)   & sub-constituents (2 chart symbols)]
s    fs [formal subject]
     cs [conjunctional subject]
     ns [negative subject]
v    ['finite or non-finite verbal'; cf. PHR_ANL aux]
o    do [dative object]
     no [negative object]
p    sp [subject predicative]
     op [object predicative]
     kp [comparative predicative]
     np [negative predicative]
a    qa [quasi-adverbial]          cf. vqa
     ra [relative adverbial]       cf. vra
     pa [predicative adverbial]
     na [negative adverbial]       cf. vna
c    uc [subordinating conjunctional]
     kc [comparative conjunctional]
     oc [objective conjunctional]
     ac [adverbial conjunctional]
x    x-variable
```

The sub-constituents are defined by the general categorial criteria as specifications or predications of the concepts they are the forms of (i.e. their syntactic functions), and only the verbal has been furnished with a minor clarification: since verbal morphemes are seen as parts of verb phrases, there are, so far, no verbal sub-phrases. And the only category that is at odds with traditional descriptions is adverbial constituents, which is split into the sub-categories 'qa', 'ra', 'pa' and 'na'; the conceptual framework of which originate in Götzsche (1993) and (1999). Furthermore, to manage the topological variation in the

Scandinavian languages it is convenient to have a dummy symbol at one's disposal for some of the constituents and this is called the 'x-variable'. This is a topological variable that can be used to substitute all constituents except the verbal and the conjunctional, and it can be formally defined as:

```
x -} zˆ¬vˆ¬naˆ¬c
```

Between the constituents of the Scandinavian languages there are a number of mutual conditions for their occurrence, both concerning constituents and sub-constituents:

```
# special rules
## special Sca occurrence rules
[categories vs sub-categories]
s°\cs
s°\ns
o°\no
p => zp
a => za
```

and concerning the relations between specific categories:

```
[different categories]
o°\sp
ʃcs°\ucʃᵇ>Ωv²_πv◊aux\vrb◊
```

These restrictions are supposed to work within the overall pattern of the Scandinavian syntax topology, i.e. the linearization of the (CST) symbols as derived from the Scandinavian syntax occurrence pattern:

```
## special Sca linearization rule
(weak subsequential implication)
[Sca STC structure: topological structure (CST-co-ordination
restricted to CST-concatenation)]

(c)ᵒsᵒvᵒ(o/p)ᵒ(a) -> }(c)ᵒs\{x}ᵒvᵒ{s}ᵒ(a)ᵒ(v)ᵒ(o/p)ᵒ(a)}
```

The latter formula is a way of expressing the empirical generalization that the subject has (under certain circumstances) an alternative place, that the normal place of the subject may be taken by another constituent (represented by the x-variable), and that adverbials may be found in two places in the sentence. Apart from the linearization rules (restrictions), this is also basically what is described by Diderichsen's sentence table. Provided these, and only these, constituents are found, this linear pattern represents a chain of constituents in which they have 'coordinated' or 'concatenated' places (cf. the terminology suggested in Chapter 3): some of the constituents may be missing and some may be found in alternative places, but from our impression of the overall pattern we know what they are, and there is little need for morphological signification of the categories. Such a pattern can be called a TOPOLOGICAL PROTOTYPE,[2] and each place within the pattern presented in Chapter 3 can be called a POSITION (in the combinatorial system called a NODE, symbol: 'Ω'). The way I see it, these were the (more or less implicit) theoretical notions Diderichsen used when he developed and elaborated his sentence table. In accordance with Diderichsen's general theoretical paradigm we can also make clusters of the eight positions, by Diderichsen called FIELDS (cf. discussion of Diderichsen in Chapter 2):

```
[cf. STC fields (FLDs):

Initial     Central     Final

STC positions (PSTs):

(c) s\{x}   v {s} (a)   (v) (o/p) (a)]
```

But, as mentioned, it is hard to ascribe any theoretical significance to this division. We might say that a field is a series of constituents in which there is at least one (quasi-) obligatory constituent, if we regard the object and the predicative as so prominent that one of them will occur in most normal sentences, and in that case the definition is based on observed frequency or calculated probability, and the fields have no consequences for the handling of the syntactic variations.

If we accept the general idea that specific languages or dialects can be variations of, more or less, the same linguistic structures, then Danish and Swedish can be said to be STRUCTURAL DEVIATIONS of a common Scandinavian syntax (to avoid any confusion: the languages mentioned are considered deviations *of* a syntactic prototype; obviously, I do not claim that one of the languages is a deviation *from* the other). It is commonly acknowledged that the syntax of each of the two languages is not as simple as that of the formulae set up above, and one way of being able to manage this diversification theoretically and analytically is to assume that there can be further alternative and also multiple CST[3]-instantiations in each position (thus creating a structural deviation; a formal definition is presented below). In my view, this variety of possible constructions of constituents cannot be controlled by the pattern of a 'coordinate' system (CST-coordination) like Diderichsen's sentence table, because I assume that human beings are not mentally capable of managing too many 'empty slots' at the same time (and this would be the consequence of the Diderichsen sentence table), but this point of view is clearly no more than an assumption. Accordingly I shall claim that both the positions of a deviation, and the constituents that may be found in each position, follow each other by necessity, and this is what I formally call 'strong subsequential implication'. When the CST-occurrences in each position have been established for each language on the basis of empirically generalized descriptions, the result can be called the TOPOLOGICAL TYPE of that language, implying a topical succession or order of all constituents in the sentences of the language. These insights can then be expressed in a formal way, for instance, for Danish:

```
EFAXDan (Danish syntax)
# special rules (1) STC_CSTs (STX)
##special Dan CST occurrence rules:
(c) => (c)
s°\{x} => s°\{x}
v => v\◊aux◊
{s} => {s}°/{o[m]}
(a) => pa°/qa°/nz
(v) => v◊{aux}/vrb/vva◊/{ra}
(o°/p) => {p}°/o°/{va}°>{o}°/p°/{s}°/kc°^kp
(a) => ra°/pa

## special Dan linearization rule
(strong subsequential implication):
[Danish structural deviation (DEV): Dan stx topological (structural)
deviation; CST-consecution]
(cf. Sca linearization rule: }(c)ºs\{x}ºvº{s}º(a)º(v)º(o/p)º(a)})

>(c)ºs\º{x}ºvº{s}º(a)º(v)º(o/p)º(a)>

# Dan CST calculus [STC formation: construction]
## parameters (>Ωz etc >: strong subseql impl):
∑>Ωc_πcΩs_πs\{x}Ωv_πv\◊aux◊Ωs₂_π{s}/{o[m*]}Ωa_πpa/qa/nz
Ωv₂_πv◊{aux}\vrb/vva◊/{ra}Ωo_π{p}/o/{vva}>{o}/p/{s}/kc^kp
Ωa₂_πra/pa>∑

special morphemic conditions:
[*mig, dig, sig, ham, hende, den, det, os, jer, dem]
```

Once again, this looks like heavy machinery but it is really not that laborious. The deviational Danish sentence structure as described by the formal deriva-tional string of symbols does not contain all the information of what has now become an EPI-FORMAL CALCULUS of (CST) symbol-occurrence: the information about which constituents are facultative is contained in the labels of the nodes (the positions), the interrelations between (CST) symbols are stated in the tables of occurrence conditions above, and the specific morphemic (i.e. concerning single morphemes) conditions are listed below the Σ-formalism, but the calculus can, in combination with this external information, predict the place of a constituent in an actual sentence. The generation of an actual sentence can be called a SYNTACTIC INSTANTIATION, a term which can be used about both the process of making a construction of constituents and about the resulting construction, and any single step, or function, of a linearization in the calculus describing a syntactic construction is (as in Chapter 3) called a PARAMETER (symbol: 'π'). The fact that the calculus is based upon what I call 'strong subsequential implication' does not mean that every single position of the construction is always instantiated to effect the setting of the value of one or more parameters in the calculus (because a sentence is instantiated by means of a number of positions (but maybe not all) being taken by constituents in accordance with the formal description, thus following a rule of 'strong subsequential implication'), but some of the positions are, according to the topological prototype, formally described as facultative, and this (occurrence) feature cancels the relation of 'strong subsequential implication' between the symbols. Thus the implication of nodes only has the effect that, if a preceding node is facultative and not assigned any of its values, then a succeeding node is tied up with the next preceding node. But if a facultative node is actually set by one or more values, then this setting is a necessary condition for a setting of the values of the succeeding node. By means of this formal apparatus, we are able to describe the syntactic differences between, for instance, Danish and Swedish by setting up the calculus for Swedish in parallel with the Danish calculus:

```
EFAXSwe (Swedish syntax)
## special Swe occurrence rules:
(c) => (c)
s°\{x} => s°\{x}
v => {na}^v°>{qa/na}°\◊aux[ha]◊
{s} => {s}°/{o[m]°\[sig]°>{s}}
(a) => pa°/qa°/nz
(v) => v◊∫cs°\uc∫°>{aux°\~aux[ha]}/vrb/vva◊°/ra
(o°/p) => {p}°/o°/{vva}°>{o}°/p°/{s}°/kc°^kp
(a) => {ra}°/pa
```

```
## special Swe linearization rule (strong subsequential implication):
[Swedish structural deviation (DEV): Swe stx topological (structural)
deviation; CST- consecution]
(cf. Sca linearization rule: }(c)ºs\{x}ºvº{s}º(a)º(v)º(o/p)º(a)})
```

$$>(c)ºs\backslash\{x\}ºvº\{s\}º(a)º(v)º(o/p)º(a)>$$

```
# Swe calculus [STC formation: construction]
## parameters (>Ωz etc. >: strong subseql impl):
```

$$\sum>Ωc\_πcΩs\_πs\backslash\{x\}Ωv\_π\{qa/na\}^{\wedge}v>\{qa\}\backslash\Diamond aux[ha]\Diamond Ωs_2\_π\{s\}/\{o[m*]\}\backslash[sig]>\{s\}$$
$$Ωa\_πpa/qa/nzΩv_2\_πv\Diamond\int cs\backslash uc\int>\{aux\backslash\neg aux[ha]\}/vrb/vva\Diamond/ra$$
$$Ωo_p\_π\{p\}/o/\{vva\}>\{o\}/p/\{s\}/kc^{\wedge}kpΩa_2\_π\{ra\}/pa>\sum$$

```
sequence constraints:
[*mig, dig, sig, honom, henne, den, det, oss, er, dem]
```

Apart from the morphemic differences in the list of pronouns in the oblique case, the calculus above shows the main differences between Danish and Swedish syntax on the CST-'level' (i.e. the parameter ('π') level): (1) some special adverbials may be found in the position of the finite verbal ('Ωv'); and (2) the second subject-position ('{s}') may include the specific reflexive pronoun [*sig*] in front of the subject. We may also (3) delete the finite verbal in its alternative position ('(v)') in Swedish (i.e. in subordinate clauses), and finally (4) the normal place of a special adverbial 'ra' is in front of the position of the object and predicative ('o/p'). These facts may be described by a calculus comparison (in which the Swedish differences are marked with bold characters):

```
EFAXDan/Swe (Danish vs Swedish syntax)
[Dan:Swe stx deviations (contrastive description):

# Dan & Swe calculus comparison:
```

$$\sum>Ωc\_πcΩs\_πs\backslash\{x\}Ωv\_π\{\mathbf{qa/na}\}^{\wedge}v>\{\mathbf{qa}\}\backslash\Diamond aux[\mathbf{ha}]\Diamond Ωs\_π\{s\}/\{o[m*]\}\backslash[\mathbf{sig}]>\{\mathbf{s}\}$$
$$Ωa\_πpa/qa/nzΩ\mathbf{v}\_πv\Diamond\int\mathbf{cs}\backslash uc\int>\{aux\backslash\neg aux[\mathbf{ha}]\}/vrb/vva\Diamond/\mathbf{ra}$$
$$Ωo\_π\{p\}/o/\{vva\}>\{o\}/p/\{s\}/kc^{\wedge}kpΩa\_π\{\mathbf{ra}\}/pa>\sum$$

```
Dan sequence constraints:
[*mig, dig, sig, ham, hende, den, det, os, jer, dem]

Swe sequence constraints:
[*mig, dig, sig, honom, henne, den, det, oss, er, dem]
```

There are, of course, other differences which may be called syntactic, in a very broad sense, but according to this theoretical paradigm they should be dealt with by morphematic (i.e. concerning morphemes in general) analysis of phrases, i.e. constituents comprising more than one morpheme (cf. Chapter 3 and below). So the number of specifically syntactic differences between Danish and Swedish can be said to be four, and a few examples will be offered below to demonstrate this fact.

How these epi-formal calculuses for Danish and Swedish can be used in the description of the structures of sentences can be illustrated by a limited number of examples,[4] and if we take as our point of departure a sentence of which the construction corresponds to the syntactic (topological) prototype it thereby fills in all the slots of the Diderichsen sentence table, provided we ignore the absence of the conjunctional:[5]

```
(1)    s\x      v     {s}     (a)     (v)       (o/p)     (a)

       derfor   har   Peter   ikke    trænet    hunden    i dag (Dan)

       qa       aux   s       na      v         o         pa---

       therefore has P not trained the dog today
```

In this example the 'qa' has taken the position of the subject, an alternative that is licensed by the representation of the 'x-variable' as a parameter of the node, and therefore the subject finds its place in the alternative subject-position: the node '{s}'. A sentence like this is a necessary prerequisite to present the whole structural prototype (except for the conjunctional), and to see the regular structure of Danish sentences within this pattern we have to choose an example with the subject in the front:[6]

```
(2)    Peter    har    ikke    trænet    hunden    i dag (Dan)

       s        aux    na      v         o         pa---

       s_       v_     a_      v₂_       oₚ_       a₂____

       Peter has not trained the dog today
```

And accordingly the alternative place for the subject is not filled in. There is another alternative position for the subject in the 'oₚ_' position, but that presupposes the instantiation of a formal subject in the node 's_' position:

```
(3)    der    er     faldet    en sten      ned    fra taget (Dan)

       fs     aux    v         s------      ra     pa-------

       s_     v_     v₂_        oₚ_____    a₂_____

       there is fallen a stone down from the roof
```

and the third option for a subject (that is negative) is the position of the first adverbial (node 'a_'):

```
(4)   der    er     ingen skade    sket (Dan)

      fs     aux    ns---------    v

      s_     v_     a_____       v
                                    2_
      there is no harm happened
```

Whereas a formal subject may be found with or without a subject later in the sentence, the negative subject excludes another (non-formal) subject from the same sentence, and this is also expressed in the rules accounted for in the formalism.

As for the verbal, the most salient feature is, basically, that it cannot be found in other places than its primary position, and the reason for that seems to be that it has a function as a specifically topological 'anchoring unit', a 'ground zero' or a 'pivot' like a reference point in a coordinate system in relation to which the other constituents find their alternative places. In my view, this holds not only for the Diderichsen 'coordination' account of Scandinavian sentence topology but also for my formal 'implication' theory, and this view can be said to be underpinned by the fact that the verbal actually has an alternative position, namely, in the subordinate clause:

```
(5)   at   Peter   ikke   har    kørt   bilen   hjem (Dan)

      uc   s       na     aux    v      o       ra

      c_   s_      a_     v      o      o       a
                           2_____      p_      2_
      that P not has driven the car home
```

The necessary precondition for the use of the alternative position for the verbal is (so far, cf. below) the occurrence of the subordinating conjunctional, ('uc' in this context called a subjunction), and when the verbal is 'moved',[7] the alternative position for the subject is blocked, because it is defined as an alternative in relation to the normal place of the verbal, and consequently the subject-position as an alternative for 'x-constants' is also blocked. Accordingly, what is left is a little variation for the adverbials. In this way the structure of sub-clauses is even more rigid than the structure of sentences (main clauses), and the order of their constituents is so fixed that the topical information as syntactic significance is not interfered with by an alternation of the verbal. But it should be noticed that the rigidity of sub-clauses does not come without costs. A perfectly stable topology covering all sentence structures is, of course, a possible feature of a language but a language user of such a language should always have a cue to be able to find the beginnings of sentences, and there would be little room for stylistic variation in the linear orientation. When Danish and Swedish have rigid sub-clause topology, language users always know where the sub-clauses begin because they are embedded in sentences and have no stylistic variation in their linear orientation.

As is well known, spoken Danish has lost much (some, including me, would say most) of its morphological signification in the inflectional paradigms. Apart from number and definiteness in the inflection paradigms of nouns, only the endings of verbs have some of their morphemic features left, but the effects of phonetic reduction are especially felt in the weak verb conjugation, and neutralization based on homophones is an abundantly found phenomenon. The only other resort for inflection is the paradigm of morphological variation in the paradigm of pronouns, and this still has certain syntactic implications:[8]

(6)	Peter	tog	ham	ikke	med	(Dan)
	s	v	o	na	ra	
	s_	v_	s_2_	a_	a_2_	
	Peter	took	him	not	with	

(7)	Peter	tog	den	ikke	med	(Dan)
	s	v	o	na	ra	
	s_	v_	s_2_	a_	a_2_	
	Peter	took	it	not	with	

(8)	Peter	tog	han	ikke	med	(Dan)
	o	v	s	na	ra	
	s_	v_	s_2_	a_	a_2_	
	Peter	took	he	not	with	

If we compare sentences (6), (7), (8) it is evident that the personal pronouns signify their syntactic function, either by using the oblique form *ham* 'him' or the nominative *han* 'he', and the way I see it this is the reason why an object can be found in the alternative position of the subject (node 's_2_' in (6)), or the reason why a subject is accepted in the same position in the highly unorthodox (in general, rephrased as a cleft construction) but acceptable example of (8). The pronoun *den* 'it' in (7) is both the nominative and the oblique form (or more correctly: there is no case differentiation), but the actual interpretation is facilitated by the lexical semantics of the pronoun, because only in special narratives would it not be counter-intuitive to assume that 'it' took 'Peter' some place, and the occurrence of inflected pronouns with the same syntactic characteristics supports the use and understanding of *den*. This pronominal deviation is incorporated in the calculus above by the formula:

```
{s}/{o[m:*]}
```

which is a constraint meaning that objects may occupy an alternative position together with the subject if they satisfy certain criteria for morphemic manifestation, i.e. the limited set of morphemes which in the formula is defined by the list below the calculus.[9]

There is no dative case in Danish, and thus we cannot use the German way of signifying the dative object, but we have other ways of doing it:[10]

```
(9)     Peter   gav   ikke    Pia    en bog (Dan)
        s       v     na      do     o-----
        s_      v_    a_      o_p_____
        Peter gave not Pia a book

(10)    Peter   gav   ikke    en bog til Pia (Dan)
        s       v     na      o----- vva do
        s_      v_    a_      o_p_____
        Peter gave not a book to Pia
```

and here the topological signification is evident. If the dative object is placed in front of the object, there is no need for further specification, but if it comes after the object, then morphological information is given about the relation between the two constituents, and in this case it is a preposition connected with the dative object. According to the assumed CST-categories accounted for above, I prefer to consider the preposition an adverb (i.e. as part of the verb phrase), and the option is written in the calculus as:

{vva}>{o}

It is a possible interpretation to analyse *til Pia* 'to Pia' as one phrase, not as an adverbial in the final (node 'a$_2$_') position the way it is done traditionally, but as a dative object with morphological signification as in German. In that language the prepositions are bound with case forms, irrespective of the syntactic functions of the connections, while cases without prepositions are used to signify syntactic functions, and so it should be possible for a language with no case forms in the noun inflections, like Danish, to use prepositions to signify syntactic functions (cf. the analyses below and the section on prepositions).

I also prefer a special interpretation of the comparative construction in Danish, e.g.:

```
(11)    Peter   er    større end mig (Dan)
        s       v     sp    c   kp
        s_      v_    o_p_____
        Peter is taller than me
```

(12)	hormonerne	har	gjort	Peter	større	end	mig (Dan)
	s	aux	v	o	op	c	kp
	s_	v_	v₂_	o_p			

the hormones have made P taller than me

In general, comparative constructions in Danish express the comparison by means of conjunctions like *end* 'than' and *som* 'like', and they offer no straightforward syntactic analysis, especially if the constituent following the conjunction is a pronoun in the oblique case. If it is found in the nominative case, the construction can be interpreted as an elliptic sentence, and this is how Diderichsen analyses these constructions (cf. Diderichsen [1946] 1966: 200), implying that the constructions containing the pronouns in the oblique case work as a kind of derivation of the sentence constructions (cf. *ibid.*: 109–10). In the traditional topical analysis, it is not evident which status the constituents of the comparison can be assigned. Diderichsen suggests *(ibid.*: 109, 200) that the constituents after the conjunction should be called 'Sammenligningsled' 'comparative constituent', but he does not explain the syntactic and topical status of such a constituent. One solution may be to place them in a position according to their most probable actual syntactic function as constituents or as parts of constituents, but then their syntactic function must be assumed to be unstable, i.e. they have in fact no STC-syntactic function as constituents because they do not have their own syntactic category. Consequently they are only morphematic constructions (like so-called 'prepositional phrases'), and if, furthermore, some of them end up in the final (node 'a₂_') position (which is a possible solution in the analyses of (11) and (12)), then the function of the conjunction is quite close to the function of prepositions. Then it will not be easy to separate them from prepositions, and Aage Hansen (1967) suggests (Vol. II, p. 243) that they should be interpreted as prepositions in constructions like (11) and (12); a solution chosen by other – also Swedish – grammarians. As an alternative I will suggest that what is found here is a reduplication of predicatives, and that the last one, the comparative predicative, is connected with the preceding predicative by a conjunctional. In traditional Danish grammars it is a general solution to categorize everything coming after the object as adverbials – also prepositional phrases like the ones I have described as dative objects and comparative predicatives. I am not in favour of this solution because, first, it implies that something, which is clearly not an adverbial, appearing after the adverbials has to be placed outside the traditional sentence table – an arrangement which has resulted in the creation of special so-called 'postpositional fields' or 'positions', by itself a contradiction in terms[11] – and, second, it is (as mentioned above), on traditional grounds, difficult to define what a preposition is without assuming that it is something that occurs in a prepositional phrase, and then one seems to be trapped in (more or less vicious) circularity (cf. also below).

As for the Swedish deviation, it can be described by the differences from the Danish syntax. There are – as mentioned – four syntactic features that are not found in Danish, and somehow (based on western alphabetical texts) they can be characterized under the heading: 'left-wing syntax'. Thus it is possible in Swedish, and normally not in Contemporary Danish but licensed in e.g. nineteenth-century Danish (cf. Diderichsen [1946] 1966: 191), to place the adverbial 'qa' to the left of a subject in its alternative position:

```
(13)    det    har  nog   Peter    sagt    någonting    om (Swe)
        op     aux  qa    s        v       o            vva
        s_     v_____    s₂_      v₂_     oₚ_          a₂_
        that has probably P said something about
```

And in the calculus I have placed it in the position of the first verbal (node 'v_'). The second possibility is the placing of the reflexive pronoun *sig* '-self' to the left of the subject, like this in the subject's alternative position:

```
(14)    då    satte   sig   Peter    i soffan (Swe)
        pa    v       o     s        pa------
        s_    v_      s₂_____     a₂_____
        then sat himself P in the sofa
```

Because the pronoun is the object of the sentence, it seems most natural to place it in the same position as the subject – and not in the verbal or the adverbial position – and then there has to be a special rule in the calculus to license the construction:

```
[sig]>{s}
```

In connection with these diverging syntactic tendencies – which cause an extension of the calculus – it can be mentioned that Swedish also allows a combination of adverbial constituents in front of a subject, i.e. a normal sentence-negation (the negative adverbial 'na') and maybe also another adverbial constituent, normally a 'qa':

```
(15a)   då    kan   väl    inte   Peter    vara    med (Swe)
        pa    mod   qa     na     s        v       ra
        s_    v_____     s₂_      v₂_     a₂_
        then/so can probably not P be with
```

```
(15b)   inte    kan    väl    Peter    vara    med (Swe)
        na      mod    qa     s        v       ra
        v_____      s₂_      v₂_     a₂_
        not can probably P be with
```

Such constructions are excluded in Contemporary Danish (but the first may
be found in Late Modern Danish): *så kan vel ikke Peter være med* (as one
reading of the Swedish sentence). Normally a negative constituent which is not
a negative adverbial in Danish and Swedish is the pronoun (Danish:) *ingen* 'no
one, nothing' (variations of it or combinations with nouns, e.g. *ingenting, ingen
penge* 'nothing, no money'), but at this point Swedish is, it seems, more liberal
than Danish and it illustrates the general 'left-wing syntax' of Swedish. Some
may offer the idea that the negation in front of the verbal in (15b) is found in the
s_ position but I do not see it this way. While it seems to be a fair description of
both Danish and Swedish syntax that certain adverbial categories – i.e. 'pa' and
some 'qa' adverbials – can be 'moved' to the s_ position – a solution that implies
that the negation, and a few other adverbials, are found there – may encounter
the problem that the s_ position is occupied:

```
(15c)   Peter   kanske   kan    vara    med (Swe)
        s       qa       mod    v       ra
        s_      v_____ v₂_     a₂_
        P maybe can be with
```

This means that the 'qa', like the negation, looks more naturally affiliated with
the verbal position, also because adverbials basically seem to be specifications
of verbals. Accordingly the v_ position in Swedish is a rather crowded place
but I suggest that all the options presented in (15a–c) are seen as one Swedish
syntactic difference, i.e. as variations of (13), meaning that a number of adverbials
may besiege the auxiliary or the verbal in the v_ position, and which adverbial
expressions does what depends on the lexical meanings of these adverbs.

The last two characteristics of Swedish syntax do not extend the number of
parameters in the calculus but only cause changes in the conditions. In Swedish
it is possible (facultative but subject to stylistic influence) to drop the auxiliary
verb in subordinate clauses (aux-deletion), i.e. it is a labile construction:

```
(16)    att    han    (hade)    kommit    igår (Swe)
        uc     s      (aux)     v         a
        c_     s_     v_        v₂_       a₂_
        that he (had) come yesterday
```

This is an option not found in Danish and I will come back to this below.

The very last feature of Swedish syntax as opposed to Danish is the regular place of the special adverbial 'ra' to the left of the object. While we can say that the aux-deletion just mentioned leaves an open slot in the structure to the left of the non-finite verb in sub-clauses, which then takes over its syntactic function, then all the other features are 'left-wing' constructions related to (but not structurally affiliated with) nominal constituents (subjects and objects). Thus, the 'ra' in:

```
(17)   Peter   har   klätt   på    barnen (Swe)

       s       aux   v       ra    o

       s_      v_    v₂_____    o_p_

       Peter has dressed on the children
```

has to be placed in front of the object, and this is an option in Danish, but it is rather seldom used, and only in constructions with very long objects. That this phenomenon is found in Danish and Swedish is clearly a part of the syntactic structure of these languages. There are no external natural causes to the phenomena, because Danes and Swedes understand each other perfectly well (provided they understand the diverging words of the other language) in spite of the difference in the placement of the 'ra' or the other 'left-wing' features, and these syntactic deviations in one Scandinavian language (seen from the point of view of the Scandinavian prototype) are, according to what I have observed – I have not studied it systematically – among the linguistic differences that immigrants, or other language students, from the other Scandinavian country learn rather quickly. This is opposed to the differences in other linguistic constructions, for instance, in the use of specific (abstract) prepositions[12] in 'prepositional phrases' (which according to my syntactic theory is not a syntactic feature but a lexical one (in FoG a morphemic one, i.e. you choose one prepositional expression (morpheme) instead of another expression)): *gå på bio* (Swedish) vs. *gå i biografen* (Danish) 'go on/in (the) cinema'. Such differences are apparently learnt much slower than syntactic and syntagmatics (phrase) features, and it may support the speculation that what I call syntactic signification is the most important feature to be learned when acquiring a new language.

The analyses above are, as mentioned, carried out in accordance with the principles of structural and formal analysis presented in Chapter 3, so they can be checked by the calculuses for Danish and Swedish respectively. As was also mentioned, this is most conveniently done by a computer program but each instance of a structural analysis can also be checked by hand. For that purpose, the 'trunk-like' form of the calculuses is not the most user-friendly, and for convenience the calculuses can be converted into another graphic form (the Danish calculus only):

```
NOTN_EFAX3 (Dan)
∑>
Ω↑0↑c_πc
  Ω↑1↑s_πs\{x}
    Ω↑2↑v_πv\◊aux◊
      Ω↑3↑s₂_π{s}/{o[m*]}
        Ω↑4↑a_πpa/qa/nz
          Ω↑5↑v₂_πv◊{aux}/vrb/vva◊/{ra}
            Ω↑6↑o_p_π{p}/o/{vva}>{o}/p/{s}/kc^kp
              Ω↑7↑a₂_πra/pa>∑
sequence constraints:
[*mig, dig, sig, ham, hende, den, det, os, jer, dem]
```

In this shape the calculus combines sentence and verb phrase formalisms, in that the verb phrase calculus has been integrated into the sentence calculus. Neither the calculuses for the noun phrases (of complex subjects ('s'), objects ('o') or predicatives ('p')) nor a calculus for the adverbial phrase ('pa') have been inserted explicitly into the sentence calculus and there are two reason for that: one is that the same phrase calculus would be found in a number of places, extending the sentence calculus in an unsuitable way; another reason is that the adverbial phrase is, apart from the occurrence of an initial preposition in the noun phrase, identical to the noun phrase. So, instead of integrating it into the sentence calculus, this part of the formalism is presented in this list of rules:

```
# special rules (1) PHR_CPNs (STGM)
##special Dan CPN occurrence rules
nom°>det,adq,adj,prp,psp
nom°\prn
vrb°>aux,vva

##V_PHR calc (Dan) — integrated into the calculus above:
>◊{aux}/vrb/vva◊>
##N_PHR calc (Dan):
>◊det/adq/adj^^/nom^^√prp/det/adq/adj/nom√psp◊>
##A_PHR calc (Dan):
>◊prp/det/adq/adj^^/nom^^√prp/det/adq/adj/nom√psp◊>
```

The specific rules for adverbial and noun phrases respectively might, of course, have been put together into one rule controlling the formation of the phrase calculus depending on the nature of the constituent, but for the sake of clarity this has not been done here. For the sake of explicitness, the verb phrase has also been listed in the special rules.[13]

This format should make it easier to carry out the formal checking of the constructions, but the figure also has some theoretical implications. It is, obviously, not a Chomskyan tree-structure and it does not depict a procedure in which some 'deep-structure' constructions are being 'transformed' into some 'surface-structure' constructions. Instead the starting point is the upper left 'corner' at the initial sigma character followed by 'jumping' some steps down the stairs towards the end of the sentence at the other sigma character, and these represent two by-products of the format: on the one hand, each node ('Ω') may be construed both as a part of the overall formalism and as separate bits of formalisms that can be applied to separate bits of constructions, which are, sort of, 'floating around' (cf. Chapter 5) in the (mental) grammars of people; on the other hand, the format illustrates the option that only fragments of what the whole formalism is intended to describe may be used in real constructions. A sentence produced by some Danish speaker may drop the conjunction and start with node number †1†[14] and end up somewhere in node number †4† having made a perfectly well-formed sentence including some adverbial specifications but without having run through the complicated algorithms of nodes †5† through †7†. It was one of Diderichsen's empirical insights that his so-called 'v n a' 'fields' reduplicate themselves: 'v n a V N A' (cf. Chapter 2), which, in due course, implies that sometimes you will not need more than the first field 'v n a', but in the end his pedagogical intuition failed since he said that, when practising sentence analysis, in case there might have been something in, for instance, the 'N' position then something naturally otherwise placed in the 'a' position should be 'moved' to the 'A' position. The EFA(X)3 format above illustrates the redundancy of this practice.

Finally, this format demonstrates the basic difference between a Chomskyan tree-structure and the EFA(X)3 calculus. In the tree-structure some expressions are supposed to be attached to branches of the tree and their placement is supposed to be a result of the process of having been there from the beginning or having been moved from somewhere else, in principle reflecting a number of rewrite rules like those found in early transformational grammar. The consequence is that the task of the grammarian is to devise rules for movements, and when sentences become even more complex – and maybe look strange because they are found in exotic languages – the rules may become even more complicated. Some of the linguists working in the Chomskyan tradition have spent a lot of time designing new rules to solve such problems. I would not claim that the EFA(X)3 solution is the one that would solve all problems, only that the problems have been relocated. Instead of saying that expressions should move around in a tree-structure, I say that for each expression the speaker wants to use it is checked by an inner mechanism that is adequately described by the EFA(X)3 calculus. In short, the complexity of the process is taken out of the tree-structure – as a kind of closed-circuit system – and put into the rules of a string of symbols in the form of a calculus, and the formal analysis is a sequential checking of whether an item (picked up from the lexicon in due order) is allowed in each single slot.

Whether the features of the EFA(X)3 formalism mentioned here make a more adequate model of what goes on in the cognitive systems of human beings may be hard to evaluate but in the concluding chapter (Chapter 5, Conclusions and Perspectives) I shall briefly present the outlines of a cognitive model that matches the EFA(X)3 formalism. The test of the cognitive model is a matter of experimental linguistics and will be carried out in future so, for the time being, the EFA(X) framework can only be justified by illustrating its adequacy in a number of analyses. In the following, I will take up a number of syntactic constructions in Danish and Swedish in order to show how the EFA(X) model is able to make adequate structural and formal descriptions of these constructions. First it will be emphasized that what concerns Danish and Swedish typology and genealogy is, somehow, two sides of the same coin. Then a reasonable number of constructions will be analysed, and finally some especially problematic issues in syntax – and grammar, in a broad sense – such as government vs. agreement and the question of what prepositions really are will be taken up in order to offer accounts that may solve problems that are particularly tricky and controversial when uncovering these patterns in the East Scandinavian languages of Danish and Swedish.

The syntax of Danish and Swedish: a more detailed survey

In the following I will present a number of syntactic descriptions – and sporadically some explanations. As to the explanations, I have to make a number of reservations. In a philosophical context the notion of explanation is an evasive idea because it is hard to offer a well-defined concept that covers all domains. On the other hand, it is used in both everyday language and scientific nomenclatures for (sometimes very) different purposes, and accordingly it has to be specified also in this context. An initial problem with explanations and causes in language descriptions is the fact that linguistic expressions are not always stable and regular entities: sounds and spellings may differ, sentences and phrases may appear fragmented, and even basic linguistic structures may be punctuated by circumstances that are seemingly accidental; and this is also the reason why only a minor part of the details of Danish and Swedish grammar can be touched upon in this context. In addition, such basic structures are seldom, according to Jespersen, 'logical'. An obvious candidate for 'logical deficiencies' in the context of Germanic and Romanic languages are gender systems, of which Danish and Swedish still have a common gender and a neuter gender as a kind of historical relic being endowed with no evident functional features in the modern versions of these languages. So, when offering explanations in the following I shall, for these reasons, use the notions of 'cause' and 'explanation' with all kinds of reservations. Also, the concept of 'proof' may technically be applied only to logic and mathematics (and in a court of law), 'causes' in the real world and 'explanations' in human minds may only be applied to cases where mechanisms are fairly well accounted for in detail.

Sentences, phrases and differences

As suggested in Chapter 3 the exhaustive analysis of a Danish or Swedish sentence will start out with annotation of the constituents (CSTS) of the sentence and the components (CPNS) of the phrases (if there are any), thereby establishing a STRUCTURAL ANALYSIS. This is done as, for instance, in (18):

```
(18)  (Dan)
      og derfor har Peter fra Kbh ikke trænet de to store hunde
      c  qa      aux s-nom⁀prp⁻nom na  v       o-det-adq-adj-nom
      i dag
      pa-prp-nom
      and therefore has P from Copenhagen not trained the two big dogs today
```

The symbols, including the connecting hyphens or broken lines, tell us that there are two constituents comprising one expression each, the conjunctional 'c' and the adverbial 'qa', that the nominal constituents 's' and 'o' are phrases and that one of the components (aux) of the verbal 'v' is ALLOCATED (ALC) to a position between the 'c' and 's'. This fully conforms to the Danish calculus, a fact that is shown by having the instantiated CSTS and CPNS displayed in bold (cf. Chapter 3), and the notation {x≈qa} means that in the string the x-variable is instantiated by the CST 'qa' :

```
    NOTN_EFAX3 (Dan)
    ∑>
Ω  †0†c_πc

  Ω  †1†s_πs\{x≈qa}

    Ω  †2†v_πv\◊aux◊

      Ω  †3†s₂_π{s}/{o[m*]}

        Ω  †4†a_πpa/qa/na

          Ω  †5†v₂_πv◊{aux}/vrb/vva◊/{ra}

            Ω  †6†o_π{p}/o/{vva}>{o}/p/{s}/kc^kp

              Ω  †7†a₂_πra/pa>∑

sequence constraints:
[*mig, dig, sig, ham, hende, den, det, os, jer, dem]
OBS x≈pa = x is instantiated by pa
```

The combination of the structural analysis above and the highlighted symbols means that the calculus has checked the parameters (and the bold ones signal occurrence while the regular ones signal non-occurrence) and that a FORMAL ANALYSIS has been carried out. Next, the phrases can be dissolved:

```
(18a-d) (Dan)

 Peter fra Kbh (N_PHR)
 nom--prp⁻nom
 >◊det/adq/adj^^/nom^^√prp/det/adq/adj/nom√psp◊>

 de to store hunde (N_PHR)
 det-adq-adj-nom
 >◊det/adq/adj^^/nom^^√prp/det/adq/adj/nom√psp◊>

 i dag (A_PHR)
 prp⁻nom
 >◊prp/det/adq/adj^^/nom^^√prp/det/adq/adj/nom√psp◊>

 har »» slået (V_PHR)
 aux    v
 >◊aux◊◊{aux}/vrb/vva◊>
```

For convenience, the corresponding calculuses have been displayed below the analyses and corresponding to the sentence analysis the combination of the structural phrase analyses and the calculuses presents a formal phrase analysis. An ellipsis in the text is, in the analysis format, marked with the French quotation marks: '»»', as in *har* »» *slået*. As for Danish and Swedish, there are, so far, no special differences between the languages:

```
(19)  (Swe)

och    därför   har    Peter från Kbh inte tränat   de två stora hundarna

c      qa       aux    s-nom⁀prp⁻⁻nom na  v          o-det-adq-adj-nom

idag

pa-nom

and therefore has P not trained the two big dogs-the today
```

The most salient differences are those concerning different words, inflections and/or spellings in that, for instance, we find the Swedish supine form *tränat* and the double definiteness *de ... hundarna*, and this sentence conforms directly to the Danish calculus. The same goes for, almost all of, the phrases:

```
(19a-d)  (Swe)
Peter från Kbh (N_PHR)
nom--⁀prp⁻nom
>◊det/adq/adj^^/nom^^√prp/det/adq/adj/nom√psp◊>

de två stora hundarna (N_PHR)
det-adq-adj--nom
>◊det/adq/adj^^/nom^^√prp/det/adq/adj/nom√psp◊>

idag (A_PHR)
nom
>◊prp/det/adq/adj^^/nom^^√prp/det/adq/adj/nom√psp◊>

har »» tränat (V_PHR)
aux     v
>◊aux◊◊{aux}/vrb/vva◊>
```

Until now the examples and analyses offered have categorized the constituents of the sentences and annotated the constituents according to the symbolic conventions proposed above. Furthermore, the annotated constituents have been furnished with annotations that showed to which node each constituent belonged, thereby yielding formal analyses. In the following, the analyses will combine identification of constituents as well as the components of the phrases according to the notational system presented above, but no formal analyses in the form of calculuses will be displayed – it will just be taken for granted that an analysis offered as an example actually will conform to the relevant calculus. First, we take up sentence analysis as above:[15]

```
(20)

og derfor  har  Peter  vist  alligevel   ikke  holdt  af  Pia  længe (Dan)

c  qa      aux  s      na----------------  v-------  o    pa

and therefore has Peter presumably anyhow not cared for Pia (for) long
```

Then sentence and phrase analysis:

```
(20a)

og derfor  har  Peter  vist  alligevel   ikke  holdt  af  Pia  længe (Dan)

c  qa      aux  s      vqa--vqa-------na   v----vva  o    pa

and therefore has Peter presumably anyhow not cared for Pia (for) long
```

Each phrase has been annotated and the extension of the phrase is, as above, marked with hyphens or a broken line. In some cases a phrase contains a sub-phrase and the subordinate relations of the components are not quite straightforward, and then the annotation will, as mentioned, look like this:

```
(20b) (Dan)

og derfor  har  Peter  fra Kbh  ikke  trænet   de to store hunde  i dag

c  qa      aux  s-nom-prp⁻nom    na    v        o--det-adq-adj-nom  pa-prp-nom

and therefore has Peter from Copenhagen not trained the two big dogs today
```

As can be seen from the examples (19) through (20) sub-phrases are marked by being connected with their embedding phrase by slashes whereas the internal components are connected by one or more horizontal bars (quotation dashes).

Now a number of fairly simple constructions will be presented in order to show the principles of analyses and to exemplify some similarities and some differences between Danish and Swedish.

```
(21)

Pia  løb    hen    ad vejen (Dan)

s    v      ra     pa-prp-nom


Pia  sprang  längs vägen (Swe)

s    v               pa-prp-nom

Pia ran along the road


(22)

Pia  kom   løbende  hen    ad vejen (Dan)

s    v     pa       ra     pa-prp-nom
```

```
Pia    kom    springande    längs vägen (Swe)

s      v      pa            pa-prp-nom

Pia came running along the road


(23)

et halvt spist æble lå på bordet (Dan)

s-det-adq-adj-nom v pa-prp-nom

ett till hälften ätet äpple låg på bordet (Swe)

s-det⌐prp⌐adq----adj--nom v pa-prp-nom

a half-eaten apple lay on the table
```

Two out of three sentences seem to be different between the two languages, but it should be observed that the different constructions are elicited by lexical differences. Where Danish prefers an adverb *hen* (approximately) 'over (direction)' and a preposition *ad* 'along' to express the relation, Swedish – like English – needs only a preposition *längs* 'along'. And Swedish needs a 'prepositional phrase' in order to express the fact that half of the apple has been eaten whereas Danish can put together the phrase from a quantificational expression *halv* in the neuter *halv-t* and, like Swedish, a past participle *spist* / *ätet*. Accordingly the Swedish 'adq' becomes a sub-phrase: *till hälften*. These differences only show that the languages have taken different historical paths making different words and collocations the preferred ways for Danes and Swedes of expressing themselves. In fact, all of the examples (21–3) would fit into the prototypical Scandinavian syntactic structure. Actually, each language might have followed the historical path of the other one and chosen the alternative constructions; they both have the sufficient parallel lexicons. I suggest that such phenomena are called NORMATIVES, i.e. FORMATIVES, or combinations thereof, that might well have been chosen otherwise in the process of language (or dialect) change.

This is not the case with the examples in the following. Take the constructions:[16]

```
(24)

han    tog    trøjen    af         (Dan)    he took the sweater off

s      v      o         ra

han    tog    av        tröjan     (Swe)    he took off the sweater

s      v      ra        o
```

and we have the different placements of the adverbial 'ra' (in the Danish and Swedish tradition called verb particles) reflected in the calculuses, and this is an obligatory structure in Swedish. Not quite so with:

```
(25)

nu   vil   læreren  ikke     svare  (Dan)   now will the teacher not answer
pa   aux   s        na       v

nu   vill  läraren  inte     svara  (Swe)   now will the teacher not answer
pa   aux   s        na       v

nu   vill  inte     läraren  svara  (Swe)   now will not the teacher answer
s    aux   na       s        v
```

As mentioned in the previous section the negation may be placed in front of the subject (and in Swedish grammar books it is emphasized that the subject must be stressed in spoken language, but this is not evident when found in written language). On the other hand, more or less unstressed pronominal objects may be found after a negation in Swedish, compare:

```
(26)

jeg   kendte  hende  ikke    (Dan)   I knew her not
s     v       o      na

jag   kände   henne  inte    (Swe)   I knew her not
s     v       o      na

jag   kände   inte   henne   (Swe)   I knew not her
s     v       na     o
```

The last of these constructions is normally not licensed in Danish, and if so then the pronoun must be stressed, but it would be perceived as pretty awkward by a speaker of Danish and it would normally be paraphrased. As also mentioned in the previous section, reflexive pronouns may be found on both sides of the 'logical subject' of the reflexive expression in Swedish:

```
(27) (Dan)

om morgenen  barberede  manden  sig
pa---------  v          s       o
(Swe)

på morgonen  rakade     mannen  sig    in the morning shaved the man
                                       himself
pa---------  v          s       o

på morgonen  rakade     sig     mannen in the morning shaved himself
                                       the man
pa---------  v          o       s
in the morning shaved (himself) the man himself
```

This is not licensed in Danish and one may wonder why. Apart from the placement of the ra-adverbial in Swedish, that language seems to accept more topical alternatives than Danish, and the infinitival marker makes no exception:

```
(28)

hun   bad   hende   om   undtagelsesvis   at forlade  klasseværelset (Dan)

s     v     do      vva  qa               o⌐ifm⌐inf--nom

hun   bad   henne   om   att undantagsvis lämna      klassrummet       (Swe)

s     v     do      vva o⌐ifm-vqa--------⌐inf---nom

she asked her (to) as-an-exception (to) leave the classroom
```

In this analysis I take no stance in the debate on what infinitives and infinitive markers are – but I will offer some clarifications below – and the word forms are only annotated with the symbols *ifm* (infinitive marker) and *inf* (infinitive) respectively. If, anyhow, one accepts the idea that the separation in Swedish of the marker from the infinitive has the effect that the adverbial expression *undantagsvis* must be perceived as a part of the verbal phrase (a reading that does not seem to be justified in Danish), then it seems as if what looks like a more liberal topology (the infinitive marker can be separated from the infinitive) actually is a symptom of a stricter phrase structure. I will come back to some principles on that below. For now, I will offer another example of what could also be seen as a more rigid phrase structure in Swedish. Participles really differ between Danish and Swedish:

```
(29)

han   havde sparket   bolden   ud (Dan)

s     aux---v          o        ra

han   hade sparkat    ut        bollen (Swe)

s     aux--v          ra        o

he had kicked (out) the ball (out)
```

These sentences display the features mentioned above that the ra-adverbials are, in general, placed differently in Danish and Swedish, and it seems to have serious effects on what could be labelled as passive constructions with participles:

```
(30)

bolden    var sparket   ud (Dan)

s         aux-v          ra

bollen    var           utsparkad (Swe)

s         v              sp

the ball was (out-)kicked (out)
```

In Danish the copula in the preterite will normally be interpreted as an auxiliary and the participle as the verbal ('the main verb') of the sentence while keeping

the ra-adverbial in place. The participle would (presumably) not be interpreted as a subject predicative, not even if the 'passive periphrastic verb' *blive*
'become' had been inserted: *bolden var blevet sparket ud*. This can be checked
by choosing the noun in the plural: *boldene var blevet sparket ud* 'the balls had
been kicked out'. Nothing inflectional happens to the participle, so it seems
most natural to see *var blevet sparket* as a verb phrase. Not so in Swedish. The
construction *bollen var utsparkad* is significant on two counts: the participle
has been inflected in that the *-d* signifies the common gender of the participle
in concord with the common gender of the moun *boll-en*, i.e. a *-d*, which is a
voiced sound in Swedish, expresses the concord with the voiced *-n* in *bollen*.
And in the plural the phenomenon becomes even more salient: *boll-arna var
utspark-ade*. This is not what happens in contemporary Danish. We have some
relics of strong verb conjugations in participles that function as attributives: *de
indskrev-ne studenter* 'the enrolled students', but these are perceived as adjectives and would not be seen as predicatives following a copula verb: *studenterne
er indskrevet/skrevet ind* 'the students are (i.e. have been) enrolled (in)'. The
second characteristic of the Danish vs. Swedish differences in the participles is
the fact that, while Danish may keep the ra-adverbial placed in its secure place
after the object, or may make it a prefix of the verb without altering the verbal
function when 'transforming' the object into a subject, Swedish seems to handle
the ra-adverbial according to strict 'rules'. It is prepositioned in front of the
object and coming after the verb form (which is a Swedish supine), but when
the object becomes the subject of an analogous sentence, then the 'ra'-adverbial,
sort of, stays in place and becomes a prefix to the verb, which in turn becomes
an inflected participle that can function as an adjective. One could (without
making any mystifying speculations) say that Swedish uses the inflectional
options in order to keep a kind of balance between syntax and morphology,
in due course in order to make the logical content explicit. Basically Danes do
not know what constituent a non-attributive past participle actually is; and one
might express the personal opinion that we can live happily without knowing.
It has, however, the effect that we are able to put together more ambiguous
constructions than Swedes. The verbs *få* 'have, make' and *lade* 'let' – which I
would prefer to call pseudo-auxiliaries (*lade* is a kind of modal verb) – behave
differently in Danish and Swedish:

(31a–d)

han	**fik**	sin bil	**repareret**	med det samme[17] (Dan)
s	v	o------	op	pa----------

```
han    fik repareret   sin bil    med det samme (Dan)
s      v-aux-v         o------    pa----------
he had (repaired) his car (repaired) directly/immediately

han    fick    sin bil    reparerad   med det samma (Swe)
s      v       o------     op          pa----------
he had his car (made a) repaired (car) directly/immediately

han    fick reparerat    sin bil    med det samma (Swe)
s      aux--v            o-----     pa----------
he had repaired his car directly/immediately
```

The last of the constructions (31d) is not excluded but is, by Swedes, characterized as 'regional (southern and western parts of Sweden) language use'.
So, while Swedish explicitly expresses the fact that, in this case, the owner
of the car got his car back in a repaired state (common gender in *bil-en* is
in concord with common gender in *reparera-d*), whatever Danish expressions are being chosen only the (event of 'repairing') meaning of the verb is
explicit and the state of 'being repaired' about the car can only be explicitly
expressed by the verb 'repair' as a participle in an attributive position: *en
repareret bil* 'a repaired car'. Then the reason for the analysis of (31a), namely,
that the syntactic function of *repareret* is as an 'op' (an object predicative,
i.e. a adjectival function) is the fact that an interpretation of *repareret* as a
verbal constituent would violate Danish syntax as described by the EFA(X)3
calculus and other grammatical description of Danish. It means that Danish,
because of morphological decay, in contexts with the verb *få*, can choose
between different constructions in which different alignments of constituents
(effecting different instantiated constituents) do not affect the meaning of the
construction or the scenario referred to (in fact, the meaning stays vague),
contrary to Swedish that offers different basic semantics, namely, verbal
semantics (the supine) vs. adjectival semantics (past participle). Even more
clear-cut is the case with the (pseudo-modal) verb *lade / låta* 'let' in Danish
and Swedish respectively:

```
(32a-c)
vi    lod    børnene    fotografere (hinanden) (Dan)
s     mod    o------    v
vi    lät    barnen     fotografera (varandra) (Swe)
s     mod    o          v
we let photograph the children each other
'we let the children take photos of each other'
```

```
vi   lät   fotografera   barnen (Swe)
s    mod   op                 o
we let (be) photograph(ed) the children (by somebody else)
'we had taken photos of the children'
```

The Swedish sentences express different scenarios in that the first one tells us that the children were allowed to take photos of each other while the second one tells us that we allowed the children to have somebody take photos of them. In this scenario the children are ascribed the feature of being photographed and this is the reason why we have the object predicative in the last construction. It has, of course, to do with the special lexical semantics of the verb *lade / låta* 'let', but in the end the difference means that in Danish the meaning of the sentence as such becomes crucially dependent on the contextual meaning of the discourse or the text because the Danish sentence can have both meanings.

The pattern that emerges from this is apparently a kind of paradox: on the face of it Swedish seems to be a language with a freer 'word order' since words can be found in a number of places where they cannot be found in parallel Danish sentences. Adverbials pop up between the two normal places of the subject in the beginning of sentences, reflexive pronouns appear in front of the subject in its alternative place, a special adverbial, 'ra', is found to the left of the object, and, finally, an auxiliary verb may be omitted in subordinate clauses. On the other hand, freedom is rather limited in that it is only freedom relative to a Diderichsen sentence table matrix. In fact, all occurrences in unusual places are strictly governed by what traditional grammars would describe as 'rules'. Certain words or functions may only be found in certain places, and from a traditional point of view one may ask whether it has to do with grammatical, semantic or pragmatic 'rules'. I do not see it quite that way. It should be kept in mind that the Diderichsen sentence table was (1) based on empirical generalizations from Danish, and (2) it was not a word-order-matrix. As for the first feature, Danish is an extremely rigid topical language: units (constituents and components) come in strict order, and minor changes in the order may have severe effects on the semantics of sentences (and this is not contradicted by the Danish ambivalence diagnosed in (31a, b) since that has to do with phrase structure). As for the second feature, the sentence table handled not only words but also what Diderichsen called *helheder* 'unities', which is what I call phrases, i.e. as constituents containing more than one morpheme. So when the sentence table is applied to Swedish, a number of things may look like abnormalities and also as liberated from the straitjacket of the sentence table. A broad view may also try to explain the differences by pointing to the more detailed morphology of Swedish, but that only suggests a vague relationship that cannot directly be accounted for. Instead, in the framework of Formative Grammar I would like to suggest that the difference lies in the different ways phrases and government/ agreement relations are organized in Danish and Swedish respectively. This will be dealt with in a following section but before that the topic of typology and genealogy will be taken up.

Typological features of Danish and Swedish: genealogical effects

If it seems plausible that the syntaxes of Danish and Swedish are conceived of as DEVIATIONAL TOPOLOGICAL STRUCTURES, then the characteristics of the deviations have to do with the stronger and weaker compulsory linear distribution of the constituents and morphemes. How this has come about is basically a matter of the historical processes from which the languages evolved from what was, presumably, the same (in a very broad sense) language about a thousand years ago; a GENEALOGICAL narrative that is an acknowledged fact in the history of the Scandinavian languages. In this section two cases concerning language type and historical processes will be taken up, and the first one can be illustrated by a sentence from a text by H. C. Andersen (1843–55). In the subordinate clause one finds a Danish construction and the corresponding Swedish translation (the notation '> ä ö ü <' marks the sub-clause):

```
jeg   saa   han       skyndte   sig   bort   med dit lille barn; (HCA Dan)

s     v     o>e s     v          o     ra     pa---------------<

s_    v_    o_>s_  v_     s_      a_____<
            p      2       2      2

jag   såg   att   han     skyndade  sig   bort   med ditt lilla barn (HCA Backm)

s     v     o>uc s        v          o     ra     pa----------------<

s_    v_    o_>c_ s_   v_     s_      a_____<
            p            2     2      2

I saw (that) he hurried himself away with your little child
(my bold typeface, HG)
```

The Danish construction has omitted the (general, neutral or semantically fairly void) subordinating conjunction (henceforth also called a subjunction in accordance with some Scandinavian traditions) *at* 'that', that otherwise signals a subordinate clause (and does so without specifying the nature of the subordination), as opposed to the way in which it is actually found in the Swedish translation. According to the topological structure of Modern Danish sub-clauses, the occurrence of the subordinating conjunction ought to be the precondition for the occurrence in the potential alternative position of the finite verbal as in: *jeg så at han ikke skyndte sig bort* 'I saw that he not hurried himself away'. The omission is very common in Contemporary Danish and in spoken Danish it is almost ubiquitous where the sub-clause is the object of the main clause (except for some particular constructions) and also in sub-clauses that are part of 'prepositional phrases'. In Swedish *att* may also be omitted but that is subject to less tolerant constraints at that point (cf. *Svenska Akademiens Grammatik,* vol. 4: 536–7) and it raises the question as to whether it is possible to explain these differences, which mostly seem to be tendencies. The mid-twentieth-century differences are described in detail by Hulthén (vol. II, 1948: 181, 183 seqq.), and an explanation may take as its point of departure two kinds of conceptual framework: first, the overall characteristics of the languages in question, and, second, what sort of influence may presumably have directed the historical orientation of the languages.

The solution to the first issue may be grasped by means of the assumption laid out in Chapter 3 that the syntactic structures of Danish and Swedish are structural deviations of the same 'proto'-structure and that they DEVIATE from each other as to the extent they use TOPOLOGICAL or MORPHOLOGICAL SIGNI-FICATION of the syntactic functions of constituents in sentences. Thus, it can be – on the basis of the analyses above – reasonably assumed that Danish is a more topological language than Swedish, and that Swedish is a more morphological language than Danish, and furthermore on the basis of the well-known facts that Danish has three inflectional categories in the class of nouns while Swedish has five, that Danish has three conjugational categories in the class of verbs while Swedish has four, and that Swedish has the syntactic features of 'double definiteness' (cf. below) in the noun phrases and, even so, the Swedish supine is governed exclusively by the auxiliary *ha(va)* in contrast with Danish. It should also be observed that Swedish has the prosodic feature of 'musical accents' that seems to provide Swedish pronunciation with more phonetic substance than Danish pronunciation. These different structural implementations of the syntax of the two languages can be characterized by the terms STRONG VS. WEAK TOPOLOGY and MORPHOLOGY. Thus Danish can be said to be a language with STRONG TOPOLOGICAL SIGNIFICATION and WEAK MORPHOLOGICAL SIGNIFI-CATION, while Swedish is a language with topological signification WEAKER than Danish and morphological signification STRONGER than Danish. These labels are, of course, just labels, and they should be justified by a way of pointing to some mechanisms that may explain the differences.

In the end it involves the interesting philosophical question of the final cause of everything, but as a topic (the second issue above) in historical linguistics – where it is assumed that synchronic states of languages are results of diachronic changes and (so-called) language development – the question is, in general, asked: what affects (and maybe effects) the process of change? In my view it is – in a simple scenario – reasonable to assume three (presumably unconscious) basic motivations for changing linguistic expressions and their relations: (1) economy, i.e. the motivation of saving energy in articulation or writing; (2) semantic distinction, i.e. the motivation of obtaining clear linguistic communication (and clear cognition); and (3) social distinction, i.e. the motivation of using linguistic features as symbols of social and psychological characteristics (cf. Götzsche 2010, on historical linguistics).[18] Of these motivations the first is in opposition to the other ones, and the results of linguistic changes may be seen as produced by the interplay and balance between them. Sometimes a language changes rapidly, and according to a quotation in Brink and Lund (1975, vol. 1: 49), the Danish linguist Karl Verner was astonished by the extensive changes in spoken Danish during the Modern Danish period because he realized the number of problems in linguistic communication between the generations. I see two acknowledged reasons for not being astonished: first, it is a well-known fact that, in general, spoken language is often phonetically relatively redundant, and when we know what we talk about, embedded in a universe of discourse, we are able to communicate, more or less successfully, with people using phonetically very different expressions like those of dialects and those of related languages like Danish, Swedish and Norwegian; and, second, it is also a well-known fact that people do not know (or are aware of) what they actually say (phonetically) or what they actually hear, i.e. the specific acoustic (in the end auditory) nature of the linguistic medium. Hence, guided by the objects in the surroundings, the imagined topics of conversation and by expectations about what they would prefer to hear, generations are able to talk with each other and understand each other (to the extent it is necessary in the discursive context) in spite of considerable variation in pronunciation.

So, then, what makes Danish delete the subjunction *at* 'that' to a larger extent than Swedish *att* 'that' as a subjunction? A preliminary answer will be that it has to do partly with pronunciation and partly with phrase structure in Danish and Swedish. The topic last mentioned will be taken up below, but as for Danish pronunciation it does not support intentions on the part of the speaker to keep the subjunction in use. A variant of the sentence above from H. C. Andersen (1843–55) may look like this with the subjunction inserted:

```
jeg sagde (at) han skyndte sig bort
```

The combination of sounds in the chain *sagde at han* after the initial -s- in standard Danish may end up as one long frontal open-mid vowel – maybe in the process getting slightly more open and thereby becoming a diphthong – and finishing up with the alveolar nasal -n-. Some Danes may object to my claim that the laryngeal in *han* is omitted but I shall maintain the claim that it is, in a context like this, very often omitted. And if I am right, it may be pretty hard to ascertain the subjunction in vernacular Danish. Which phonemes are actually involved is, then, a good question.

Another instance of historical change leaving typological traces is what is above described as auxiliary-deletion in Swedish subordinate clauses. The option of Swedish aux-deletion emerged in the last part of the seventeenth century, probably as a result of influence from German (cf. Malmgren 1985), and in my view there may be a connection between this phenomenon, the development of a special supine form in Swedish and the development of the special subordinate clause construction in the Central Scandinavian languages (cf. Götzsche 1990).[19] According to Platzack (1988), it can be reasonably assumed that the subordinate clause construction emerged in the sixteenth and seventeenth centuries (cf. also Pettersson (1988) and Svanlund (1988)), and according to Diderichsen (1944), there are indications of the special supine in the strong verb conjugation in the Old Swedish period (1500–1700). The verb form – the history of which is described in detail by Ekbo (1943), and put into context by, among others, Ljunggren (1934) and Johannisson (1945) – was, according to the tradition, allegedly labelled as 'supine' by the Swedish grammarian Sahlstedt (1769) (but the term is mentioned by Ihre (1745)), and the phonetic (and orthographic) basis of the category is the special ending in the strong verbal conjugations: -*it*, for instance, in *han har komm-it* 'he has come', in connection with the auxiliary *ha* 'have', and how these phonemes came about is an interesting story but it will not be taken up here. There is a 'government' relation between the auxiliary and the verb form and, as opposed to Danish constructions, the supine cannot be combined with *vara* 'be'. The (assumed) fact that the emergence of the supine and the aux-deletion partly coincide may lead to the conclusion that there is a connection between them. The spreading of the aux-deletion was (according to Johannisson (1960)) very rapid (ca. 25 years), and the speed cannot be explained only linguistically and has to be seen as an effect of the social motivation of the high status in the seventeenth century of the Germans and the German culture and language; which, by then, had aux-deletion. But the syntactic structure of a language can hardly change without the existence of a structural basis for the change in question, and this basis was probably the emerged existence of both the subordinate clause construction (which Danish also has) and the verb paradigm of the supine exclusively connected in syntax with the auxiliary *ha* 'have' (a feature which Danish, like German, does not have; till now, cf. Götzsche 1997,[20] and cf. also Götzsche (2007) on the historical development of Danish syntax).The effect is, as mentioned above, that in Swedish the subordinate clause construction has the option of letting the non-finite verbal constituent of the supine function as a finite verbal, i.e. as a sentence-generating constituent, and, again, this supports my point of view that subordinate clauses are extremely fixed constructions and that Scandinavian sentences are established according to what I describe formally as 'strong subsequential implication'. But why, then, does Swedish and not Danish allow aux-deletion in sub-clauses? Again, it has to do with pronunciation and auxiliary functions in Danish, and a model for a kind of explanation will be offered in the section on government and agreement.

On government and agreement: and double definiteness

I shall not go into the deeper details of the theoretical problems associated with government and agreement, but in general one can say that these relations have grammatical functions in many languages – and also in Danish and Swedish – and one way of explaining these functions is the one chosen by Källström (1993) in his doctoral thesis. His basic question is:

Vilken information till mottagaren innehåller de böjningsformer som är utslag av kongruens?

What kind of information to the recipient do the inflectional forms effected by agreement contain?

(Källström 1993: 6)

I strongly agree that this pragmatic perspective is essential in explaining the grammatical phenomena. His notion of government is accounted for on p. 21, and in a concise form it says: there is a word that governs a unit (Källström: 'led'), the unit is inflected, and the property expressed by inflection belongs to the governed unit. In accordance with this, Källström's notion of agreement is in a condensed form: the grammatical phenomenon that some properties of a controller (Källström: 'kontrollör') are marked by inflection of an agreeing unit which has a syntactic relationship to the controller (p. 32). This seems fair enough, but, from a theoretical point of view, it may not fully answer the question. The problem is that these definitions presuppose that expressions have inherent grammatical (including morphological) and semantic properties in the traditional sense, and if my line of reasoning propounded in Chapter 3 is, so far, accepted, this is not likely to be the case; and furthermore it is not totally in accordance with the pragmatic point of view expressed by Källström in the quotation above. Finally, in Källström's model, these relations seem to hold between words, but according to the FoG principles words are not syntactic or syntagmatic entities. If government and agreement should be incorporated in my syntactic theory, I would propose notions of (1) GOVERNMENT as: CST-EXTERNAL MULTIPLE MORPHOLOGICAL SIGNIFICATION; and (2) AGREEMENT as: CST-INTERNAL MULTIPLE MORPHOLOGICAL SIGNIFICATION.[21] The definitions have the advantage that nothing is said about the morphemic forms involved; only that the syntactic signification is expressed by morphemes, and that more than one morpheme (in Formative Grammar: a part of more than one morpheme) is used to express the same syntactic function. Theoretically this is an advantage because the fact that expressional forms are similar or identical does not by itself imply any syntactic significance, and then it is, theoretically, more satisfactory to try to describe a (defined) general function – which may be instantiated by means of similar or identical forms, but also may be instantiated by other means – without any presumptions about the forms of the expressions. It is more or less obvious that this multitude of expressions is, in principle, redundant, but on the other hand there can be said to be some reason for their occurrence, because this morphemic overload contributes to what I see as basic characteristic features of syntactic unities and units: INTERNAL COHESIVENESS, EXTERNAL LIMITEDNESS and FUNCTIONAL INDEPENDENCE. This can be illustrated by some specific (some of them historical) constructions (excerpt from the Swedish translation 1877 of Hans Christian Andersen, 'Historien om en Moder') (Backm: 395)

```
(HCA Swe)
men sjön lyfte henne, som om hon (hade) sutt-it i
'but the lake lifted her, as if she (had) sat in'
```

In this case the relation (mentioned above) between the auxiliary verb and the supine ending can be described as government. The reason for keeping the basic notion of government, namely, that something governs something else (according to the proposed definition), is that morphological signification is a syntactic function expressing the category of one single constituent (in which there is a primary morpheme expressing the morphological signification). If so, signification of the same category in another constituent (in which there is a secondary (part of a) morpheme expressing the same morphological signification) can be said to be a little paradoxical, but not if it is assumed that the signified constituent triggers (i.e. governs) the signification in the other constituent. Thus there is no obvious reason why an auxiliary verb should be followed by a verbal form with a specially created inflectional ending (cf. neutralization in the preterite and the past participle: *sit, sat, sat* in English). But that it is in fact, in the case of this excerpt in Swedish, followed by a supine ending can be accounted for by saying that they not only co-occur, but that the occurrence of the supine is governed by the occurrence of the auxiliary verb, and that the function of the occurrence of the supine is to signify the status of the auxiliary verb as the morpheme (in EFA(X) so far: the allocated component) expressing finiteness; a property the supine ending of the non/ finite verb does not have. Evidently the supine also (redundantly) signifies the status of the non-finite verb as a non-finite verbal constituent (in EFA(X): that it is the verbal ('main verb') of the sentence), or, conversely, 'marks' that it is not the finite morpheme and that it lacks something expressing finiteness. But because the supine, in Swedish, occurs only in connection with the verb *ha(va)* these are only secondary effects of the basic function of the multiple morphological signification of the finite verbal constituent. Expressed in the technical language of Formative Grammar, the basic mechanism of the auxiliary-supine government in Swedish is, of course, not the relation of government between specific morphemes but the relation of government between, on the one hand, the merged syntactic and semantic signification of all the members of the morphemic paradigms of the finite verb morpheme and, on the other hand, all the members of the morphemic paradigm of the supine, but in this case the group of finite verb morphemes contains only two paradigms (the present tense paradigm and the preterite tense paradigm), and there is only one member in each paradigm (namely,. *har* and *hade*). At the morphematic 'level' the mechanism could be described as the relation that in the occurrence logic of constituents above is called consequential 'implication', i.e. the governed morpheme occurs if and only if the governing morpheme occurs – in this case, except for sub-clauses.

The claim that it is a multiple way of expressing the same syntactic function has *per se* nothing to do with the 'basic' semantics of the verbal forms – neither with their 'isolated' meaning nor with the 'combined meaning' of the two constituents – since the auxiliary has 'lost' the meaning of possession of the verb *ha(va)* 'have', and the only meaning of the supine is the (governed) morphological signification. But the syntactic functions may influence the paradigmatic (tense) semantics of the forms, and this, in turn, may enhance certain government effects on the syntactic application of verb forms. Which tenses the combination expresses – the past perfect tense or the present perfect tense – is, of course, determined by the tense of the auxiliary and its combination with the supine, and this may be facilitated or modified by the interpretation of the remaining part of the specific sentence – especially the adverbials – and the context. In the process of combination, the tense semantics of the finite verb paradigms (i.e. in this case either the present tense or the preterite tense of the auxiliary *ha(va)* 'have') is applied to all of the multiples of morphemes (in this case, so far, two morphemes: the finite aux and the supine) involved in the government relation. Thus, the actual tense meaning of the combination of the verbal constituents is expressed both by the auxiliary and the supine ending, and accordingly the paradigmatic semantics of the finite auxiliary may be transferred partly or totally to the governed morpheme, facilitated by the other constituents of the sentence. The way I see it, this semantic process is possible primarily on the basis of a previous transfer of morphological signification to the governed morpheme through frequent use. In Swedish, the mechanism may be described by saying that there is a primary partial transfer of the morphological signification of the auxiliary *ha(va)* 'have' to the supine, resulting in a secondary transfer of finite verb paradigmatic semantics, so that the auxiliary may be deleted in sub-clauses (a result which cancels the consequential 'implication' mentioned above and requires another description of the phenomenon), and seen in the perspective of this account, the relation of government between the auxiliary and the special supine ending – in combination with the fixed sub-clause-structure – seems to be the basis of this labile construction in Swedish sub-clauses.

So, in sum: the basic prerequisites for aux-deletion in Swedish are, first, a clear-cut expression for the auxiliary, in this case *har, hade* 'has, had', and a clear-cut inflectional ending for the Swedish supine, in the strong verb conjugation *-it* and in the weak conjugations endings that may to some extent be identical to those of the past participles but in general are contextually distinctive so that confusion does not take place. Danish is, compared to Swedish, something of a mess: there are, like in German, two auxiliaries, *er, var* 'is, was' and *har, havde* 'has, had', and the so-called non-finite form used as the 'main verb' cannot in its verbal constituent functions be distinguished from other syntactic functions. That there is a current tendency in Danish to drop the copula verb as an auxiliary and replace all instances with *har, havde* 'has, had' does not solve the Danish problem. And, again, it has to do with pronunciation. In spoken Standard Danish the only difference between the two is a minimal vowel distinction: *har* 'has' is a more open allophone of -a- while *er* 'is' is a more closed and fronted allophone of -a-; and the preterite pronunciation does not fully make the problem evaporate: *havde* 'had' is a vowel like the one in the present tense in front of an alveolar voiced fricative, while *var* 'was', in some manifestations, is almost identical to *har* 'had', leaving it to the non-occurrence of an object to make the distinction. Older people's pronunciation and more distinctive speech may, so to speak, be more distinctive, but the phonetic substance of Contemporary Danish does not leave much room for morpho-logical signification that would make aux-deletion in sub-clauses possible.

I would also prefer a government analysis of this Swedish excerpt (from the Swedish translation 1877 of Hans Christian Andersen 'Historien om en Moder', Backm: 395):

```
(HCA Dan / Swe)
Sø-en var ikke fross-et nok til …(Dan)
Sjö-n var icke tillräckligt frus-en för …(Swe)
'the lake (had)/was not (been) frozen sufficiently / sufficiently frozen for'
```

This is because it is an instance of the relation between two basic constituents, the subject *sjö-n* 'the lake' and the predicative *frus-en* 'frozen'. A traditional analysis will claim that there is agreement between the two words on the grounds that the inflectional endings are the 'same', or at least sufficiently similar (common gender *(e)n*), but if one can find no background for the sameness then it cannot be said to be significant in accounting for the phenomenon. If, on the contrary, we can say that the morphemic reduplication is an extra feature expressing the status of the subject, then the 'sameness' of the morphemes is functional, but then we cannot say that it is a mere 'identity' of inflectional endings. We have to say that the 'sameness' is triggered by an extra morphological signifi-cation of the subject in the subject predicative, by which this signification is then governed. Thus, the inflection of a subject predicative, like the use of the nominative case affixed to the subject predicative which is found in a number of languages, seems not to have much to do with 'agreement', and does not neces-sarily have much to do with the syntactic signification of the predicative. The labelling of the subject predicative is sufficiently done in most cases by means of the topological construction, the copular verb and the semantics of the logical predicates of the 'underlying' statement, and if an inflectional ending is

needed, one might readily invent a *precusative suffix for this purpose. That the
inflection of the predicative is often in concord with that of the subject may be
motivated by the intuitive understanding of some kind of 'identity' or 'equivalence' between the two constituents, but the fact that this is not a compulsory
construction is indicated by the abundant counterexamples, and accordingly, in
my view, it is a misconception to believe that these constituents are in a stronger
or weaker sense 'correlated' by agreement. On the contrary, the basic function
of the inflection seems to be multiple morphological signification of the subject,
i.e. to tell the language user where to find the subject that is predicated in this
specific construction. This also entails that the identity or the similarity of the
morphemes is not the criterion of agreement as opposed to government, and
this fact can be illustrated by an example from Finnish:

```
(33)    Sitka on iso-ssa punaisi-ssa talo-ssa (Fin)
        Sirkka is in the big, red house
        'Sirkka is big-in, red-in, house-in'
```

The noun phrase 'the big, red house' is an adverbial, and both the tradition and
I will be inclined to call the morphemic (inflectional) 'sameness' agreement,
but for different reasons. What is important here is, in my view, not the identity
of the forms of the (illative) case endings meaning 'in' but the fact that the
multitude of morphemes occurs within a phrase functioning as a constituent.
It has a cohesive and delimiting function in telling the language user what
belongs to the constituent and what does not (what makes it independent), and
it may be debated to what extent it is in fact redundant, especially seen from
the perspective that Finnish sentence constituents are to some extent freely
distributed.

The same thing can be said about the Swedish double signification of the
definite meaning of nouns in certain constructions mentioned above as double
definiteness (which, in Standard Swedish is expressed in combinations of *den*
[noun], *den där/här* [noun] and *den* [adjective][noun]; and also in the neuter
and in the plural inflections):

```
(34)    den stor-a hund-en (Swe vs Dan:) den stor-e hund)
        'the big dog-the'

        den hund-en (Swe)
        'the dog-the'
```

In the Swedish examples the definite meaning is expressed by the definite article
den 'the' and the inflectional ending *-en* '-the', and because the phenomenon occurs

within a constituent (a phrase), it follows from what is said above that it is an instance of agreement, the function of which is to signify the internal cohesiveness, external limitedness and functional independence of the phrase.[22] Why it is so in Swedish and not in Danish was the question asked above. Now the question can be rephrased: if agreement is a way of holding the expressions of a phrase-formed constituent together and separating it from other constituents, why is that necessary in Swedish and not in Danish? The answer is that Danish syntax has a rigid topological structure, meaning that the constituents have to come in a certain linear order (which is, cf. Chapter 2, something different from word order) while Swedish has a more FLEXIBLE topological structure, meaning that constituents and/ or (phrase) components can be found (or may be missing) in places where they cannot be found in Danish sentences, as has been illustrated above. The reason for this seems to be that spoken Danish has very little morphological signification left (very few inflectional endings) so if a listener is to interpret what is said in terms of which expressions are, or belong to, which constituents, then he has, almost exclusively, the chain of sounds that can be decrypted as lexical expressions as the basis for his process of interpretation. Swedish has a – not RIGID but FIXED – syntactic topology and noun phrases may be found in obscure places where parts of them may be confused with other combinations of expressions if they are not held together by means of double definiteness, and it is more vital in Swedish in order to be able to identify what series of expressions really is a separate noun phrase.

Anyhow, this may not be the end of the story. In the first decade of the twenty-first century I have observed a tendency in Danish to create a kind of double signification of noun phrases in the plural:

```
(35)    jeg tager bestemt klimaproblemerne alvorlige (Dan)
        'I take definitely the climate problems serious'
        Nordjyske Stifstidende (Danish newspaper), 6 Sept. 2010

        et musikstykke der er klassikerne værdige
        'a piece-of-music that is the classics worthy'
        Danish Radio, 15 Dec. 2009

        de sociale udsatte
        'the social exposed' [not socially]
        (no reference)

        Den bureaukratiske etniske udrensning
        'the bureaucratic ethnic cleansing'
        Kristeligt Dagblad (Danish newspaper), 13 Nov. 2010
```

The first construction includes an object followed by an adverbial expression, and in the tradition – and according to Danish orthography – an inflectional -*t* suffixed to *alvorlig* should tell us that the adjective had become an adverb. Instead *alvorlig* has become a plural form by having the -*e* ending suffixed: *alvorlig-e*. The second construction displays an analogous problem in that the adjective *værdig* should have been furnished with a -*t* in order to show us that it works as a predicative in concord with *musikstykke*, that is a word in the neuter gender in Danish, cf. *musikstykke-t*. Instead *værdig* has been furnished with a plural ending: *værdig-e*, so that it is in agreement with the plural word *klassiker-ne*. The third construction is a noun phrase in that the adjectival derivation *udsat* 'exposed' from a verb, *udsætte* 'expose', has been derived once more and has become a noun *(en) udsat* '(an) exposed (person)'. It has a plural inflection, *udsatte* 'exposed (persons)', but an attributive adjective like *social* 'social' should, in that context, not be an adjective but an adverb and should therefore be provided with a -*t* in order to signify this (it should equal *socially*). Instead the adjective *social* is found inflected in the plural: *social-e*. The last one of these constructions actually has two readings: either it may mean 'the bureaucratic and ethnic cleansing', but in that case it ought to follow Danish orthographic conventions and insert a comma between *bureaukratiske* and *etniske*. On the other hand, a reading like that does not look more logical than an understanding saying that the newspaper headline deals with 'ethnic cleansing carried out in a bureaucratic way'. What is at stake is the delicate balance between different kinds of signification: what is more important? That we are able to ascertain the syntactic functions left over from the historical process, albeit in a fragile phonetic substance, or that the basic lexical semantics is able to transfer the logical content of the constructions and that phrases should signal how they are held together by agreement (as defined above)? If that last option is the more important phenomenon, then Danish seems to have embarked on a journey developing 'double plural inflection', something that looks like a version of Swedish double definiteness.

I shall not go into the historical background of Swedish double definiteness. Only point to the fact that Swedish and Danish seemingly use – or are about to use – double forms as what I call multiple morphological signification, but do it for different purposes and reasons. While Swedish may be said to have, and maintain, morphology and use it for making noun phrases identifiable even though their units may be spread out a little, then Danish may be said to 'invent' new noun phrases by altering syntactic and phrasal functions of expressions and thereby expressing logical information in a way that differs substantially from, for instance, Swedish. An extreme in multiple morphological signification is Finnish, as illustrated above, and it seems to be needed in that language because of a relatively 'free' constituent order. Swedish is a little mixed while Danish may end up creating peculiar forms of combining morphology and strict topology.

On prepositions and infinitives: the remains of the day

In order to answer the question asked above as to why there are differences between Danish and Swedish tendencies to omit the initial subjunction in sub-clauses, it will be convenient to see the phenomenon in connection with the infinitive marker and the overall question of prepositional functions. To begin with, I shall, in line with the account in the preceding section, also characterize the traditional 'prepositional government' found, for instance, in German as agreement:

```
(36)    für mich 'for me'(Ger)
        außer mir 'without me'
```

I see no reason for claiming that a preposition governs a specific case form, because the occurrence of the case forms, the accusative and the dative respectively, adds no new information to the semantics of the prepositions, and the case forms have in these phrases no function in the syntax (as opposed to their functions as signification of the object and the dative object respectively). In the technical language of Formative Grammar, what the case forms actually do when joined with prepositions, is that they signify, by extraordinary means, the fact that this is a preposition belonging to certain paradigms of prepositions, and apart from the specific (semantic signification or lexical) meaning of the preposition, it is the same thing the preposition does, and accordingly this is multiple morphological signification within a constituent. The argument is also valid for the German prepositions with 'double case government', because the information embodied in these prepositions is a further specification of the basic spatial (directional or locative) information of the verbs (in the concrete senses):

```
(37)    Peter legte den Schlüssel auf den Tisch (Ger)
        'Peter laid the key on the table'
        Der Schlüssel lag auf dem Tisch
        'the key lay (was lying) on the table'

(38)    Peter ging in den Park
        'Peter went into the park'
```

```
Peter ging in dem Park spazieren
'Peter went in the park walking'
```

If the verb is unchanged (e.g. *ging*) then the case form may 'disagree' with the verb meaning (in the last example in (38)), and then the case form is 'balanced' by the addition of an adverbial (*spazieren*). Thus, the case forms add no new information, neither to the verbs nor to the prepositions. If one wishes to apply a government analysis to the phenomenon, it ought to be the 'government relation' between the verbs and the case forms, but such a solution is not in accordance with the definitions proposed by me above. In the scope of FoG principles I cannot consistently say that the syntactic function of the verb is signified morphologically by the case forms. Therefore, I would prefer the agreement analysis also in these cases, implying that – provided the basic spatial and/or temporal verbal meaning in an sentence has been determined – the actual case form 'facilitates' the specific meaning of the preposition under the special circumstances determined by the verbal, i.e. agreement as CST-internal morphological signification. The way I see it, this line of reasoning can also be applied to the abstract and 'metaphorical' use of prepositions and case forms. Furthermore, the relation between, for instance, a subject and a verbal by 'agreement of person' (cf. Källström 1993: 25 seqq.):

```
(39)    du geh-st    (Ger)    'you go-you'
```

should, in my view, be analysed as government. It is evident that the morphemes are not similar but have a corresponding meaning, because one of them could be dispensed with, but it is equally evident that when they both occur on an obligatory basis, it is the occurrence of the specific subject that 'elicits' the occurrence of the personal ending of the verb. The significational task of the ending is a multiple and redundant signification of the CST-function of the subject, and why German has an extensive use of such sentence and phrase redundancy remains to be explained. One way of doing it may be to discuss – briefly – what prepositions actually are beyond 'the syntax of prepositions and prepositional phrases' (the entry by Jaworska (1999) in Brown and Miller 1999: 304).

This is not the place for an historical overview of the emergence of prepositions in some Western European languages, or for a review of theoretical positions on the issue. This is only an attempt to find a way to interpret the grammatical functions of prepositions within the theoretical framework of Formative Grammar and the EFA(X) technical nomenclature, especially in Danish and Swedish. If we recall the FoG claim that this kind of grammar rejects the idea that 'words' are made of morphemes like 'roots', 'inflections' and 'prefixes' that are somehow glued together and instead holds the idea that what resembles a word in texts, for instance, the English expression *bewildered* (which in the tradition is considered having the prefix *be-* and the preterite and past participle ending *-ed*), is regarded as one, and only one, morpheme, then prepositions are, so far, in FoG actually seen as morphemes, but maybe as truly 'bound morphemes' (a characteristic normally ascribed to inflectional endings or derivational prefixes). In a Jespersen way of seeing things, prepositions are clearly 'free expressions' (cf. Jespersen 1924: 18–24), albeit as members of the class of 'particles' (*ibid.*: 87), but it is an acknowledged problem that they, by definition, only occur in front of some nominal expression or some sub-clause. If they are found elsewhere as isolated morphemes then they can, from a FoG point of view, adequately be analysed as adverbs that are isomorphisms relative to prepositions. So an EFA(X) occurrence formula for prepositions may look like this:

```
nom\∫subclause∫°>prp
```

And this means that a preposition occurs if, and only if, there is an adjacent nominal expression or a sub-clause. Then prepositions sit uneasily between morphemes that can function as constituents (they can only be components) and totally locked 'morphemes' like prefixed items. One solution to this problem may be to see prepositions as morphemes that are labile (unstable) and may diffuse into other syntactic functions. They occur in phrases in front of a nominal item or a sub-clause, and they have the effect of forming a syntagmatic derivative: if the nominal item is a noun, then the combination of morphemes alters the function of the noun to the effect that the noun can no longer function syntactically as a noun, i.e. as a subject, an object or a predicative, only as an adverbial or as a subphrase. This means that prepositional constructions and nominals or nominal phrases are in complementary distribution, and this is just the syntactic signification of prepositions: they tell the language user that this noun is not a nominal sentence constituent. Apart from this, prepositions have, evidently, some lexical semantics, often something that has to do with temporal and spatial meanings, but in abstract contexts the semantics may be, so to speak, very abstract and subject to rapid changes. Thus there seems to be a tendency in Contemporary Danish to let the preposition *på* 'on' in abstract contexts spread into the domains of other prepositions. In essence, so-called postpositions, which are found in, for instance, Finnish, function in exactly the same way apart from their position after a nominal expression; and in accordance with the

FoG principles they would also be analysed with the nominal expression as the habitat (the 'head') and not the pre- or postposition. This morpheme would be seen as a specification of the nominal expression, yielding a complex semantics that can be used as, for instance, an adverbial specification or as post-positioned specification in a nominal phrase. And this leads us back to the question why subjunctions are more easily dropped in Danish as compared with Swedish and why infinitive markers are allowed to be separated from their infinitives in Swedish and not in Danish.

It is a well-known fact that while, in Danish and Swedish, the subjunction and the infinitive marker have identical language-specific spellings (Danish *at* and Swedish *att* respectively), it is an historical accident in that the subjunction goes back to Old Norse *þat* (a demonstrative pronoun) and the infinitive marker goes back to the preposition *at* (which can be seen in parallel with English *to* and German *zu* as infinitive markers), from which maybe the Swedish preposition *åt* 'to, direction' developed. Out of this has become, on the one hand, the subjunctional function of signifying a sub-clause and, on the other, the infinitive marking function of signifying an infinitive in certain contexts. These contexts are, in Danish and Swedish, characterized by the feature that the infinitive works as a noun:

```
(40)

Peter     prøver     at læse bogen (Dan)

s         v          o⁀prp⁻nom-nom

Peter tries to read the book
```

In this reading the infinitive marker is seen as a preposition and the infinitive as a noun, and if the analysis of prepositions proposed above is accepted, then the effect is that a verbal form functioning as a noun is signified as not being a noun, in due course making the combination of the infinitive marker and the infinitive eligible as specifications of the noun that comes after them (in FoG, basically a noun that is not part of a compound cannot specify another noun).

So far, this goes for Danish. As mentioned above, Swedish looks a little different:

```
(41)

Peter     försöker     (att) läsa boken (Swe)

s         v            o⁀prp⁻nom--nom

Peter tries to read the book


Peter     försöker     att inte läsa boken (Swe)

s         v            o⁀prp⁻vna⁻nom-nom

Peter tries to not read the book
```

In general, Swedish will omit the infinitive marker in the first case while keeping it in the second case when a negation has been inserted. The construction is, then, very much like that in a sentence in Swedish in which a negation, among other things, may be inserted in front of a verbal or an auxiliary, and if the infinitive construction might be mistaken for a sentence (a sub-clause) because of that, then the infinitive marker is in place to tell us that the infinitive is not, *per se*, a noun, only in combination with the infinitive marker is it a noun functioning as a non-noun that is licensed to specify another noun. Or licensed to function as a nominal constituent:

```
(42)

att läsa      är    bra (Swe)

s-ifm-ifv     v     sp

s-prp-nom     v     sp

to read is good
```

Even though the infinitive marker is not always obligatory:

```
(43)

(att) äta gröt     är    gott (Swe)

s-ifm-ifv-nom      v     sp

s-prp-nom-nom      v     sp

eat(ing) porridge is good
```

Swedish seems to let a noun (in the form of an infinitive without an infinitive marker) specify a noun when the two are adjacent to each other, and it may have to do with the pronunciation of the infinitival ending vowel in Swedish: -a-; which clearly differs in pronunciation from the rest of verbal morphology. And it is not in opposition to some expressions being placed between the infinitive and the infinitive marker in Swedish because it only shows that the Swedish infinitive is, by and large, identifiable without the infinitive marker in front of it. Whereas Danish, in which infinitives may, in pronunciation, be confused with other verb forms, needs the infinitive marker as part of its morphological signification.

And this brings us all the way back to subjunctions in Danish and Swedish. Jespersen (1924: 89) claims that: 'The so-called conjunction is really, therefore, a sentence preposition.' Hence, if prepositions are morphemes that cancel the nominal syntactic and syntagmatic (phrasal) functions of nouns, then one might be tempted to suggest that the 'dummy' subjunction *at/att* 'that' in Danish and Swedish cancels the 'normal' sentence structure and creates a kind of sentential derivation in the form of a sub-clause. The salient features of Danish and Swedish sub-clauses respectively have been outlined above and the main pattern reveals that Danish sub-clauses are topologically very strict, no obligatory constituents can be 'moved' and/or omitted in a Danish sub-clause, whereas in Swedish the auxiliary may be deleted, thereby transferring finiteness to the non-finite verb form; the mechanism being this: Swedish has an identifiable non-finite verb form, the supine, which in sub-clauses can take over the function as a finite verb and let the auxiliary be dropped, and therefore Swedish sub-clauses need the subjunction *att* to be in place. Accordingly, a Danish language user will be able to ascertain a sub-clause even though a subjunction is omitted whereas a Swedish language user may need a subjunction and combine it with a finite non-finite verb form in order to identify a sub-clause.

The occurrence of the subjunction as well as the omission of the auxiliary is an instance of what in FoG is called morphological signification, i.e. the shapes of morphemes and their occurrences (and sometimes their non-occurrences) tell the language user which status as sentence constituents they have or are part of. This feature is to a higher degree significant in Swedish, as opposed to Danish, which for its part as a language has not much morphology to assist the language user in finding out what is what, and therefore has to let the morphemes come in strict order. The prepositional and subjunctional examples just discussed above are only details expressing these general language types as derivations of one common Scandinavian language prototype, and so are the previously details taken up as analyses by means of the Formative Grammar principles and the technical apparatus of EFA(X)3.

Accordingly, the final overall pattern that emerges from this is: (1) the uncovering of the syntactic structures of the two languages, Danish and Swedish, pointing to their structural differences as they are displayed by their respective calculuses; and (2) a number of variational features shared by both languages and a number of unstable features not common between them as they are displayed by the analyses.

Particles and other minor expressions: a way out?

The problems scrutinized above ended up offering some structural explanations for the way some special syntactic constructions look in Danish and Swedish respectively, and the account also illustrated some differences between the languages. But the analyses did not solve the problem concerning what the different kinds of expressions 'word classes' 'really are'. In this section I will offer an alternative approach to these problems.

If some of the basic contentions of FoG are accepted, namely, that linguistic expressions are morphemes, that morphemes are the minimal expressions with (sometimes complex) meanings, and that morphemes are 'chunks' incorporating features signifying morphology and not 'roots and stems' glued together with each other and with 'inflectional endings' and 'derivational morphemes', then some unconventional solutions to the problems of the minor parts of language can be put forward. Assuming the basic insights of morphology and word formation studies, namely, that expressions may be reshaped in different ways in order to adjust meaning and/or adjust their syntactic (and syntagmatic) functions, I suggest that the notions of inflection and derivation are redefined:

```
§ inflection def
a morpheme is inflected when one or more features (phonological and/
or orthographic segments) have been changed and/or added to (also as
segments *dislocated from) the morpheme, resulting in the morpheme
having had its paradigmatic signification (paradigmatic semantics)
altered, thereby creating sub-paradigms.
# notation :, : (») :,
```

And

```
§ derivation def
a morpheme is derived when one or more features (phonological and/
or orthographic segments) have been changed and/or added to (also as
segments *dislocated from) the morpheme, resulting in the morpheme
having had its syntagmatic signification (categorial function) altered,
thereby being transferred to other — or creating new — paradigms.
# notation ., . (») .,
```

If we are open to the possibility that there are no derivational changes of the morpheme and that it only undertakes another syntactic function like conversions (which is a common phenomenon in English, where, e.g. deverbals are often made out of nouns and vice versa), then this is not far from the traditional way of doing things, but the basic criteria are being clarified in that the difference has to do specifically with function, and in that the units are specifically morphemes in the FoG understanding. If, in line with traditional nomenclature, the morphemic features are called affixes in both inflection and derivation, then languages like Danish, Swedish and English expose the traditional pre- and suffixes, but in general no infixes, and my approach is, so far, just another way of analysing and describing what is well known. But I would like to propose the idea – that is introduced in the definitions above – that features can be allocated (cf. above on auxiliary verbs as allocated morphemes). This means that certain parts of expressions that are not seen as separate morphemes are anyhow 'displaced' and found separated from their 'base'. Actually, auxiliary verbs could be conceived of in this way (in the following, punctuation marks, etc. are, for convenience, inserted also in the texts):

```
og    derfor   har:    Peter   ikke   :trænet   hunden   i dag
c     qa       auxl:   s       na     :v        o        pa---
```

The analysis (in which the colons in auxl: and :v mean that this is considered one morpheme that has been split) means that the auxl is an allocated (or maybe '(*) DISLOCATED' would be a better term) feature of the morpheme expressing the verbal constituent, and it works in the same way as inflectional endings while allowing other expressions to be inserted between these parts of the morpheme. I would like to call such a 'dislocated' expressions an *ABFIX.[23] The advantage is, then, that the traditional opposition between morphology as inflection vs. 'free words' like auxiliaries – according to which we normally say that the present and the preterite tenses are matters of verbal conjugation while we may disagree whether the 'past participle' is a tense or not – has been dissolved: all verbal constituent expressions are conceived of as conjugational categories. If so, the Danish declarative verb forms would be seen as an opposition between the present tense and the preterite tense, including a number of variations of verb meaning depending on the meanings of the auxiliaries:

jeg kører 'I drive'	present tense
jeg kørte 'I drove'	preterite (imperfective meaning)
jeg er/har kørt 'I am/have driven'	preterite (perfective meaning)
jeg var/havde kørt 'I was/had driven'	preterite (past perfective meaning)

Accordingly what is sometimes called a compound or complex tense[24] is no longer perceived as a compounding form but as one form that is 'spread out', maybe with some distance between its parts. The background of the phenomenon in Danish and Swedish seems to be the fairly fixed syntactic topology that is characteristic of these Germanic languages, namely, the so-called V2 rule saying that the verbal constituent should always be found in the second position of the main clause, and, as argued above, this has to do with possible (basically stylistic) variation in the sequence of constituents pointing to the slot in front of the verbal as the position where different constituents can be placed.

This line of reasoning can also be used when handling other expressions, and those which have not been seriously integrated into the EFA(X) framework are prepositions and infinitive markers. They have, so far, been apprehended as separate morphemes (in EFA(X) called components) and merged with nouns and verbs forming phrases. I am not especially happy with the widespread idea that prepositions are 'heads' of 'prepositional phrases' because, if we do not really know what a preposition is, apart from calling it a particle,[25] it may be a little odd to assume that it has a specific syntactic function. Instead I will propose the idea presented above, namely that a preposition is an *abfix and that what happens when it is (normally) prepositioned is that the outcome is a derivative (the punctuation marks indicate, like the colons at verbs, that it is one, maybe split, morpheme):[26]

```
på.bordet     'on the table'
prep.nomn

i.            store     .biler     'in big cars'
prep.         adjv      .nomn
```

When the prepositions are placed in front of these nouns, then the nouns can no longer function as nominal constituents, meaning that this is a case of complementary distribution of morphemes. The resulting combined forms can function as postpositioned specifications of nouns, like *kagen på.bordet* 'the cake on the table' or as (parts of) adverbial constituents like in *bogen ligger på.bordet* 'the book lies on the table', but a 'prepositional phrase' cannot be a subject, an object or a predicative constituent, in short: a nominal constituent. Thereby the noun is derived, since it no longer belongs to the nominal 'word class' and it becomes an adjective or an adverb, and, consequently, the preposition becomes a derivational affix; or rather, what I would prefer, an abfix, because the parts of the morpheme, as in *i. store .biler* 'in big cars' can be split.

The approach can also be useful when discussing the infinitive marker, and we need not ponder the depths of diachronic insights. When it is only a matter of how the infinitive marker behaves today, it has been demonstrated above that in Danish the *at* is closely prefixed to the verb form whereas the Swedish infinitive marker *att* may be separated from the verb form, and the solution in the previous section was to interpret it as a preposition. This may have worked well, apart from the fact that we, by then, still did not know exactly what a preposition was, and apart from the fact that infinitive markers cannot make nouns become non-nouns. So, instead I would like to bring up the idea just applied to prepositions and apply it to infinitive markers in a reversed categorial fashion, namely, acknowledging the fact that, whatever it looks like, the effect of prepositioning an infinitive marker is the detail that the verb can no longer work as a verbal constituent: a verb becomes a non-verb. Instead it can only function as a nominal (cf. (42)) or an adjectival (with optional infinitive marker, cf. (43)) constituent (or a phrase component), as is illustrated by taking up some previously offered examples (in which the inserted punctuation marks indicate that the text words connected by them are seen as single morphemes):

```
(40)

Peter    prøver     at.læse bogen (Dan)

s        v          o-adjv--nom

Peter tries to read the book


(41)

Peter    försöker   (att.).läsa boken (Swe)

s        v          o------adjv-nom

Peter tries to read the book


Peter    försöker   att. inte .läsa boken (Swe)

s        v          o-ajdv.--vna--.adjv-nom

Peter tries to not read the book


(42)

att.läsa    är    bra (Swe)

s-nom       v     sp

to read is good


(43)

(att.).äta gröt    är    gott (Swe)

s------adjv-nom    v     sp

eat(ing) porridge is good
```

Instead of the *ad hoc* solutions presented above – which made the infinitive marker a preposition and which were not able to clarify what a preposition was – these analyses perceive the phenomena from the perspective of syntactic functions, which was the basic principle in developing the EFA(X) approach. But of course, one objection from the viewpoint of word formation might be that derivatives are relatively 'solid' expressions whereas the proposed derivative forms made of a noun and a preposition may be relatively 'transient'. My answer will be that – as pointed out in Chapters 3 and 4 – we do not know much about how 'solid' or 'transient' the entities that make expressions really are; and, furthermore, that the borderline between 'solidness' and 'transience' as characteristics of linguistic expressions is, at best, nebulous. As is the case with so-called 'bound' and 'free' morphemes (or words).

What is left over, now, is the group of determiners, traditionally comprising articles, demonstratives, possessives and, sometimes, quantifiers. As is apparent from the account above, I will, based on analyses of Danish and Swedish phrases, maintain the categories of quantificational expressions (morphemes as phrase components) while I would be inclined to say that articles, demonstratives and possessives function as inflectional features of nouns (illustrated with the example from Chapter 3):

```
den:    store,   gule   :hund   med   de:    dårlige    .:tænder
nom:    adj      adj    :nom    nom.  nom:   adj        .:nom
the big yellow dog with the bad teeth
```

Also when furnished with some quantifiers:

```
den: tredje  store,   gule  :hund  med.  de:   mange  dårlige  .:tænder
nom: adq     adj      adj   :nom   nom.  nom:  adq    adj       .:nom
the third big yellow dog with the many bad teeth
```

What is now seen as a split morpheme, for instance *den: ... :hund* 'the dog' – and was previously in Chapter 3 seen as a determiner and a noun – can have the 'definite article' part replaced by a possessive or a demonstrative; which, accordingly, become inflectional features:

```
min: tredje  store,   gule  :hund  med.  disse:  mange  dårlige  .:tænder
nom: adq     adj      adj   :nom   nom.  nom:    adq    adj       .:nom
my third big yellow dog with these many bad teeth
```

Hence, in this construction the noun *hund* 'dog' is inflected by means of the 'dislocated' morphemic feature *min* 'my' carrying the possessive meaning, and the noun *tænder* 'teeth' is inflected by means of the morphemic feature *disse* 'these' carrying the demonstrative meaning, while at the same time becoming a derivative by means of the morphemic feature (the'preposition') *med* 'with' so that it can function as a postpositioned (actually adjectival) specification of the habitat of the phrase, the noun *hund* 'dog'.

One may ask: what is the advantage of this kind of analysis? The answer is that it solves two problems: (1) there is the basic categorial problem that there are a number of minor expressions that apparently cannot fit into the major grammatical categories; and this is the theoretical problem; and (2) there is, accordingly, a (too?) large number of grammatical categories, that sometimes makes it hard to decide which categories to annotate when being presented with real-life linguistic materials, and which may, furthermore, not be easily handled by whatever cognitive systems do the job in the brain, and, finally, make the analyses less aesthetically satisfactory; and that is the analytical problem. This approach solves both problems by suggesting a process of dissolution: the task is not to look carefully at a series of 'words' and try to figure out what their characteristics are as a prerequisite for their coming together in this arrangement. The task is to make fathomable the fact that a chain of sounds or a series of letters can possibly be grasped as something meaningful by humans, and my approach assumes that it can be done by connecting things in the world with what can be called concepts in the mind and with sounds and letters. The essential way of making this connection is to assume that there are constituents in sentences reflecting the concepts in the mind, and the next step is to conceive of all expressions as a minor number of consistently defined categories (the theoretical problem) that can be applied to the data in a uniform way (the analytical problem). And, what's more, the number of phrase categories (components) will be reduced in an appropriate manner:

```
# component categories
con [conjunction]
nom [noun: notion]
det [determiner: specification of referential in/determination]
adq [adjective: specification by quantification]
adj [adjective: specification by qualification]
prn [pronoun: referential in/determiner]???
prp [preposition: specification by special semantics]
psp [postposition: specification by special semantics]
vrb [verb: notion]
aux [auxiliary verb: specification by finiteness]
mod [modal auxs: specification by special semantics]???
vqa [quasi adverb: specification by presupposition] cf. qa
vna [negational adverb: specification by negation] cf. na
vra [relational adverb: specification by relation] cf. ra
vva [variational adverb: specification by variation of verb lexcl semantics]
```

If possessives can be excluded then (as indicated by the ???), the rest of the pronouns could be seen as nouns (with a special blurred lexical semantics), and some adjustments to the understanding of infinitives may skip modal auxiliaries. All this will, of course, increase the number of inflectional and derivational paradigms – and such paradigmatic information may suitably be annotated in the analyses above – but the tendency to reduce syntactic and syntagmatic categories at the expense of increasing the inflectional and derivational paradigms (as understood in the EFA(X) framework) will, by nature, make syntactic analysis less complicated, and this elaboration of the theory may be called EFA(X) version 3.1. A lexicon, be it on paper, in an electronic version or handled mentally, is a complicated affair, but humans do it, almost effortlessly, and machines are fairly good at it, whereas machines are, for now, rather bad at putting words together in meaningful ways.

Summary

This has not been an exhaustive account of the grammatical differences between Danish and Swedish according to the principles of Formative Grammar. In order to undertake such an endeavour one would have to write a new grammar of Danish, a new grammar of Swedish, and a grammar recording all the details that differ between the languages. And a key question would be: what to include and what to exclude? Just one example:

```
ambassade overvågning ikke strafbart
'embassy surveillance not punishable'
TV2 NEWS (Danish semi-commercial public service TV) text, 16/11-2010@20:01

I middelalderen var hellige kvinder helt normalt …
'in the Middle Ages were holy women fully normal'
Kristeligt Dagblad (Danish newspaper), 10 November 2010
```

What is peculiar here (apart from the misspelling of the compound *ambassade overvågning* that should have no space between its parts) is the *-t* endings of *strafbart* and *normalt*. According to Danish orthography, there should be (traditional) subject/predicative agreement between the common gender of *ambassadeovervågning* and *strafbar* (with no *-t*) and between *kvinder* and *normal-e* (with an *-e* to signify the plural). Instead we find the *-t*. There may be two kinds of explanation for this: either the predicatives have been reanalysed as adverbials, even though such a solution would require a copula (an elliptic one in the first case) without a predicative, or the inflectional ending of the Danish past participle has spread by analogy to adjectives like these. What has happened is hard to say, because, on the one hand, these adjectives end with an occlusive *-d* (not voiced in standard Danish), whereas the *-t* in *repareret* (cf. above) is a fricative *-d*. Whatever the future end product will be, it will be fairly easy to incorporate in what has been laid out in this chapter.

It will not challenge the Danish calculus presented in the beginning of the chapter on the background of the formal system presented in Chapter 3. On the contrary, it can be analysed in line with the examples taken up from Danish and Swedish in order to illustrate some differences between the languages. On the other hand, it might encourage some severe contemplation on how to choose between the different solutions for description, analysis and explanation of the phenomenon, in parallel with the deliberations on Government and Agreement and on Prepositions and Infinitives above.

So far, the Formative Grammar theory, the EFA(X) calculuses and the structural and formal analyses have offered an alternative way of uncovering the structures of sentences and phrases. But the basic paradox remains unsolved: how can a language both be used in speech with extreme speed under fragile circumstances and also continuously offering new grammatical traits, and, against all odds, keep its essential traits stable – sometimes over centuries? In Chapter 5, I will offer a cognitive model of syntax that may suggest some of the answers.

5

Conclusions and Perspectives

Take care of the sense, and sounds will take care of themselves.
(Lewis Carroll, Alice in Wonderland*)*

Conclusions

In the previous chapters I have presented a theory of syntax based on, partly, the ideas and principles that lie in the heritage of what I call the Classical Danish Tradition in Grammatical Analysis and, partly, in the background of what may be called the Chomskyan contributions to linguistic theory. The theory takes as its starting point a number of basic assumptions about how things in the world are built and put together (a metaphysics and an ontology) and about what kind of entity a language is (a philosophy of language). Then a formal system – based on what I propose as a new kind of logic: Occurrence Logic – is devised in the form of a combinatorial system (Epi-Formal Analysis in Syntax (EFA(X)) of which the essential property is its ability to describe and (to a certain extent) explain the alignment and the form of expressions in, at least, two natural languages: Danish and Swedish. In the process it has been acknowledged that the theoretical apparatus will need further elaboration and that the analytic methodology may need further development, but for those interested in an alternative analytic instrument like this, the theory is offered as an option. Whether it will prove its adequacy as a better theoretical solution in understanding human languages is, of course, a matter of potential applications to a number of languages, especially some languages that are not Germanic or even Indo-European, and an attempt has been made to apply the apparatus to Finnish, and Russian, Slovak and Basque may be next in line for a Formative Grammar application.

Another way of testing the explanatory power of the approach is to set up an experimental model that aims at simulating the cognitive systems that run the linguistic processes of humans. A possible model will be presented next.

Perspectives

In order to account for a potential set-up in experimental linguistics it is necessary to recapitulate the basics of the theory. The basic assumption is that when people use language for cognition and communication, they have to tell the interlocutors which of the units (parts of speech) are used for what purposes in transferring information, a phenomenon in the context called SIGNIFICATION. The theory then presumes that the main problem in describing linguistic expressions is to find out which phenomena are used for which information purposes, or: what (kind of expressions) occurs where? In order to characterize the systems determining these occurrences, the theory has created a new kind of logic, called OCCURRENCE LOGIC, by means of which a formal (EFA(X)) calculus for describing (and predicting) the specific instantiations of expressions in sentences in a language can be elaborated. By way of illustration, this is, once more, the formula for Danish:

```
NOTN_EFAX3 (Dan)
∑>
Ω↑0↑c_πc                                        Ω
  Ω↑1↑s_πs\{x}                                  Ω
    Ω↑2↑v_πv\◊aux◊                             Ω
      Ω↑3↑s₂_π{s}/{o[m*]}                       Ω
        Ω↑4↑a_πpa/qa/nz                         Ω
          Ω↑5↑v₂_πv◊{aux}/vrb/vva◊/{ra}         Ω
            Ω↑6↑o_p_π{p}/o/{vva}>{o}/p/{s}/kc^kp   Ω
              Ω↑7↑a₂_πra/pa>∑                    Ω
sequence constraints:
[*mig, dig, sig, ham, hende, den, det, os, jer, dem]
```

The next step, which was presented at the conference, 'Cognitive Dynamics in Linguistic Interactions: Theoretical and Applied Perspectives', Irkutsk, 17–20 June 2010, is the idea that – since the format of the calculuses has a specific shape – a calculus could be transformed from the two-dimensional presentation into a three-dimensional figure. To do this, the formula is converted into a kind of 'rope ladder' by connecting the omega characters to the left and imaging a corresponding connected chain of omega characters to the right, and by this it has been made into a double helix (Figure 5.1).

Next, one option is to suggest that the cognitive system of syntax is such an idealized infinite double helix that rummages through the mental space of the

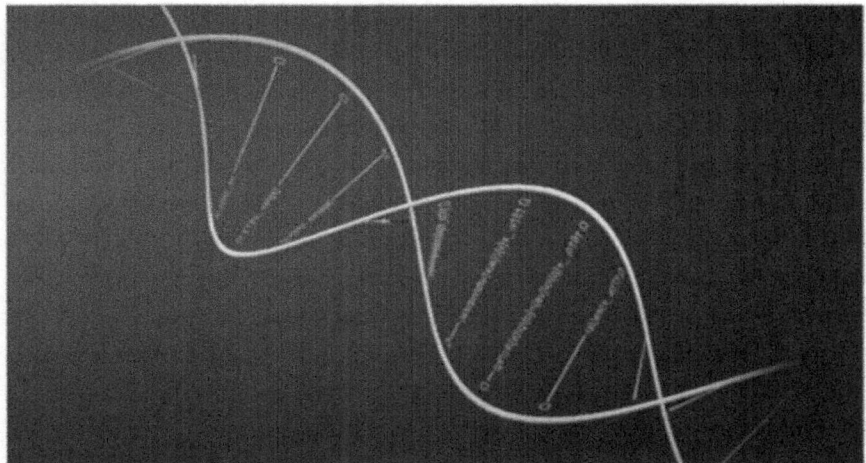

Figure 5.1 The double helix of syntax

individual through its human lifetime, thus suggesting that the brain is able to run systems that function as a mechanism doing this job. With these reservations in mind, then maybe a more convincing model would be the figure created by the double helix if it is turned into a Möbius strip (Figure 5.2).

Thereby it is achieved that the end of the calculus is connected directly to the beginning of the calculus, at the sigma characters, and, if conceived of as a running system, it is an infinite and iterative system.

Figure 5.2 The Möbius strip of syntax

In that case the cognitive system of syntax could be seen as an idealized Möbius strip running extremely fast all the time in the mental space, and the sentences of speech could be seen as being produced by the interference between this system and the mental lexicon. Which, in turn, could be conceived of as a number of idealized 'normal and plain' (i.e. cylindrical) non-Möbius strips also running extremely fast and calibrated with the syntactic strip. This might explain how people are able to talk at the high pace of normal speech they actually speak, because linguistic expressions stored in a number of strips corresponding to paradigms of morphemes would be able to meet the adequate points in the syntactic processing strip at the adequate points in time.

By this move the formula has been transformed into a mechanism that can be seen as a model of a cognitive system. What is needed, then, is a theoretical elaboration of how the mental lexicon can be characterized as a number of (idealized) plain strips, i.e. how morphemes (in the FoG sense) are assumed to be 'attached to' different strips in a way so that they are able to 'cooperate with' the constituents in the syntactic mechanism, how they interact, and how linguistic variation is assumed to work. Most people have at least more than one language and one linguistic register and are able to 'switch codes' in seconds.

As for the Möbius strip, the critical issue is whether this specific model is the most adequate image of the cognitive system running the syntactic functions. An elaboration of the idea will comprise a technical account of the mechanics of the system and a mathematical proof of the system's efficiency compared with other solutions. This – in the form of a lengthy presentation of a number of steps in the line of reasoning – will be offered in the future. But some indications can be presented.[1]

Using a Möbius strip for the cognitive system of syntax instead of a cylindrical strip has several advantages. Some of them can be explained briefly: (1) the interaction between the cognitive system and a lexical string, both of which are represented by two-dimensional manifolds, can be thought of bringing together both kinds of strings for a short time interval in a smooth manner, i.e. during the contact of the strings, the normal vectors of both strings at the line they share at that time coincide up to the sign (plus or minus). Thus, one criterion for the acceptance of a lexical string to be processed by the syntactic cognitive system is the direction from which the lexical string is moving towards the Möbius strip (thereby bringing the lexical items in contact with the syntactic system). The normal vectors of a cylindrical strip form a two-dimensional real vector space (a plane, which after an adequately chosen parallel movement is, consequently, orthogonal to the surface of the cylindrical strip, or rather, its generating line), whereas the normal vectors of a Möbius strip span a three-dimensional space. Although the cardinality for both vector spaces is equal, the dimension for the Möbius strip is higher by one, which enables a rotating syntactic system to process lexical strings coming from all directions of three-dimensional space. Therefore, a Möbius strip as a cognitive system has a much higher capacity in processing and clearly is superior to a model with only a cylindrical strip as the cognitive system of syntax. (2) The middle line of both a Möbius strip and a cylindrical strip forms a circle and defines a plane, which we denote here as the middle plane for short. Under an adequate coordination, e.g. taking the centre of gravity of the respective strips as their coordinate origin, in the case of the cylindrical strip its normal vectors are always parallel to the middle plane, but for the Möbius strip in general the normal vectors meet the middle plane under an angle between 0 and 360 degrees (or 180 degrees, according to definition). This angle will serve as a parameter in modelling various kinds of interaction between the syntactic system and lexical strings, additionally depending on the loci of interaction at the syntactic system.

In sum, the idea of such a model implemented in experimental linguistics would be to find out how language works in the mental space of humans as one or more detailed cognitive systems and to develop a cognitive linguistic model that is able to explain why humans are able to speak at the relatively high pace observed in normal conversations.

One could say that this is the ultimate quest of all kinds of linguistics, and this approach shares the quest. As has been presented in this book, the approach builds upon ideas from different kinds of linguistics, but it brings together the theoretical notions in a specific way, and the approach integrates them in special ways into frameworks of certain ideas on language and cognition, which may be justified by being tested experimentally.

The objective of an experimental project like the one implied above would be to build a 'virtual language user' (VLU) that can both generate grammatically well-formed sentences and interpret such sentences in real-time set-ups, also connected with modules that can translate the VLU output into speech synthesis and, conversely, by means of adequate devices, can translate speech recognition into VLU input. The wider perspective aims at building a VLU that can also acquire one or more languages and at building a number of different VLUs processing (between them) common and different languages. Maybe such an artificial language user will be able to shed light on how people use languages, and maybe thereby the discrepancy between de Saussure's '*langue*' and '*parole*' and between Chomsky's 'competence' and 'performance' as system and process respectively could be, somehow, dissolved, i.e. there is no *'langue'* and no *'parole'*, no 'competence' and no 'performance'. What there is, is language use: continuous language use and accidental language use, and how this works is the ultimate objective of linguistics. But for that purpose one will, at least initially, have to take care of the sounds and let sense take care of itself.

Appendix A
Glossary of Technical Terms

The aim of the definitions below is not to summarize the theory but to clarify the meanings of words used with special meanings (terms), and therefore there may be some minor inconsistencies in the vocabulary of the definitions. As for the formal system of EFA(X), only a basic selection of definitions are offered here since most of them are integrated into formalisms displayed in the EFAX Appendix (Appendix B in this volume).

*Abfix a dislocated expression; see *dislocation*.
*Adverbate the concept which is either a specification or a predication of the *verbate.
Adverbial (constituent) form of the *adverbate.
Agreement CST-internal multiple morphological signification.
Algorithm the stratification of the configurations of a formal sentence and statement; see *stratification* and *configuration*.
Allocation (alc) the phenomenon that a component is separated from 'its' phrase.
Artificial system a system made by human beings.
A-specification (assertive specification) the concept in a statement that subclassifies another concept, see *s-specification*: a subclassified concept.
Assignment the act of producing linguistic sounds (and writing) and the human interaction with the world manipulating objects giving sense and meaning to the sounds (and writing); see *medium assignment* and *object assignment*.
Calculus (calc) a formal system for making theorems for empirical applications.
Categorial unit constituent belonging to a specific syntactic function or a component belonging to a specific syntagmatic function.
Category a syntactic or syntagmatic function in a sentence or phrase; the set of linguistic expressions that belong to the same syntagmatic category is called a paradigm.
Cognitive system a set of processes in the brain that takes care of our understanding (comprehension) of the world (and our bodies) and contributes to the organization of our behaviour.
Cohesiveness a relative term describing one of the basic characteristic features of syntactic unities and units; see *independence* and *limitedness*.
Combinatorial system a formal system, the rules of which control the distribution and substitution of symbols.
Comparison predication by class intersection.

Component a morpheme that is the unit of a phrase.

Concept (cpt) a mental connection between one specific linguistic expression and the configuration(s) of one or more (kinds of) objects, states, or events, etc. which are observable, assumed or fictive; or a connection between two or more linguistic expressions and the configuration of one (kind of) object, state, or event, etc.

Configuration mental figures (images) representing (aspects of) material or mental objects.

*Conjection a relation between two concepts by a third concept.

Conjunction the concept which may connect different statements or, within a statement, concepts of the same category, or concepts related by comparison.

Conjunctional (constituent) form of the conjunction

Constituent (cst) an expression of a concept.

Content the information of a linguistic sign, i.e. the mental representation of the human acts, etc. that build the explications made by the expressions.

Derivation a formal procedure by means of which a string of symbols are replaced by another string of symbols in accordance with some formal rules.

Descriptivism the theoretical approach in linguistics (and other academic subjects in the humanities) that leads to the most detailed account of the structure of an object of investigation.

Deviation the phenomenon that languages share basic structural features while being different on certain other basic points.

Deviational topological structures assuming that (typologically) two or more languages share basic topological features but differ on certain basic points, then their topological structures can be said to deviate.

Dislocation (dlc) the phenomenon that a part of a morpheme is separated from 'its' morpheme.

Diversity a metaphysical concept referring to the assumption that we experience the world as different units.

Element an ontological concept referring to the presumption that the world is made out of units of some kind.

Entity a metaphysical concept referring to the assumption that we experience the world as units of some kind.

Epi-formal analysis (efa) the empirical application of an epi-formal system.

Epi-formal system (efs) a formalism in which (1) the formalism as a set of concepts has a limited extension; (2) it has, as a set of concepts, a limited intensional value; and (3) at least one of the expressions has a specified semantics.

Equation predication by class identification (the claim that they are identical).

Explication the interrelation between expressions and the content of linguistic signs; explications build the concepts of statements.

Expression ordered (ascertainable) linguistic sounds or writing; expressions have meaning (semantics) and build the constituents of sentences in the form of morphemes and build the form of languages.

Facultative occurrence by non-necessity.

Fixed (syntactic topology) a feature of a syntactic structure in a language meaning that its constituents have by necessity certain positions, but this allows anomalies in accordance with specific conditions; see *flexible (syntactic topology)* and *rigid (syntactic topology)* .

Flexible (syntactic topology) a feature of a syntactic structure in a language meaning that its constituents do not by necessity have certain positions, and also this allow anomalies in accordance with specific conditions; see *fixed (syntactic topology)* and *rigid (syntactic topology)* .

Form structural limits of perceptible phenomena.

Form (linguistic) structured expressions.

Formal language one subset of (artificial) formal systems; see *formal system* and *technical system*.

Formal logic the semantics of a formal (artificial) language.

Formal system a set of characters and rules for their combinations.

Formalism (1) the theoretical approach in linguistics (and other academic subjects in the humanities) that leads to the most consistent explanation of the structure of an object of investigation; (2) a formal system.

Formative (from Chomsky) an expression that is a morpheme (in the tradition 'a word') in a syntagm (a sentence); see *morpheme*.

Formula (fml) a sentence in a formal (artificial) language.

Generate the process of producing syntactic constructions (sentences) in a language.

Generation the production of a sentence in a language; see *syntactic instantiation*.

Glosseme (from Hjelmslev) an expression that is a morpheme (a word) in (a paradigm in) a lexicon.

Government constituent-external multiple morphological signification; see *morphological signification*.

Habitat (symbol 'h') a component that is the nucleus (expression of a notion) of a phrase.

Identity the relation between two entities that have all their properties in common.

Independence a relative term describing one of the basic characteristic features of syntactic unities and units; see *cohesiveness* and *limitedness*.

Index (symbol 'j') a component that is a specification of a habitat (nucleus) of a phrase.

Indicating object assignment of material objects in the local perceivable environment in a situation (a setting).

Information the meaning of the linguistic sign, i.e. the mental representation of (at least aspects of) things in the world as mental images (configurations in stratification) created by the human perceptual apparatus; animals are not supposed to have languages (except in a figurative sense), and therefore they have no concepts, but any organism that has a neuronal system is supposed to process and store information. In order to clean up the nomenclature, one might differ between human cognition vs. animal recognition, human action (based on linguistically facilitated planning) vs. animal reaction, and human comprehension vs. animal apprehension. In that perspective animals may have thoughts, but they cannot think. But there need not be a clear borderline here, rather a continuum.

Interpret the process of comprehending syntactic constructions (sentences) in a language.

Interpretation the perception of a sentence in a certain language; see syntactic instantiation.

Language, artificial a language which (1) is created out of a natural language; which (2) serves a specific purpose according to the demands of a specific group of people; and which (3) is systematic and discrete in such a way that one is able to clearly identify and demarcate its expressions and their combinations.

Language, natural a language that is spoken by human beings and may be encoded in writing systems.

Limitedness a relative term describing one of the basic characteristic features of syntactic unities and units; see *independence*.

Linearization a basic theoretical principle in the EFA(X) approach saying that the linear distribution of expressions can signify their syntactic functions.

Logic in natural languages, the relations between concepts in statements; the sense of the linguistic sign.

Magnitude an ontological concept referring to the presumption that structures have certain measures.

Material what is outside the human mind.

Meaning (linguistic) structured content, i.e. the mental representation of the human acts (in the material environment) which give sense (semantics) to the form of a language.

Medium assignment the mental and material processes of producing (creating or utilising) articulation and writing.

Mental what has to do with the human mind.

Mental figure (image) perceptual and cognitive patterns of discrete stimuli.

Mentioning object assignment of mental objects

Metaphysics (metaphysical) assumptions about what is beyond actual knowledge but within possible knowledge, i.e. potential knowledge.

Minimal linguistic sign the smallest linguistic sign in communication and cognition.

Morpheme a minimal expression in a language.

Morphological signification a term referring to the phenomenon that a language may signify its constituents (totally or partly) by means of morphological features.

Morphology the phenomenon that (and the field of knowledge about) the different features of morphemes.

Multitude an ontological concept referring to the presumption that structures are found in certain numbers.

Natural system relatively independent and identifiable physical structures.

Negation a-specification or predication by complementary classification.

Node see *position (syntax)*.

Normative a morpheme that is, presumably on the basis of semantic and pragmatic features, the preferred contextual use in a language even though there are other morphemes in that language that could have communicated an analogous meaning.

Notion a concept instantiated as a constituent in a sentence.

Object assignment the processes of activating (creating or retrieving) one or more concepts (of mental objects or (as mental representations of) material objects), so that they are part of the conscious mental universe, connected (as reference) with related interactions with the world.

Object (conceptual) the concept which is a specification of the *verbate.

Object (grammatical) form (as expression) of the object.

Obligatory occurrence by necessity.

Occurrence logic the logical principles and rules of a formal system that can describe the occurrence of entities.

Operation the mechanical processes effected by the 'instructions' executing the controlling actions of humans interacting with a mechanism or a machine by means of a technical system.

Paradigm the set of expressions (morphemes stored in the mental lexicon, and here called glossemes) that belong to that same category.

Parameter a value in an epi-formal calculus; each parameter ('π') will be set by an instantiation.

Perception (natural language) the process of interpreting sounds (and writings) as linguistic expressions; see *production (natural language)*.

Philosophical physicalism the basic metaphysical assumption that the world (physics) is what we can know about it; see *physics*.

Phrase a constituent built of more than one morpheme; see also *component*.

Physicalism epistemological physicalism, i.e. the ontological claim that everything that is within the domain of possible knowledge is what we call physical.

Physics everything that is, or can be, known.

Plurality a metaphysical concept referring to the assumption that we experience the world as numbers of units.

Position (syntax) a point in a syntactic structure that defines the ordering of a syntactic unit in relation to the other units of a sentence, in the formalism called a node ('Ω').

Pragmatic universals basic assumptions about how humans understand (comprehend) the world and their own behaviour in the world, put together as the background for describing human behaviour in the world.

Predicate the concept which is a predication of the subject by *conjection.

Predication the concept that (re-)classifies another concept (cf. *specification*).

Predicative (grammatical) form of the predicate.

Process an ontological concept referring to the presumption that the world is made out of transitory connected units of some kind.

Production (natural language) the process of making articulatory sounds (or correspondent writings) that function as linguistic expressions; see *perception*.

Property a metaphysical concept referring to the assumption that we experience the world as units with characteristics of some kind.

Proposition a statement in a formal (artificial) language.

Prototype see *topological prototype*.

Quality an ontological concept referring to the presumption that structures have certain characteristics.

Quantity an ontological concept referring to the presumption that structures are found in different numbers.

Reference object assignment of material objects; see *assignment* and *object assignment*.

Referent material object in the world that can be talked (and written) about by means of object assignment.

Referring object assignment of material objects from common or shared experience.

Relation an ontological concept referring to the presumption that the world is made out of connections (of some kind) between units.

Rigid (syntactic topology) a feature of a syntactic structure in a language, meaning that its constituents have by necessity certain positions, and it does not allow for anomalies; see *fixed (syntactic topology)* and *flexible (syntactic topology)* .

Semantic signification the meaning (content, information) of linguistic expressions.

Sense structured explications.

Sentence (stc) the form of a minimal linguistic sign, built of constituents.

Sentence table the graphic (column designed) topological description of Danish sentences developed by the Danish linguist Paul Diderichsen.

Setting a continuous space–time specific situation.

Signification the structural relation between the 'levels' of the linguistic sign; in a broad sense, the mechanism that makes linguistic sounds mean something.

Similarity the relation between two entities that have some of their properties in common.

Society coherently organized economic activity of a group of people.

Specification a concept that subclassifies another concept; see *predication*.

S-specification (stipulative specification) a subclassified concept; see *a-specification*.

Statement (stm) the sense of a minimal linguistic sign, built of concepts.

Stratification the content of a minimal linguistic sign, a construction of configurations in a minimal linguistic sign built of mental figures (images).

Strong implication a relation in occurrence logic, see the section 'Excursus on Occurrence Logic' in Chapter 3.

Strong morphological signification a relative term referring to the phenomenon that a language signifies its constituents primarily by means of morphological features.

Strong topological signification a relative term referring to the phenomenon that a language signifies its constituents primarily by means of topological linearization.

Structural analysis the investigative process of identifying the constituents and other units of a number of linguistic expressions.

Structuralism the ontological claim that everything is structures, i.e. there are structures built of elements, relations and processes in the world.

Structure an ontological concept referring to the presumption that the world is made out of units of some kind connected in certain ways.

Style the form of a linguistic sign.

Sub-habitat a habitat that is also an index (symbol 'hj').

Subject the concept which is (in a setting) the mental object (i.e. a configuration) of the act of linguistic communication (i.e. transfer of information) or cognition (i.e. transformation of information) of the interlocutor uttering the statement.

Subject (grammatical) form of the subject.

*Subjection assertive (a-)specification, or predication.

Syntactic function expressions (morphemes) as constituents in a sentence.

Syntactic instantiation production of a construction of constituents making a sentence; also the processing of such a construction in a calculus.

Syntactic signification the way constituents in a sentence express their syntactic functions, i.e. which syntactic categories they belong to.

Syntagm a set of linear order of morphemes picked up from paradigms; the form of an utterance is always a series of morphemes; when the morphemes, alone or grouped, fit into syntactic categories, they have syntactic functions.

*Taxiology a theoretical set of terms expressing the presumed insights in a field of knowledge.

Technical system one subset of (artificial) formal systems, i.e. a system operating (handling and controlling) mechanisms and machines; so-called 'programming languages' can be seen as technical systems.

Term an expression used in a field of knowledge in a sufficiently precise manner in order to ease the understanding of reasoning in that field.

Theoretical what has to do with theories.

Theory a set of propositions or statements referring to how things in the world experienced as phenomena can be understood as structures.

Topological prototype a linear syntactic structure that is common to two or more languages.

Topological signification a term referring to the phenomenon that a language may signify its constituents (totally or partly) by means of topological linearization.

Topological type a linear syntactic structure characteristic of a language.

Topology the phenomenon of (and the field of knowledge about) the different kinds of linearization of morphemes.

Tradition (in science) the basic, theoretical and methodological assumptions shared by a group of scientists.

Utterance a linguistic sign produced at a certain time and place.

Verbal (constituent) form of the *verbate.

*Verbate the concept that *subjects and/or *conjects the subject.

*Verbation the *subjection or *conjection which constitutes a statement.

Weak implication/strong implication a relation in occurrence logic, see the section 'Excursus on Occurrence Logic' in Chapter 3.

Weak morphological signification a relative term referring to the phenomenon that a language signifies its constituents insignificantly by means of morphological features.

Weak morphology the phenomenon that a language may have a minor set of morphological features.

Weak topology a relative term referring to the phenomena that a language signifies its constituents insignificantly by means of topological linearization.

Appendix B
The EFA(X)3 (EFA(X)3.1) Formal System

EFA(X)3rd_vers/CTNM_PUBLC

(EFA(X): Epi-Formal Analysis in Syntax)

STRUCTURAL CATEGORIZATION

(01) Sentence Theory [cf. The Linguistic Sign]

syntactic defs & axioms (paragraph notation §):

§Statement def:

a statement (STM) is the explication of the minimal linguistic sign

§ statements & concepts

the standard form of a *statement* (stm) is a *structure* (forms as
functions) of *concepts* (cpt):

(1)SUBJECT(2)*VERBATE(3)*ADVERBATE(4)OBJECT/PREDICATE(5)CONJUNCTION

S, V, A, O/P, C (capitals are symbols for CPTs)

CPT-defs:

SUBJECT: the concept which is (in a situation (a setting)) the
mental object [conceptual entity] (i.e. a configuration) of the act of
linguistic communication (i.e. transfer of information) or cognition
(i.e. transformation of information) of the interlocutor uttering the
statement

*VERBATE: the concept which *subjects and/or *conjects the subject

*ADVERBATE: a concept which is either a specification or a predication
of the *verbate

OBJECT (or *SPECIFICATE): a concept which is an assertive specification
of the subject by *conjection

PREDICATE: a concept which is a predication of the subject by *conjection

CONJUNCTION: a concept which may connect different statements or,
within a statement, concepts of the same category, or concepts
related by comparison

CPT-relations, defs:

subjection: assertive (a-)specification, or predication

a-specification: a CPT subclassifies another CPT

[cf. stipulative (s-)specification: a subclassified CPT]

predication: a CPT (re-)classifies another CPT

*conjection: a relation between two CPTs specified by a third CPT

**verbation:* the *subjection or *conjection which constitutes a STM

equation: predication by class identification

comparison: predication by class intersection

negation: a-specification or predication by complementary classification

§Sentence def:

a sentence (STC) is the form of the minimal linguistic sign

§ sentences & constituents (syntax (STX))

a *sentence* is (*generated* as) the form [cf. ling sign] of a statement,
i.e. the *constituents* are (generated as) the forms of the concepts.

The standard form of a sentence (STC) is a *structure* of constituents
(CSTs); the structural functions of the constituents are *syntactic
functions* establishing *CST-categories* as sets of *categorial units*:

(1)subject (2)verbal (3)object/predicative (4)adverbial (5)conjunctional

s, v, o/p, a, c (symbols for CSTs)

CST defs:

subject: form of the subject of the statement

verbal: form of the *verbate of the STM

adverbial: form of an *ADVERBATE

object: form of an Object of the STM

predicative: form of a Predicate of the STM

conjunctional: form of a Conjunction of the STM

The *formation* of a STC is a *construction* of actual CSTs *expressed* as
morphemes (MPHs) in *syntagms* (STGMs); *syntagmatic functions* establish
paradigms (PDGMs), i.e. sets of MPHs.

(02) COMBINATORIAL SYSTEM

efs (epi-formal system)

combinatorial symbols and rules for distribution (distr) and substitution (subst), i.e. combinatorial system (CMB SYS) (paragraph
notation #, ## &)

 # combinatorial substitution rules

combinatorial *production* (i.e. 1 symbol substb n symbols) rule:

>> is produced as

combinatorial *occurrence derivation* (i.e. 1/n symbol(s) substb 1/n symbol(s)) rule:

=>   occurs as

=}   may occur as

combinatorial *linearization* (linear vs non-linear occ) *derivation* (i.e. 1/n symbol(s) substb 1/n symbol(s)) rule:

->   is linearized as

-}   may be linearized as

combinatorial distribution rules: occurrence
occurrence *symbols* (combinatorial *vocabulary* [constituent symbols = 1 character symbols]):

s   [subject

v   verbal

o   object

p   predicative

a   adverbial

c   conjunctional

z,y,

ä,ö,ü   any symbol (symbol variables)

zy   sub-category of y (subconstituent= 2 character symbols)

e   ellipsis

occurrence *lists*, *sets* & *strings*
occurrence symbol lists & strings (non-/vs occurrence relations):
(• any operator, ° any occurrence operator, cf. below)

z,y,ä etc.list (combinatorial)

     (list, def: any collection of unrelated symbols)

z•y•ä   set (combinatorial)

     (set, def: any collection of related symbols

z°y°ä   string (combinatorial)

     (string, def: any set of occurrence related symbols)

occurrence *markers*
occurrence symbol markers (of *absolute* occurrence *values*):

z   obligatory (OBL)

(z)   facultative (FAC)

{z}   labile (LAB)

(lability, def: occurrence value may be indefinable)

occurrence *operators*
occurrence symbol operators (*relative* occurrence *values* (indicates symbol co-occurrence (condition) relations)):

°   any occurrence operator

~   occurrence negation

connectives (binary occurrence operators):

°^   conjunction

°\   exclusive disjunction

°/   inclusive disjunction

°>   strong implication; def: z °> y, y occ iff z occ

°}   weak implication; def: z °} y, if z occ then y occ

consequential (relation of necessary co-occurrence in) strings:

°>z°y°zy°>   strong consequential implication

°}z°y°zy°}   weak consequential implication

combinatorial distribution rules: linearization
(def: linear vs non-linear occurrence, i.e. dimensionality)

linearization *symbols* (combinatorial *vocabulary* [CST symbols])

s   [subject

v   verbal

o   object

p   predicative

a   adverbial

c   conjunctional

z,y,

ä,ö,ü   any symbol (symbol variables)

zy   sub-category of y

e   ellipsis

linearization *strings* sets and lists (linear vs non-linear occurrence relations):

(° (º, ª)   any occ operator (linear, non-linear), cf. below)

…z°y°ä…   linearization string (linear vs non-linear)

…zºyºä…   linear string

…zªyªä…   non-linear string

linearization *markers*

linearization symbol markers (of *absolute* linearization *values*, i.e. *sequentiality* (def: initial state definition (i.e. un/vs defined starting point)):

          obligatory initial state definition:

zºyºzy   linear sequence (LSQ)
          [topological signification (CST-coordination)]

zªyªzy   non-linear sequence (alignment by frequency) (NSQ)
          [morphological signification]

(*sequence*, def: a linear or non-linear string with a defined initial state)

    facultative initial state definition:

z°y°ä…   linearization string (undefined initial state)

zºyºä…   linear string (undefined initial state)

zªyªä…   non-linear string (undefined initial state)

    labile initial state definition:

…z°y°ä…   linearization string (no initial state)

linearization *operators*

linearization symbol operators (*relative* linearization *values*
(indicates symbol linearization (condition) relations)):

º any linearization operator

(cf. ° any occ operator, ª any non-linearization operator)

¬ linearization negation

connectives (binary operators):

^ conjunction

\ exclusive disjunction

/ inclusive disjunction

> strong implication; def: z > y, y occ iff z occ

} weak implication; def: z } y, if z occ then y occ

subsequential strings:

>zºyºzy>   strong subsequential implication

}zºyºzy}   weak subsequential implication

(*subsequence*, def: a linear sequence of implications)

special linearization value *constraints*

linear sequence constraint:

[topological signification (TPL SFC)]

zºyºäº etc. {z}   alternative (labile) position

linear and non-linear sequence constraints:

[morphological signification (MPL SFC)]

z[μ]   symbol and morphemic expression (MPH XPR)

z[μ]   obligatory (OBL)

z[(μ)]   facultative (FAC)

z[{μ}]   labile (LAB)

(04)FORMAL CALCULUS (THEORETICAL APPLICATION)

efc (epi-formal calculus)EFAXGnl (general syntax):

general symbols

##calculus conventions:

∑   sequence [sentence]

Ω   node, def: a derivation in a string [position]

π   parameter, def: a derived symbol [constituent]

∫ ∫   parenthesis: insertion of formulae in calculus

[ ]   brackets: insertion of non-formal information

[μ]   morpheme

[m]   morphematic paradigm

[*sig*] morphemic ex (morpheme)

##calculus notation:

∑ >> ΩΩ = ∑Ω

Ω => z etc = Ωz etc.

π => y etc = πy etc.

general rules

production (general formal system production rule):

∑ >> z°y°ä

[S,*V,*A,O/P,C generates s,v,a o/p,c]

[Z,Y generates z,y]

derivation (general occurrence rule):

z,y,ä => z,y,(ä),öy,(üy) etc.

derivation (general linearization rules)

[syntactic signification: structural deviations]:

either

linear sequence

[topological signification]:

z,y,(ä),öy etc -> z°y°{z}°(ä) etc.

or

non-linear sequence

[morphological signification]:

z,y,(ä),öy etc -> z[μ]ªy[(μ)]ª(ä[{μ}]) etc.

[syntactic functions generate syntactic signification, either morphological or topological]

[morphematic expression: z is expressed as z[μ]]

special rules

special occurrence rules:

[CST definitions & relations]

s°>v

s°^v°>o°/p

s°^v°>a

s°^v°>c

y =} zy

y°/zy

z°^z°^z etc (simplified notation: z^^)

z°^z =} z°^c°^z

special linearization rules:

[syntactic signification: structural deviations]

either

non-linear sequence:

[morphological signification]

cᵃsᵃvᵃo/pᵃa

or

linear sequence

(sequential linear derivations):

either

c⁰s⁰v⁰o/p⁰a (linear sequence)

[topological signification (CST-*coordination*)]

or

}c⁰s⁰v⁰o/p⁰a} (weak subsequential implication)

[topological signification (CST-*concatenation*)]

or

>c⁰s⁰v⁰o/p⁰a> (strong subsequential implication)

[topological signification (CST-*consecution*)]

(05)FORMAL CALCULUS (THEORETICAL APPLICATION)

efc (epi-formal calculus)

EFAXSca (Scandinavian syntax)

[SENTENCE CALCULUS]

 # general rules

production (general Sca production rule):

∑ >> c°s°v°o°/p°a

derivation (general Sca occurrence rule):

c°s°v°o°/p°a => (c)°s°v°(o°/p)°(a)

symbols

additional symbols:

[constituent categorization (structural categorization):

constituents (1 chart symbols) & sub-constituents (2 chart symbols)]

notn: sub-constituent substitution of constituent zy≈y

s   fs [formal subject]

    cs [conjunctional subject]

    ns [negative subject]

v   ["finite or non-finite verbal"; cf. PHR_ANL aux]

o   do [dative object]

    no [negative object]

p   sp [subject predicative]

    op [object predicative]

    kp [comparative predicative]

    np [negative predicative]

a   qa [quasi-adverbial]   cf. vqa

    ra [relative adverbial]   cf. vra

    pa [predicative adverbial]

    na [negative adverbial]   cf. vna

c   uc [subordinating conjunctional]

    kc [comparative conjunctional]

    oc [objective conjunctional]

    ac [adverbial conjunctional]

x   x-variable

special rules

special Sca occurrence rules

[categories vs sub-categories]

s°\cs

s°\ns

o°\no

p => zp

a => za

x -} $z^\neg v^\neg na^\neg c$

[different categories]

o°\sp

$\int cs°\backslash uc\int°>\Omega v_2\_\pi v\Diamond aux\backslash vrb\Diamond$

special Sca linearization rule

(weak subsequential implication)

[Sca STC structure: topological structure (CST-coordination restricted to CST-concatenation)]

```
(c)ºsºvº(o/p)º(a) -> }(c)ºs\{x}ºvº{s}º(a)º(v)º(o/p)º(a)}
```

[cf. STC fields (FLDs):

Initial   Central   Final

STC positions (PSTs):

(c) s\{x}   v {s} (a)   (v) (o/p) (a)]

(07) Phrase Theory

syntagmatic defs & axioms:

§Phrase def:

a phrase (PHR) is a constituent expressed in two or more morphemes

§ PHR-functions (categories): structure & components

the standard form of a phrase (PHR) — as a part of the syntagm (STGM)
making a sentence — is a morphematic structure of *components* (CPNs);
the structural functions of the components are *phrasal functions*
establishing *phrase categories* as sets of *categorial units* (components); expressions functioning as categorial units are accumulated in
paradigms (PDGMs) in the lexicon in accordance with their categorial
features; a phrase may integrate *sub-phrases* (SUB_PHRs).

§ Structural Phrase Analysis

structural PHR-analysis: categorization of expressions rendering
a structural description of a construction, i.e. categorization of
morphemes in constituents as syntagms

OBS: stipulative (s-)specification ['attribution']

           (vs

           stc anls: assertive (a-)specification ['declaration'])

formal PHR-analysis: an instantiation of certain parameters (of a
calculus) and the deletion of others executed by the calculation of the
structural analysis rendering a formal description of a construction.

§ Formal Phrase Analysis

EFA(X) PHRASE CALCULUS EFA(XPC)

#general symbols

##calculus conventions

Σ◊   sequence [phrase]

æ   parameter, def: a derived symbol [component]

∫∫   parenthesis: insertion of formulae in calculus

[]   brackets: insertion of non-formal information

 # general rules

production (general Sca [PHR] production rule):

∑◊ >> æ°ø°å [PHR]

s, o, p, pa≈a =} N_PHR

derivation(general Sca [PHR] occurrence rule):

æ,ø,å => æ,ø,(å) etc

combinatorial strings, markers, operators and constraints apply

symbols

additional calculus symbols

æ,ø,å; æøå   any CPN (component)

◊   PHR_parentheses/boundaries

√   SUB_PHR-parentheses/boundaries

◊æ◊   allocated (ALC) CPN (vs ◊æ•ø•å◊ attributed (ATB) CPNs)

analytic notation:

æøå‾‾‾æøå‾‾‾æøå   SUB_CPN markers (SUB_CPNs in SUB_PHRs)

æøå⁻æøå‾‾‾æøå   SUB_PHR marker (postpositioned SUB_PHR)

æøå--æøå‾‾‾æøå⁻‾‾æøå   SUB_PHR markers (postpositioned SUB_PHRs)

æøå⁻æøå‾‾æøå‾‾æøå--æøå   SUB_PHR markers (prepositioned SUB_PHRs)

component categories

symbols & definitions (empirical generalizations)

[component categorization (structural categorization):

components (CPNs) & subcomponents= 3 character symbols]

nom [noun: notion]

det [determiner: specification of referential in/determination]

adq [adjective: specification by quantification]

adj [adjective: specification by qualification]

prn [pronoun: referential in/determiner]

prp [preposition: specification by special semantics]

psp [postposition: specification by special semantics]

vrb [verb: notion]

aux [auxiliary verb: specification by finiteness]

mod [modal auxs: specification by special semantics]

vqa [quasi adverb: specification by presupposition] cf. qa

vna [negational adverb: specification by negation]   cf. na

vra [relational adverb: specification by relation]   cf. ra

vva [variational adverb: specification by variation of verb lexcl semantics]

con [conjunction]

[# component categorial (specification) *hierarchization:*]

not EFAX-anls [cf. Gen Gram tree-structures]

symbols & definitions: categorial subordination

h   habitat [CPT notion]

j   index [CPT specification]

hj   indexical habitat [CPT specfc & notion]

(08)MORPHOLOGY: Categorial Morpheme Theory

syntagmatic defs & axioms

§ Morpheme def

§ a morpheme (MPH) is an expression that in a syntagm (STGM) can function
as (fc) a constituent (CST) in a sentence or as a component in a phrase.

§ morphemes are categorized in *paradigms* (PDGMs).

 # symbols

symbols & definitions (empirical generalizations):

categorial symbols (morphematic categorization [structural categori-
zation] in morpheme paradigms= 4 character symbols= æøåæ)

[[cf. "word classes"]]; fc= functions as

conj conjunctions [def fc conjunctional)

nomn nouns [def fc nominal CSTs & nom]

prop proper name [fc nominal CSTs & nom]

pron pronouns [def fc underspecified nominal CSTs & nom]

artc articles [def fc det]

adjv adjectives [def fc specification of nom]

adqv adquantors [def fc specification of nom]

prep prepositions [def fc specification of nom]

post postpositions [def fc specification of nom]

verb verbs [def: fc vrb]

infv infinitives [def non-finite verb & nomn]

part participles [def non-finite verb & adjv]

auxl auxiliary verbs *være, have* [def fc verb tense & topological
reference point]

modv modal auxiliary verbs: [lexcl semantics]

    kan, skal, bør, tør, må vil; få; lade

advp predicative adverbs [def fc pa]

advq quantificational adverbs[def fc aq or vqa]

advr relational adverbs [def fc ra or vra]

advv variational adverbs [def fc va or vva]

(09) MORPHOLOGY: Morpheme Formation Theory-*EFAX3.1*

morphematic defs & axioms:

*# notation: *dislocated morpheme segments* ('pseudo-morphemes'): 4
character symbols= æøåæ:, æøåæ., æøåæ·

§ inflection def

a morpheme is *inflected* when one or more features (phonological and/
or orthographic segments) have been changed and/or added to (also as
segments *dislocated from) the morpheme, resulting in the morpheme
having had its paradigmatic signification (paradigmatic semantics)
altered, thereby creating sub-paradigms

notation :, : (») :,

§ derivation **def**

a morpheme is *derived* when one or more features (phonological and/
or orthographic segments) have been changed and/or added to (also
as segments dislocated from) the morpheme, resulting in the morpheme
having had its syntagmatic signification (categorial function) altered,
thereby being transferred to other — or creating new — paradigms

notation ., . (») .,

§ modification def

a morpheme is *modified* when one or more features (phonological and/
or orthographic segments) have been changed and/or added to (also as
segments *dislocated from) the morpheme, resulting in the morpheme
having had its lexical semantics altered

notation ·, · (») ·,

(51)FORMAL CALCULUS (THEORETICAL APPLICATION)

EFAXDan (Danish syntax) efc (epi-formal calculus)

 # special rules (1) STC_CSTs (STX)

##special Dan CST occurrence rules:

(cf. Sca linearization rule: }(c)ºs\{x}ºvº{s}º(a)º(v)º(o/p)º(a)})

(c) => (c)

s°\{x} => s°\{x}

v => v\◊aux◊

{s} => {s}°/{o[m]}

(a) => pa°/qa°/nz

(v) => v◊{aux}/vrb/vva◊/{ra}

(o°/p) => {p}°/o°/{va}°>{o}°/p°/{s}°/kc°^kp

(a) => ra°/pa

special Dan linearization rule

(strong subsequential implication):

[Danish structural deviation (DEV): Dan stx topological (structural)
deviation; CST-consecution]

>(c)ºs\º{x}ºvº{s}º(a)º(v)º(o/p)º(a)>

Dan CST calculus [STC formation: construction]

parameters (>Ωz etc >: strong subseql impl):

∑>Ω(c)πcΩs\{x}πs\{x}Ωvπv\◊aux◊Ω{s}π{s}/{o[m*]}Ω(a)πpa/qa/nz
Ω(v)πv/◊{aux}/vrb/vva◊/{ra}Ω(o/p)π{p}/o/{vva}>{o}/p/{s}/kc^kp
Ω(a)πra/pa>∑

special morphemic conditions:
[*mig, dig, sig, ham, hende, den, det, os, jer, dem]

simplified notn:
∑>Ωc_πcΩs_πs\{x}Ωv_πv\◊aux◊Ωs₂_π{s}/{o[m*]}Ωa_πpa/qa/nz
Ωv₂_πv◊{aux}\vrb/vva◊/{ra}Ωo_π{p}/o/{vva}>{o}/p/{s}/kc^kp
Ωa₂_πra/pa>∑

NOTN_EFAX3 (Dan)
∑>
Ω †0†c_πc
  Ω †1†s_πs\{x}
    Ω †2†v_πv\◊aux◊
      Ω †3†s₂_π{s}/{o[m*]}
        Ω †4†a_πpa/qa/nz
          Ω †5†v₂_πv◊{aux}/vrb/vva◊/{ra}
            Ω †6†o_π{p}/o/{vva}>{o}/p/{s}/kc^kp
              Ω †7†a₂_πra/pa>∑
sequence constraints:
[*mig, dig, sig, ham, hende, den, det, os, jer, dem]

special phrase rules
##special Dan CPN occurrence rules
nom°>det,adq,adj,prp,psp
nom°\prn
vrb°>aux,vva

Dan PHR calculuses [PHR formation]
##V_PHR calc (Dan) — integrated into the calculus above:
>◊{aux}/vrb/vva◊>
##N_PHR calc (Dan):
>◊det/adq/adj^^/nom^^√prp/det/adq/adj/nom√psp◊>
##A_PHR calc (Dan):
>◊prp/det/adq/adj^^/nom^^√prp/det/adq/adj/nom√psp◊>

(52)**FORMAL CALCULUS (THEORETICAL APPLICATION)**
EFAXSwe (Swedish syntax) efc (epi-formal calculus)

special rules

special Swe occurrence rules:

(cf. Sca linearization rule: }(c)ºs\{x}ºvº{s}º(a)º(v)º(o/p)º(a)})

(c) => (c)

s°\{x} => s°\{x}

v => {qa/na}^v°>{qa/na}°\◊aux[*ha*]◊

{s} => {s}°/{o[m]°\[*sig*]°>{s}}

(a) => pa°/qa°/nz

(v) => v◊ʃcs°\ucʃ°>{aux°\~aux[*ha*]}/vrb/vva◊°/ra

(o°/p) => {p}°/o°/{vva}°>{o}°/p°/{s}°/kc°^kp

(a) => {ra}°/pa

special Swe linearization rule (strong subsequential implication):

[Swedish structural deviation (DEV): Swe stx topological (structural) deviation; CST- consecution]

>(c)ºs\{x}ºvº{s}º(a)º(v)º(o/p)º(a)>

Swe calculus [STC formation: construction]

parameters (>Ωz etc >: strong subseql impl):

∑>Ω(c)πcΩs\{x}πs\{x}Ωvπ{qa/na}^v>{qa/na}\◊aux[*ha*]◊Ω{s}π{s}/{o[m*]}\

[*sig*]>{s}Ω(a)πpa/qa/nzΩ(v)πv◊ʃcs\ucʃ>{aux\¬aux[*ha*]}/vrb/vva◊/ra

Ω(o/p)π{p}/o/{vva}>{o}/p/{s}/kc^kpΩ(a)π{ra}/pa>∑

sequence constraints:

[*mig*, *dig*, *sig*, *honom*, *henne*, *den*, *det*, *oss*, *er*, *dem*]

simplified notn:

∑>Ωc_πcΩs_πs\{x}Ωv_π{qa/na}^v>{qa}\◊aux[*ha*]◊Ωs$_2$_π{s}/{o[m*]}\[*sig*]>{s}

Ωa_πpa/qa/nzΩv$_2$_πv◊ʃcs\ucʃ>{aux\¬aux[*ha*]}/vrb/vva◊/ra

Ωo$_p$_π{p}/o/{vva}>{o}/p/{s}/kc^kpΩa$_2$_π{ra}/pa>∑

NOTN_EFAX3 (Swe)

∑>

Ω ↑0↑c_πc

  Ω ↑1↑s_πs\{x}

    Ω ↑2↑v_π{qa/na}^v>{qa/na}\◊aux[ha]◊

      Ω ↑3↑s$_2$_π{s}/{o[m*]}\[*sig*]>{s}

        Ω ↑4↑a_πpa/qa/nz

          Ω ↑5↑v$_2$_πv◊ʃcs\ucʃ>{aux\¬aux[*ha*]}/vrb/vva◊/ra

            Ω ↑6↑o$_p$_π{p}/o/{vva}>{o}/p/{s}/kc^kp

              Ω ↑7↑a$_2$_π{ra}/pa>∑

sequence constraints:

[*mig, dig, sig, honom, henne, den, det, oss, er, dem*]

special phrase rules
##special Swe CPN occurrence rules
nom°>det,adq,adj,prp,psp
nom°\prn
vrb°>aux, vva

Swe phrase calculuses [PHR formation]
##V_PHR calc (Swe) — integrated into the calculus above:
>◊{aux}/vrb/vva◊>
##N_PHR calc (Dan):
>◊det/adq/adj^^/nom^^√prp/det/adq/adj/nom√psp◊>
##A_PHR calc (Dan):
>◊prp/det/adq/adj^^/nom^^√prp/det/adq/adj/nom√psp◊>

(52)FORMAL CALCULUS (THEORETICAL APPLICATION)
EFAXDan/Swe calculus comparison
Danish vs Swedish syntax)

[Dan:Swe stx deviations (contrastive description):

Dan & **Swe** *calculus comparison*(Swedish in **bold**):
$\sum$>Ωc_πcΩs_πs\{x}Ωv_π{**qa/na**}^v>{**qa**}\◊aux[***ha***]◊Ωs_π{s}/{o[m*]}\[***sig***]>{**s**}
Ωa_πpa/qa/nzΩ**v**_πv◊∫**cs\uc∫**>{aux\¬aux[***ha***]}/vrb/vva◊/**ra**
Ωo_π{p}/o/{vva}>{o}/p/{s}/kc^kpΩa_π{**ra**}/pa>

Dan sequence constraints:

[*mig, dig, sig, ham, hende, den, det, os, jer, dem*]

Swe sequence constraints:

[*mig, dig, sig, honom, henne, den, det, oss, er, dem*]

simplified notn:
$\sum$>Ω**c**_πcΩ**s**_πs\{x}Ω**v**_π{**qa/na**}^v>{**qa**}\◊aux[***ha***]◊Ωs$_2$_π{s}/{o[m*]}\[***sig***]>{**s**}
Ω**a**_πpa/qa/nzΩ**v2**_πv◊∫cs\uc∫>{aux\¬aux[***ha***]}/vrb/vva◊/ra
Ω**op**_π{p}/o/{vva}>{o}/p/{s}/kc^kpΩ**a2**_π{ra}/pa>

Notes

Preface

1 An overview of the academic field of contemporary linguistics as perceived by the author is not uncommon in monographs that present new approaches, cf. Hudson (1990) who offers a list of approaches in linguistics comprising: 'Lexicalism', 'Wholism', 'Trans-constructionism', 'Poly-constructionism', 'Relationism', 'Mono-stratalism', 'Cognitivism' and 'Implementationism'.

2 According to de Beaugrande (1991: 224) this is Halliday's view on functional vs. formal grammarians: 'Despite some "cross currents" and "borrowing" of "insights", the two sides have found it "difficult to maintain a dialogue" or "exchange ideas" (IF xviii)'.

3 As opposed to Halliday, who is referred to by de Beaugrande (1991: 223): 'Halliday finds "the question 'what is language?'" unduly "diffuse" and "disingenuous"', I actually find this question meaningful. But, as argued in this book, I do not find the idea of 'language as such' productive – or adequate for that matter. I prefer to talk about 'languages' and sometimes 'a language'.

4 Or the technical 'approach', cf. below. The use of the term naturalistic should not cause confusion with Chomsky's 'language as a natural object' ontology in his 1995a article, which deals with the question whether language can be studied in the same way as objects in the natural sciences, cf. below.

5 The main reason why I refer to Kristeva (1989) in this context, is that she is – in my view – a person who has profound knowledge of language and linguistics, but who draws rather dubious conclusions about what the central concern of linguistics is or should be: 'psychoanalysis' (p. 265) and 'semiotics' (p. 295 seqq.), the latter field to include structural anthropology, music, etc. Accordingly, Kristeva (1989) can be used, both as a rather broad reference in the history of linguistics, and as an illustration of the literary delusion that linguistics is ultimately about the individual human being's emotional experiences with linguistic phenomena.

6 From a slightly different – and maybe not as biased – perspective the basic current approaches in the language sciences can be said to be:

- *The approach of technical interest*, which tries to uncover the internal 'hard core systems' of languages in general, the different systems of the languages of the world and the regularities of the external interaction of such 'systems' with the 'environment' of culture and society. The traditional disciplines of linguistics – phonetics and phonology, syntax and morphology, and semantics – and the recently developed disciplines of pragmatics, sociolinguistics and psycholinguistics, presumably belong to this category. The kinds of approach mentioned by Hudson (1990) in note 1 can be seen as sub-approaches in this category.

- *The approach of human concern*, which tries to identify the 'anthropological' functions of language and languages. Applied linguistics and discourse analysis are typical sub-fields in this category.
- *The approach of cultural heritage*, which tries to establish the national linguistic history as an essential part of the cultural identity. Traditional national philology and the fields of modern and classical languages (as 'Bildungswissenschaften') are typical candidates in this category.

One might also claim the existence of a special approach (the 'literary approach'), namely that of individual understanding, which tries to yield existential exegeses of linguistic experiences. Literary and cultural studies, on the one hand, and some versions of philosophical hermeneutics, existentialism and phenomenology, on the other, are the most productive academic fields of this approach. It is questionable whether this approach belongs to the language sciences.

The three approaches first mentioned pursue the finding of natural or cultural 'laws' or regularities, or they record interesting linguistic evidence, and they do so by means of formal or descriptive methods, while the 'literary approach' seeks patterns of subjective meaning using methods of empathy applied to words and texts.

I want to emphasize that the theories and methods applied in this book are in accordance with the general ideas and principles of the three approaches in linguistics, while the 'literary approach' plays no role in the following.

Chapter One

1 Henceforth all translations into English are by the author unless other information is explicitly given.
2 See Bertelsen (1926).
3 Both texts were published in the compilation of seventeenth- and eighteenth-century Danish grammarians: *Danske Grammatikere I–V*, and this work was republished as a reprint in 1979 by Det danske Sprog- og Litteraturselskab (Berthelsen, 1915 (reprint 1979)).
4 At this stage, Brøndal apparently had no interest whatsoever in syntax, but later it looks as if he changed his mind, and in 1932 he published a book on syntax: *Morfologi og Syntax* 'Morphology and Syntax' (Brøndal 1932), as mentioned above.

5 I take no stance on the nature of the Aristotelian Categories, neither on the Kantian ones, but I present my own views on ontology and how to conceptualize the world in Chapter 3.

6 For a discussion of the philosophical status of Aristotle's categories, cf. Jones (1970: 214–54), and for a presentation of the Kantian categories: 'Tafel der Kategorien', '1. Der Quantität', '2. De Qualität', '3. Der Relation', and 'Der Modalität', cf. Kant ([1781] 1924: 150 seqq.).

7 For now I shall not engage in a discussion on the notions of verification and falsification but merely refer to Popper (1934) and (1989).

8 I will come back to prepositions in Chapter 4.

9 Cf. the so-called Sapir-Whorf hypothesis, on which I shall make no comment here.

10 For a more detailed account of Hjelmslev's life and work, see note 11.

11 Cf. Götzsche 'Louis Hjelmslev', in Chapman and Routledge (2005: 124–7).

12 That is, European Structuralism, cf. Götzsche: 'Structuralism', in Chapman and Routledge (2009: 219–25).

13 Cf. Götzsche: 'Roman Jakobson', in Chapman and Routledge (2005: 142–7).

14 Which, at this point, should not be confused with the deductive system of the theory.

15 A technical term that is, as mentioned above, introduced earlier.

16 The notation of the negations is not the same as the one in Uldall (1957) but the logical functions are the same.

17 This is – in my view – the case, for instance, in Aa. Hansen (1967).

18 Which may not be a bad idea, see below.

19 'Scheme' is the term used in most English translations; for theoretical reasons (cf. below) I prefer the term TABLE, and accordingly I call the model a SENTENCE TABLE.

20 The formula has been taken from Diderichsen ([1946] 1966): 186, the field labels have been left out, and the sentence has been slightly changed.

21 The notion of 'markedness' is much debated but I am inclined to hold the same view as those of Haspelmath, namely, that 'the term "markedness" is superfluous' (2006: 25).

22 This is what Sigurd characterizes as 'a grammatical system which consists of a general word order or constituent schema supplemented with co-occurrence restrictions' (1994: 57).

23 But, as is illustrated by the thematic issue of *Linguistic Typology* 9(3) (2005), the question of whether categories of linguistic expressions should be called word classes or not, has not been answered yet.

Chapter Two

1 I had the privilege of meeting Noam Chomsky at MIT on 19 April 2005, and I can confirm the impression of others that he is a very kind and pleasant person.

2 So, I will not mention other important works by Chomsky like his 1975 *The Logical Structure of Linguistic Theory*, his 1964 *Current Issues in Linguistic Theory*, or his (with Morris Halle) *The Sound Pattern of English*, or his 1981 *Lectures on Government and Binding*. For a brief overview and bibliography, see Poole, 'Chomsky', in Chapman and Routledge (2005).

3 I take no stance concerning the issue to what extent Chomsky read (or misread) Descartes or whether he misconceived the historical background of the notion 'rationalism' in linguistics as the background to his 'mentalism' and his ideas about 'universal grammar', cf. the extremely critical assessment in Aarsleff (1970): 'I must conclude with the firm belief that I do not see that anything at all useful can be salvaged from Chomsky's version of the history of linguistics' (p. 583) and 'Universal grammar is profoundly important in the history of linguistics, but Chomsky's account fails to grasp both the nature and the history of that importance' (*ibid.*). In the actual context of twentieth-century American Structuralism, it is interesting to note that for Bloomfield, the word 'mentalism' was used almost as an insult, cf. A. Harris (1989: 112).

4 For the notion of 'the language faculty' in a broader context, see Hauser, Chomsky and Fitch (2002).

5 In the context of 'linguistics and biology' Jackendoff's (2011) discussion note in *Language*, 87 (3): 586–624, and the exchange of arguments with Pieter van Seuren on this and other theoretical topics in (Jackendorff 2012) *Language*, 88 (1): 174–8, offer an update of some core disagreements in this field.

6 No doubt, some scholars regard Chomsky's achievements as 'a revolution in linguistics', cf. A. Harris (1989: 108) in his almost hagiographic presentation of Chomsky: '*Syntactic Structures* was the cornerstone of a scientific revolution in linguistics.'

7 In doing this, Ouhalla follows the principles of Bloomfieldian methodology in the form of 'immediate constituent analysis', cf. Bloomfield ([1914] 1934: 209, 221 *et passim*).

8 These principles are still the recourse when identifying constituents in syntax, cf. the clear and pedagogical presentation in Moro (2008: 65 seqq.). Cf. also note 7 on Bloomfield's 'immediate constituent analysis' and the remarks below on textbook presentations of grammar and syntax.

9 On the contrary, subj-verb-obj and subj-verb-pred structures – and also those containing complex constituents like those in (4a, b) – must be assumed to be intrinsic to the constructions most frequently presented to a child speaking, for

instance, Western European languages, including American English. As is well known, the words 'eager' and 'easy' may not have been randomly chosen, cf. Chomsky (1970: 187–8).

10 As for Fromkin et al. (2011), it was a strange experience to receive the book from the publisher with an enclosed invoice ('Gratis – Payment not required') displaying the phrase 'Thank you for your interest in this title … ' because I had, to my knowledge, expressed no interest in the book.

11 The question whether there is (or should be) a theoretical distinction between constituent order and/or word order is, as is well known, not particular to Moro. The volume *EALT / EUROTYP 20-1* has the title *Constituent Order in the Languages of Europe* (Siewierska 1998), and it contains 14 contributions out of 19 with the phrase 'word order' in their title. But Siewierska states clearly in the endnote to her Introduction that 'In this volume the terms "constituent order" and "word order" are used as synonyms.'

Chapter Three

1 The following presentation of a number of basic philosophical notions is identical to the point of departure of the paper by Götzsche and Filatova (2012) on cognitive linguistics.

2 Mandler (2007) differentiates between five different notions of 'mind': 'Mind as soul', 'Mind as faculty', 'Mind as brain function', 'Mind as summary term for complex thought and action' and 'Mind as consciousness' (pp. 2–3), and from the following it should be clear that I do not use the term in the first meaning, that I do not select one of the other meanings as the most adequate one, and that I may sometimes refer to specific mind functions as cognitive systems.

3 I do not take it for granted that physicalism is a clear-cut and uncontroversial theoretical concept. Vicente (2011) offers an extensive discussion of how the use of this notion may avoid being trivial or devoid of meaning.

4 Even though some phenomena may become fairly complex 'physical' entities, like the human brain and the behaviour of humans in societies, which may give rise to somewhat complicated theories. Accordingly this is not traditional reductionism but rather an attempt to contribute to scientific unification.

5 Meaning that what was previously considered impossible knowledge becomes potential knowledge.

6 I do not know whether this will solve the psychophysical problem of traditional dualism taken up by Crane (1991), but I suppose it may solve the problem concerning what we talk about when we talk about things in the world.

7 So, PHYSICS, in this context, is:

> concerned with the basic principles of the Universe. It is the foundation upon which the other physical sciences – astronomy, chemistry and geology – are based. The myriad physical phenomena in our world are a part of one or more of the following areas of physics: 1. Classical mechanics … 2. Relativity … 3. Thermodynamics … 4. Electromagnetism … 5. Quantum mechanics …
>
> (Serway 1996: 1).

I shall not take up the intriguing question taken up by Vicente (2011) of the relationship between 'current physics' (p. 3) and the philosophical idea of physicalism.

8 Since it is a doctrine, i.e. a preparatory theory in the form of a set of axiomatic propositions, I suggest that the (invented neoclassical) term is *taxiology, namely, a 'logy' as a field of study instead of a '-nomy' as a field of knowledge on law-governed phenomena.

9 In this context, metaphysical concepts refer to physical things about which we may in the end have ultimate knowledge, ultimately about the principles and characteristics of the whole universe. For the time being we only have assumptions about such things. Accordingly, for now, metaphysics is a set of fundamental assumptions about the principles and characteristics of everything within the realm of possible knowledge as the necessary prerequisite in building ontological theories about the world. As for the lists of metaphysical and ontological concepts proposed by me, it is interesting that they are analogous to the notions that Vicente (2011) thinks will survive current physics, among them 'energy', 'momentum', 'electrical charge', 'bodies' and 'the forces' (p. 3), and 'process' (p. 14). For the correspondence with Kantian categories, see Kant ([1781] 1925: 944–95) *et passim*.

10 This does not mean that I think that syntax is the specific or main linguistic capacity as a feature of human beings that make us differ from animals (cf. Hauser, Chomsky and Fitch 2002). On the contrary, I think that our capacity of being able to learn unlimited numbers of expressions for things in the world is our specific and main human characteristic; i.e. the lexical and semantic capacity.

11 Cf. Copi (1982: 334 seqq. and 348) on consistency, completeness and effectiveness, Tarski (1937, pp. 87–95) on 'Willkürlichkeit … von Axiomen … . Postulate der Unabhängigkeit', 'Wiederspruchsfreiheit und … Vollständigkeit', and McCawley (1981, p. 76) on 'deductive completeness' and (*ibid.*: 40) on 'consistency'. The characteristics of the current standard notion of 'formal system' are accounted for in *The MIT Encyclopedia of the Cognitive Sciences* (1999: xxxii–xxxiv) *et passim*. I am aware of the fact that Gödel points to the problem that not all formal systems can be effective.

12 Accordingly, as for the formal system presented in the following, no further criteria will be considered other than that it has been meticulously examined by

my learned colleague Norbert Endres, and he has stated that its formal rigour is sufficient for its purpose.

13 I shall emphasize that by this I say nothing about the mathematical scientific field of Complexity Theory and the like.

14 This claim is, of course, my personal view, but even though it might seem relevant, I feel no urge to comment on the different viewpoints of physicists arguing for either so-called 'top-down' or 'bottom-up' methodologies concerning the problems of causality and explanation in physics and other sciences; neither do I wish to comment on so-called inductive vs. deductive methodologies; beyond mentioning Hjelmslev's remarks above. On the contrary, my way of seeing things seems to be in line with Chomsky (2007 (1979): 58): 'There is a constant interaction between the definition of the domain of research and the discovery of significant principles.'

15 Evidently not so in the social context of functionalists, but I would like to stress that my position is not a functionalist one like that of Boye and Harder (2012). Their approach is discourse-based, and it might be characterized as a 'weak' version of the EFA(X) approach, but in my view it is not able to account for the finer and more obscure details of the grammars of the world's languages.

16 I chose Lorentzen and Schwemmer, not because they could be assumed to be the only ones who had proposed a use- and dialogue-based procedure for establishing categories – on the contrary, this has been suggested by many – but because they offer a clear conceptual framework.

17 I emphasize that by using the term 'semiotics' I do not express any approval of the ideas of the American mathematician Charles S. Peirce.

18 The notion of 'sense' is not used here in a Fregean understanding. In his lengthy discussion of the notions 'sense' and 'reference' (or 'meaning') in the Fregean tradition, Kripke (2008) makes clear that these notions are not particularly transparent – even though they have, since Frege introduced them, become widely used. It should be noted that substituting 'sense' for 'meaning' does not undermine my reasoning above. If somebody is to determine the truth-value of a sentence (assuming that truth-values do not exist without human-made sentences), then one has to know what it means in order to compare it with its truth conditions, and to call what it means 'sense' does not solve this problem. And, as is well known, the notion of 'sense' is not quite transparent. In their discussion of linguistic communication, Dickie and Rattan (2010) offer the following clarification: 'On a standard understanding of the explanatory role of the notion of sense, an expression's sense is its "meaning" in the sense of "meaning" in which expressions differ in meaning iff they occupy different roles in our rational cognitive lives.' (pp. 141–2); in which you have to know what a 'role in cognitive life' is in order to find it appropriate.

19 If there are so-called one-word-sentences, their expressions must be portmanteau
    morphs, i.e. have more than one morpheme (and therefore two or more meanings)
    attached to them.

20 I am aware of the fact that this is not in accordance with the widespread use of
    the term in linguistics, cf. Crystal (1997: 350). Signification, in my sense of the
    theoretical concept, is explained in the context, and the term has been chosen
    because of the etymological relation between the words *sign* and *signification*, the
    last word meaning, in a broad sense, 'the making of signs'.

21 The 'lower levels' of this tripartite model resemble Frege's semantics (cf. Frege
    1892) in that SENSE equals *Sinn* and MEANING equals *Bedeutung*, but I want to
    avoid the confusion of meaning and reference.

22 By emphasizing that reference as the basis of linguistic meaning is human
    interaction with (and action in) the world I suggest that it is possible to achieve what
    Searle (1999: 2077) sets up as one of the goals for the philosophy of language:

> What we require in order to resolve the dispute between internalists and
> externalists is a more sophisticated notion of how the mental contents in
> speakers' heads serve to relate language in particular, and human agents in
> general, to the real world of objects and states of affairs.

I shall stress the fact that this is not a naïve updating of the common sense idea
that there is some of 'leash between words and things on the world', criticised by
many, and among them Chomsky, in a number of contexts.

23 Which should not be confused with the philosophical problem of universal
    meaning.

24 The pragmatic structures are, then, characteristics of the mental universe (stored in
    the memory) of an individual, and common characteristics of the mental universes
    (stored in the memories) of a number of individuals utilized in the interpretation
    of actual linguistic communication and cognition. In my view, this is the subject
    of pragmatics, but I am well aware of the fact that this notion is not in accordance
    with much of the theoretical and analytic work done under the label 'Pragmatics'
    (cf. the standard account of Levinson 1983 and the monograph, Levinson 2000).
    Thus it seems to be a characteristic feature of much 'Pragmatics' that it does not
    distinguish clearly between what people do and their perceptions of what they do.

25 Or expressed in a more technical way: meaning as pragmatic structures is
    accumulated experience of human action and interaction with humans and nature
    stored in memory.

26 This seems to be in accordance with Husserl's point of view: 'the reference to
    an object is a peculiarity belonging to the act-experience in accordance with its
    essential constitution (*Logische Untersuchungen*, Investigation V, § 20)', quoted in
    Dummett (1993: 227).

27 The category of performatives makes a special case, cf. Searle (1971) and (1992), and Götzsche (1995).

28 I will make no comment on the meaning of sentences like *the unicorn doesn't exist*, a problem that has caused philosophers much trouble.

29 If he 'speaks to himself', the universe is not a universe of discourse but a universe of consciousness.

30 This is, of course, also the aim of so-called 'functional approaches' (i.e. 'functional' traditions) in linguistics presenting theoretical grammatical frameworks and grammatical descriptions of specific languages. One such 'functional grammar' is the recent *Grammatik over det Danske Sprog* 'Grammar of the Danish Language' by Hansen and Heltoft (2011). This publication is, needless to say, a laudable feat, especially because of the huge amount of data they scrutinize, but from a theoretical point of view, the 'functional mindset' has a tendency to build monumental (and not always totally consistent) conceptual frameworks, because almost everything people can think of when using linguistic expression is included in the descriptions. Apart from the scientific unease this may give rise to, my main concern is the fact that such descriptions may in the end be conceived of as normative conventions, which is at odds with the general 'human concern' attitude of 'functionalists', namely, that the 'language user' and his/her needs are in focus.

31 Evidently, this does not conform to the Saussurean notion of the minimal linguistic sign of which the expression is a word or a morpheme.

32 It is hard to find an expression that has not yet been used in the language sciences for the purpose of saying that something is prior to something else in linguistic constructions since, for instance, words like 'pivot', 'nucleus', 'kernel' and 'head' mean certain things in the contexts of specific traditions, so I have chosen the term 'juncture' in the sense that it is both a point of departure in generating sentences and a place in space and time where things coincide.

33 This is not to be confused with notions like topic, theme, or focus, which I regard as terms describing discourse functions.

34 This is not quite in accordance with the standard notion of 'statement' in linguistics, cf. Crystal (1997: 361), and in traditional logic.

35 To some extent this distinction corresponds to the basic insights of the traditional descriptive (school grammar) distinction between lexical word-classes containing 'content words', and grammatical word-classes containing 'function words' (cf. the textbook by Hurford (1994: 151), in modern linguistics often labelled as the categories 'lexical' vs. 'grammatical' expressions, but since the notion of word is abandoned in this syntactic theory, the resemblance is only superficial, and the theoretical framework presented in the following will dissolve the lexical/grammatical-expression opposition.

36　Actually, I never understood the idea of truth conditions as the meaning of
　　sentences (cf. Higginbotham 2001). The problem is accounted for in Götzsche
　　(2009), in the entries 'Correspondence Theory' (pp. 42–3) and 'Possible Worlds
　　Semantics' (pp. 164–9; quoted here):

> [I]t may not be evident how the meaning of sentences is identical with the
> question of whether they are true or false. Intuitively one may think that in
> order to decide the truth value ... one has to understand it, and to understand
> it is to know its meaning. But, it is claimed, to know its meaning is to know its
> truth value based on its truth conditions, which, it follows, is the same thing as
> its meaning.
>
> 　　　　　　　　　　　　　　　　　　　　　　　　　　　　　(*ibid.*: 165)

　　So, if, by understanding the meaning of a sentence, I compare the sentence's
　　meaning with its truth conditions, then apparently I compare its meaning with
　　its meaning. Therefore I find it quite worrying that the 2012.04.12 *Notre Dame
　　Philosophical Review* by Adam Konopka (http://ndpr.nd.edu/news/30265-
　　variations-on-truth-approaches-in-contemporary-phenomenology/) starts out
　　with the following statement: 'In a 2009 online survey by PhilPapers, almost half
　　(48.9%) of the 1803 philosophy faculty or PhD participants answered that they
　　"accepted or leaned toward" a correspondence theory of truth'; of course assuming
　　that they also adhere to truth conditional sentence semantics.

37　The term 'algorithm' is, in this context, used in the broad sense about processes or
　　rules that must be followed in calculations and other problem-solving activities.

38　The technical acronym *EFA(X)* is made out of the letters in the upper case in the
　　expression *Epi-Formal Analysis in SyntaX*.

39　I shall emphasize that I do not claim to be the first to have come up with the
　　idea of defining the syntactic subject in this way. Actually, many linguists have
　　suggested thoughts quite similar to this idea of a 'starting point' in grammar, and
　　Jespersen (1937: 135) mentions two forerunners:

> What is a subject? How to define it? That the grammatical subject can be
> sufficiently defined as 'that about which we speak' has already been mentioned
> by H. G. Wivel (Synspunkter for dansk sproglære. 1901) and has been stated,
> independently, by P. B. Ballard (Thought and language. 1934: 90) in a passage
> which I transcribe: 'The subject of a sentence ... is supposed to state what the
> speaker is going to speak about. ... '.

　　There are, of course, two problems concerning this: one is the question of the
　　difference between 'subjects' in traditional logic (and that is dealt with in this
　　theory), and the other is that there seem to be sentences without a subject in some
　　languages (a problem which will not be dealt with in this context; apart from

suggesting that such sentences are kinds of 'syntactic derivations' that can only be interpreted as sentences relative to sentences with a subject).

40 The following technical account has been revised a number of times and may, on certain points, differ substantially from the one offered in the first and second editions of my doctoral thesis (Götzsche 1994). In the actual context only the necessary information is given, and an overview of the formal components of the current version of the theory (EFA(X)3): structural categorization, combinatorial system (EFS), and the general and special calculuses, is offered in Appendix B. In order to mark that these are technical presentations I use the '§' character for definitions and the '#' character for formalisms.

41 When evaluating the artificial terms '*conject' and '*conjection' cf. the analogous term 'converb', see Haspelmath's entry: 'Converb', in Brown and Miller (1996: 110–15) and Høysgaard (1752: 465).

42 I am aware of the fact that I use the notions 'syntagm(atic)' and 'paradigm(atic)' not quite in accordance with the ideas of de Saussure (1916, pp. 170–5): 'Rapports syntagmatiques et rapport associatifs', and p. 175 'paradigmes de flexion', but these theoretical concepts are ubiquitous in contemporary linguistics, and I define their technical meanings in this context.

43 As mentioned above, this is only a rudimentary display of the necessary technicalities. Appendix B offers a full list of the current notation and rules of the combinatorial system. Some of the principles of the occurrence logic on which it is based are mentioned below. Future updated versions can be found on the URL http://www.cfl.hum.aau.dk/linguistics/index.html.

44 It should be emphasized that this has nothing to do with so-called dependency grammars. In my view, such grammars assume that linguistic expressions (predominantly words) have some intrinsic properties that regulate the kind and the number of relations between them and other expressions, and the way I see it this is some kind of hypostatizing sound phenomena.

45 While standard notation often uses characters in the upper case to represent grammatical categories, I want to make explicit the fact that categories in the EFA(X) system are based on other definitions and therefore are represented by characters in the lower case.

46 A paper with the title 'The Logic of Occurrence' (1986; no information about its publication is offered) by Kenneth D. Forbus, Professor of Computer Science, is available at www.qrg.northwestern.edu/papers/Files/loo(searchable).pdf. http://citeseer.ist.psu.edu/viewdoc/summary?doi=10.1.1.55.4080.

It deals with: 'A general problem in qualitative physics is determining the consequences of assumptions about the behavior of a system.' I had no previous knowledge of this paper when I outlined my 'occurrence logic', and I have found no other suggestions about creating an 'occurrence logic' of the kind I propose in this context.

47 The symbol '°' in combination with traditional symbols denotes the occurrence
    logic functions of the symbol in question.

48 In the formalisms the square brackets cancel the application of rules until the
    information in the brackets has been used.

49 The term was initially borrowed by me from Chomsky (1965: 3): ' the
    well-formed strings of minimally syntactically functioning units (*formatives*)', but
    it has apparently gained some recognition as a technical term, cf. Trask (1993),
    who has one of his definitions as: '**formative** … *n.* 1. A **morpheme**, particularly
    one which plays part in syntax' (p. 107), which is in line with my use of the term,
    while it is not included in Brown and Miller (1999). Haspelmath (2011) offers
    the definition: 'a minimal coherent set of phonological features that play a role
    in a language system' (p. 70), and this is not inconsistent with my definition,
    in particular when he joins it with the definition of a 'morph': 'a formative that
    biuniquely expresses a meaning' (*ibid.*). Provided meanings can only be expressed
    in sentences, this is also consistent with my use of the terms morpheme and
    morph.

50 Cf. Kristensen (2001).

51 In general, I use examples, the scenarios of which may look a little nasty. I also do
    so when giving lectures. And therefore I often use the example *Peter has beaten
    the dog.* The idea is to make people remember the examples and the grammatical
    analyses. I would not dream of beating a dog, and my relationship with my wife's
    late dog, named Chomsky, was the best of all. But in order not to offend anybody I
    have, in this book, replaced the word *beat* with the word *train*.

52 In EFA(X) a MORPHEME is, as mentioned above, a minimal expression that can
    function as a constituent or a component and is connected with one or more
    general (paradigmatic) and particular (lexical) meanings, including derivational
    and inflectional information, while roots, stems and inflectional endings are not
    considered morphemes. This means that the notion of morpheme is closer to what
    we normally identify as words in texts (written language). I would like to stress the
    point that, in my view, the notion of 'word' is very hard to defend as a technical
    term in linguistics, a view also held by other linguists, cf. Haspelmath (2011), and
    I am not in favour of the idea that we are, in fact, able to identify word boundaries
    (cf. Basbøll (2000)). Morphemes as lexical items are, in the spirit of Hjelmslev,
    called GLOSSEMES.

53 In EFA(X) this implies that when morphemes are picked up from paradigms and
    put into a chain of morphemes, they form a SYNTAGM, and when they do so they
    are called FORMATIVES (cf. above), so they function either as constituents or as
    components.

54 To a certain extent, Jespersen's notion of 'Rank' (Jespersen 1937: 119 seqq.)
    corresponds to my idea of the component (specification) 'hierarchy' in phrases,

and my analysis of phrases as structures of specifications is not far from Moro's (2008) account of phrase structures, but we have different reasons for arriving at corresponding conclusions.

55 What I call the 'habitat' of a phrase looks much like a 'head' in traditional frameworks, and the reason for not choosing the term last mentioned is that my theoretical definition is not the same. The fact that both terms have an initial h- may make it easier to read this context.

56 Cf. Kristensen (2004: 189).

Chapter Four

1 Since this book is a presentation not only of one but also of different versions of the EFA(X)3 theory, then different ways of analysing the same phenomena are also presented. In this case, one approach was the EFA(X)2 way of doing things, i.e. all adverbial expressions were conceived of as csts (annotated with two-character symbols), while in the EFA(X)3 version – to a certain extent suggested by Susanne Annikki Kristensen – adverbial expressions are seen as either components (cpns) of the verb phrase (annotated with three-character symbols) or as constituents.

2 It should be noted that I do not use the term 'prototype' in the traditional sense used in, for instance, Historical Linguistics and language acquisition studies.

3 To some extent, and where there will no confusion about it, the abbreviations suggested in Chapter 3 will be used.

4 What these analyses do is that they match a structural description (ascribing cst-symbols to parts of a text) with the nodes of the Danish and Swedish calculuses and each symbol is then checked by the parameters of the actual position, resulting in the setting of the values of the parameters thereby offering a formal description. If a symbol from the structural description is not licensed by the parameters, the description will be rejected. This can be verified by comparing the analyses with the calculus above, but in the end a computational system should do the job; with the caveat that the formal system has demonstrated its formal rigour by mathematical proof.

5 The English glosses below the analyses are not marked by single quotation marks.

6 Henceforth the positions are annotated below the examples and with the simplified notation.

7 As mentioned elsewhere in this book, I do not approve of a notion of 'movement' in syntax. What happens is that expressions are found in different places in different positions in different sentences. I reject the Chomskyan (initial) idea that 'surface structure' sentences are an outcome of 'transformations' (i.e. among other things 'movements') of expressions. In my view any sentence is a unique entity and I only use the word 'move' in a metaphorical sense.

8 It should be noted that topological analyses of verbals and adverbials are – in Danish and Swedish – a particularly tricky thing in that we may have the original Diderichsen ambition that all constituents should be placed in the positions they have in expanded sentences construction, meaning that constituents found in 'v$_2$_' and 'a$_2$_' in sentences with no empty slots should be annotated with these symbols in sentences where there are no preceding verbs or adverbials. In my view, this is redundant information, but for practical reasons I use this 'Diderichsen'-inspired annotation in the analyses.

9 It should be observed that these short remarks on pronouns are far from satisfactory because complex kinds of use of pronouns in Danish and Swedish are rather complicated. I assume that all such constructions can be incorporated in the FoG matrix.

10 Standard grammars often use the term 'indirect object' while I prefer the notion 'dative object'. In my view the expressions 'indirect object' and 'direct object' signal a kind of grammatical mirroring of the scenarios that sentences describe and that may lead to an unfortunate confusion of sentence meaning and reality.

11 It is contradictory, actually, since if one maintains that linguistic expressions occur in a spatial orientation, i.e. topology, then one has to assume a certain spatial ordering of the expressions and that the ordering is significant for the syntactic interpretation of the set of expressions. It follows, then, that one cannot say both that the order is significant and that something may pop up outside the order that is also significant because in that case one will undermine the significance of the order.

12 As is well known, abstract prepositions are vulnerable to change in language use.

13 A special feature of the verb phrase in the EFA(X)3 version is the integration of the auxiliary and the adverb 'vva'. This means that these units are considered (phrase) components and not (sentence) constituents. As for the auxiliary it is a tricky expression, theoretically and analytically, and a straightforward definition is not easily arrived at. For an attempt to handle these problems, see Anderson (2006: 4–5) (definition) *et passim* (a large number of languages). Some possible solutions to the problems are offered below in the sections On Government and Agreement and On Prepositions and Infinitives.

14 I use the symbol '†' to separate numbers (like '†2†') here in order to avoid confusion with the symbols in the calculus.

15 The constructions used for these initial analyses have kindly been given to me by my colleague Susanne Annikki Kristensen.

16 These examples are in line with the ones presented by Christensen and Christensen (2004).

17 These examples have been quoted directly from Christensen and Christensen (2004).

18 In Götzsche (2010), I suggest that the 'linguistic gene' creating morphs and may be subject to pronunciation changes, which may effect language changes, is the syllable.

19 I make one reservation concerning Swedish. Thus, I take no stance in the debate on how the kind of Swedish that I investigate here has emerged; for instance, whether written Swedish historically has had an influence on pronunciation or whether (and how) a specific social class of people has come to dominate the Swedish dialectal landscape. I just stick to the idea that there is something that can be called Standard Swedish: notably what has been encoded in the reference work *Svenska Akademiens Grammatik*.

20 As pointed out by Götzsche (1997), the result of the latest development in the verb structure of Danish is the Swedish solution: *have* 'have' is the only future auxiliary in Danish.

21 This seems to be in line with what in Haspelmath (2011: 54) is called 'multiple exponence'. It should be observed that the following government analysis of the aux/main verb relation only applies if the aux is seen as a constituent.

22 Inspired by a remark made by my learned colleague Professor Kersti Börjars, University of Manchester, I am now inclined to say that so-called double definiteness is also a 3rd person label, i.e. in the EFA(X) theory: morphological (paradigmatic) signification of 3rd person.

23 I shall stress the fact that this has nothing to do with 'clitics', an analytic notion that I am not quite happy with.

24 I agree with Trask (1993: 277) that 'Traditional grammar often uses the term "tense" in a very loose manner that covers not only distinctions of tense but also those of aspect and sometimes even further distinctions.' The way I see it, my idea should solve this problem.

25 Trask (1993) has it that particles are, apart from the criterion of uninflectedness and the affiliation with the 'preposition-like items … in **phrasal** verbs' (p. 201) it is 'A label typically applied to some more-or-less well-defined class of uninflected words in the grammar of some particular language when no more obvious label presents itself.' I take it that this means that we may have no idea of what the syntactic function of a particle is.

26 The groundwork of this approach was presented in Kristensen and Götzsche (2007) and Kristensen (2010) that suggested that infinitive markers are actually prepositions and that prepositions work as derivational expressions, whereas the ultimate solution to what infinitive markers and prepositions 'really are' presupposes the idea of 'split morphemes' put forward here.

Chapter Five

1 The exact formulation of the following (brief) technical account has, through personal communication, been generously provided to me by my learned colleague Dr. habil. Norbert Endres, working with Professor Dr. Hans Fix Bonner, Ernst-Moritz-Arndt-Universität, Greifswald, on projects about Old Norse Morphology. (Cf. Also Götzsche and Filatova 2012).

Bibliography

Aarsleff, H. (1970), 'The History of Linguistics and Professor Chomsky', *Language*, 46 (3), 570–85.

Acta Linguistica vols. 1–8. Copenague: Einar Munksgaard, 1939–1960. (From 1965 (vol. 9) *Acta Linguistica Hafniensia.*)

Ahrenberg, L. (1992), 'The formalization of field grammar', in *The Nordic Languages and Modern Linguistics 7*. Tórshavn: Føroya Fróðskaparfélag, pp. 119–30.

Andersen, P. (1958), *Fonemsystemet i østfynsk, på grundlag af dialekten i Revninge Sogn*. Udvalg for Folkemaals Publikationer. Serie A Nr. 14. København: J. H. Schultz Forlag.

Anderson, G. D. S. (2006), *Auxiliary Verb Constructions*. Oxford: Oxford University Press.

Andresen, J. T. (2010), 'Review of E. F. K. Koerner, *Toward a History of American Linguistics*', *Language*, 86, 1.

Arens, H. (1969), *Sprachwissenschaft. Der Gang ihrer Entwicklung von der Antike bis zur Gegenwart*. Freiburg: Verlag Karl Alber.

Ballard Ph. B. (1934), *Thought and Language*. London: University of London Press.

Bandle, O. *et al.* (eds) (2005), *The Nordic Languages: An International Handbook of the History of the North Germanic Languages*, Vol. 2. Berlin: Walter de Gruyter.

Basbøll, H. (2000), '40. Word boundaries', in *Handbücher zur Sprach- und Kommunikationswissenschaft* Band 17.1. Berlin: Walter de Gruyter, pp. 377–88.

Bertelsen, H. (1926), *Jens Pedersen Høysgaard og hans Forfatterskab*. København: Gyldendalske Boghandel, Nordisk Forlag.

—(ed.) (1915), *Danske Grammatikere fra Midten af det syttende til Midten af det attende Aarhundrede, I–VI*, reprint 1979. København: det Danske Sprog- og Litteraturselskab and C. A. Reitzels Boghandel.

Bjerre, T., E. Engels, H. Jørgensen and S. Vikner (2008), 'Points of convergence between functional and formal approches to syntax', in *Working Papers in Scandinavian Syntax* 82. Lund: Lund University.

Bjerrum, A. (1944), *Fjoldemålet*. Ejnar Munksgaard.

Bjerrum, M. (1959), *Rasmus Rasks afhandlinger om det danske sprog*. København: Dansk Videnskabs Forlag.

Blevins, J. P. (2008), 'The post-transformational enterprise' (review article on Peter Cullicover and Ray Jackendoff: *Simpler syntax*), *Journal of Linguistics*, 44, 3.

Bloomfield, L. (1914), *Language*. London: George Allen & Unwin Ltd.

Bohm, D. (1996), *On Dialogue*. London: Routledge.

Bostock, D. (1979), *Logic and Arithmetic. Vol. 2. Rational and Irrational Numbers.* Oxford: Oxford University Press.

Botha, R. P. (1989), *Challenging Chomsky: The Generative Garden Game.* Oxford: Basil Blackwell.

Boye, K. and P. Harder (2012), 'A usage-based theory of grammatical status and grammaticalization', *Language,* 88, (1), 1–44.

Branquinho, J. (ed.) (2001), *The Foundations of Cognitive Science.* Oxford: Oxford University Press.

Brink, L. and J. Lund (1975), *Dansk Rigsmål* vol. 1. København: Gyldendal.

Brown, K. and J. Miller (eds) (1996), *Concise Encyclopedia of Syntactic Theories.* Oxford: Pergamon, Elsevier Science.

—(eds) (1999), *Concise Encyclopedia of Grammatical Categories.* Oxford: Pergamon, Elsevier Science.

Brøndal, V. (1928), *Ordklasserne.* Kjøbenhavn: G. E. C. Gad.

—(1932), *Morfologi og Syntax.* København: Bianco Lunds Bogtrykkeri.

Chambers Dictionary of Science and Technology (2007), Edinburgh: Chambers.

Chapman, S. and C. Routledge (eds) (2005), *Key Thinkers in Linguistics and the Philosophy of Language.* Edinburgh: Edinburgh University Press.

—(eds) (2009), *Key Ideas in Linguistics and the Philosophy of Language.* Edinburgh: Edinburgh University Press.

Chomsky, N. (1951), 'Morphophonemics of modern Hebrew', Master's thesis, University of Pennsylvania.

—(1956), 'Three models for the description of language', *Institute of Radio Engineers, Transactions on Information Theory,* IT-2, (3), 113–24.

—(1957), *Syntactic Structures.* The Hague: Mouton.

—(1959), 'A Review of B. F. Skinner's *Verbal Behavior*', *Language,,* 35, (1), 26–58.

—(1965), *Aspects of the Theory of Syntax.* Cambridge, MA: The MIT Press.

—(1966), *Cartesian Linguistics: A Chapter in the History of Rationalist Thought.* New York: Harper & Row.

—(1970), 'Remarks on Nominalizations', in R. Jacobs and P. Rosenbaum (eds) *Readings in English Transformational Grammar.* Waltham, MA: Blaisdell, pp. 184–221.

—(1995a), 'Language as a Natural Object', *MIND,* 104, (413), 1–61.

—(1995b), *The Minimalist Program.* Cambridge, MA: The MIT Press.

—(2000), *New Horizons in the Study of Language and Mind.* Cambridge: Cambridge University Press.

—(2007), *On Language, Language and Responsibility (1979) and Reflections on Language (1975).* New York: The New Press.

—(2012), *The Science of Language.* Cambridge: Cambridge University Press.

Chrisomalis, S. (2010), *Numerical Notation.* New York: Cambridge University Press.

Christensen L. and R. Z. Christensen (2004), '60 svensk-danska syntaxskillnader', in *På godt dansk.* Festskrift til Henrik Galberg Jacobsen i anledning af hans 60 års fødselsdag 4. februar 2004. København: Wessel og Huitfeldt, pp. 105–12.

Copi, I. M. (1982), *Introduction to Logic*. New York: Macmillan.

Crane, T. (1991), 'All God has to do', *Analysis*, 51, (4), 235–44.

Crystal, D. (1997), *A Dictionary of Linguistics and Phonetics*, 4th edn. Oxford: Basil Blackwell.

de Beaugrande, R. (1991), *Linguistic Theory: The Discourse of Fundamental Theory*. London: Longman.

de Saussure, F. (1916), *Cours de Linguistique Générale*. Paris: Payot.

Dickie, I. and G. Rattan (2010), 'Sense, communication, and rational engagement', *dialectica* 64, (2), 131–51.

Dictionary of Computing (1996), 4th edn. Oxford: Oxford University Press.

Diderichsen, P. (1936), 'Prolegomena til en metodisk dansk Syntax', in *Forhandlinger paa det ottende nordiske Filogimøde i København 1935*; republished in *Helhed og Struktur. Udvalgte sprogvidenskabelige afhandlinger*. København: G. E. C. Gads Forlag (1966), pp. 21–4.

—(1941), *Sætningsbygningen i Skaanske Lov*. København: Ejnar Munksgaard.

—(1944), 'Perfektparticipium – Supinum – Verbaladjektiv i Dansk og Svensk', *Arkiv for nordisk filologi*, 58, 263–83.

—(1946), *Elementær Dansk Grammatik*, 3rd edn, 1966. København: Gyldendal.

—(1960), *Rasmus Rask og den grammatiske Tradition*. Historisk-filosofiske Meddelelser udgivet af Det Kongelige Danske Videnskabernes Selskab, Bind 38 nr. 2.

—(1964), 'Sætningsleddene og deres stilling tredive år efter', in *Danica, Studier i dansk sprog. Til Aage Hansen 3. september 1964*; republished in *Helhed og Struktur. Udvalgte sprogvidenskabelige afhandlinger*. København: G. E. C. Gads Forlag (1966), pp. 364–79.

—(1968), *Sprogsyn og sproglig opdragelse*. København: Nyt Nordisk Forlag.

Dummett, M. (1993), *The Seas of Language*. Oxford: Clarendon Press.

Ejskjær, I. (1954), *Brøndum-Målet. Lydsystemet i en Sallingdialekt*. København: J. H. Schultz Forlag.

—(1970), *Fonemsystemet i Østsjællandsk, på grundlag af dialekten i Strøby Sogn*. Udvalg for Folkemaals Publikationer, Serie A Nr. 24. København: Akademisk Forlag.

Ekbo, S. (1943), *Uppkomsten av supinum i de germanska språken*. Uppsala: Appelbergs Boktryckeriaktiebolag.

Eriksson, U. (1971), *Åselesvenska, 1 A and 1 B*. Lundastudier i nordisk språkvetenskap, serie A nr. 20. Lund: Studentlitteratur.

Frege, G. (1892), 'Über Sinn und Bedeutung', *Zeitschrift für Philosophie und philosophische Kritik*, 100, 25–50.

Fromkin, V., R. Rodman and N. Hyams (2011), *An Introduction to Language*. 9th edn. Belmont, CA: Wadsworth International Edition.

Gärdenfors, P. (1990), 'The emergence of meaning', working paper. Cognitive Science, Department of Philosophy, Lund University.

Gianto, A. (2005), 'Aristotle', in S. Chapman, and C. Routledge (eds) *Key Thinkers in Linguistics and the Philosophy of Language*. Edinburgh: Edinburgh University Press, pp. 1–7.

Götzsche, H. (1990), 'Non-Formal Analyse i svensk og nordisk syntaks', in *Svenskans beskrivning* 18. Lund: Lund University Press, pp. 143–9.

—(1991), 'On the logic and syntax of numerals in Danish and Swedish', in *Papers from The Twelfth Scandinavian Conference of Linguistics*, Reykjavìk 1990. Reykjavìk: Linguistics Institute, University of Iceland, pp. 78–89.

—(1993), 'Adverbialer – sprogvidenskabens adoptivbørn', in *4. Møde om Udforskningen af Dansk Sprog*. Århus: Institut for Nordisk Sprog og Litteratur, Aarhus Universitet, pp. 96–107.

—(1994), 'Deviational syntactic structures: contrastive linguistic studies in the syntax of Danish and Swedish.' Doktorsavhandling (Doctoral Thesis). Göteborg: Institutionen för svenska språket, Göteborgs universitet.

—(1995), 'Some remarks on the ontology of performatives', in *Papers from the XVth Scandinavian Conference of Linguistics*. Oslo: Department of Linguistics, University of Oslo, pp. 193–9.

—(1997), 'Forklaringsmodeller i sproghistorien belyst med et eksempel fra den aktuelle sprogudvikling', in *6. Møde om Udforskningen af Dansk Sprog til minde om Peder Skautrup 1896–1996*. Århus: Institut for Nordisk Sprog og Litteratur, Aarhus Universitet, pp. 86–98.

—(1999), 'Om satsadverbial i svenska', in *Svenskans beskrivning 23*. Lund: Lund University Press, pp. 143–50.

—(2005a), 'Louis Hjelmslev', in S. Chapman and C. Routledge (eds) *Key Thinkers in Linguistics and the Philosophy of Language*. Edinburgh: Edinburgh University Press, pp. 124–7.

—(2005b), 'Roman Jakobson', in S. Chapman and C. Routledge (eds) *Key Thinkers in Linguistics and the Philosophy of Language*. Edinburgh: Edinburgh University Press., pp. 142–7.

—(2007), 'Die Bibel Christian III: Zwischen Morphologie und Topologie – eine vorläufige Hypothese', in H. Fix (ed.) *Beiträge zur Morphologie. Germanisch, Baltisch, Ostseefinnisch*. Odense: Syddansk Universitetsforlag (University Press of Southern Denmark), pp. 361–82.

—(2009a), 'Correspondence theory', in S. Chapman and C. Routledge (eds) *Key Ideas in Linguistics and the Philosophy of Language*. Edinburgh: Edinburgh University Press, pp. 42–3.

—(2009b), 'Possible World Semantics', in S. Chapman and C. Routledge (eds) *Key Ideas in Linguistics and the Philosophy of Language*. Edinburgh: Edinburgh University Press, pp. 164–9.

—(2009c), 'Structuralism', in S. Chapman and C. Routledge (eds) *Key Ideas in Linguistics and the Philosophy of Language*. Edinburgh: Edinburgh University Press, pp. 219–25.

—(ed.) (2010a), *Memory, Mind and Language: Proceedings from the 22nd Scandinavian Conference of Linguistics*. Newcastle: Cambridge Scholars Press.

—(2010b), 'Language as history and memory: challenges for historical linguistics', in H. Götzsche (ed.) *Memory, Mind and Language: Proceedings from the 22nd Scandinavian Conference of Linguistics*. Newcastle: Cambridge Scholars Press.

Götzsche, H. and K. Filatova (2012), 'On the ontology and cognitive processing of languages', in *Cognitive Dynamics in Linguistic Interactions*. Cambridge: Cambridge Scholars Press, pp. 81–106.

Griffith, S.(ed.) (1999), *Predictions*. Oxford: Oxford University Press (*The Times Higher Education Supplement*), pp. 149–54.

Halliday, M. A. K. (1985), 'Dimensions of Discourse Analysis: Grammar', in T. A. van Deuk (ed.) *Handbook of Discourse Analysis*. London: Academic Press.

Hansen, Aa. (1933), *Sætningen og dens Led i moderne Dansk*. København: Nyt Nordisk Forlag – Arnold Busck.

—(1967), *Moderne Dansk* vols I–III. København: Grafisk Forlag.

Hansen, E. and L. Heltoft (2011), *Grammatik over det Danske Sprog* vols I, II and III. Odense: Syddansk Univesrsitetsforlag.

Harris, A. (1989), 'Argumentation in Chomsky's syntactics structures. an exercise in rhetoric of science', *Rhetoric Society Quarterly*, 19, (2), 105–30.

Harris, R. (2003), *Saussure and his Interpreters*, 2nd edn. Edinburgh: Edinburgh University Press.

Haspelmath, M. (2006), 'Against markedness (and what to replace it)', *Journal of Linguistics*, 42, (1), 25–70.

—(2011), 'The indeterminacy of word segmentation and the nature of morphology and syntax', in *Folia Linguistica. Acta Societas Linguisticae Europaeae*. The Hague: De Gruyter Mouton, pp. 31–80.

Hauser, M. D., N. Chomsky and W. Tecumseh Fitch (2002), 'The faculty of language: what is it, who has it, and how did it evolve?', *Science*, 298, 1569–79.

Higginbotham, J. T. (2001), 'On referential semantics and cognitive science', in J. Branquinho (ed.) *The Foundations of Cognitive Science*. Oxford: Oxford University Press, pp. 145–56.

Hinzen, W. (2006), *Mind Design and Minimal Syntax*. Oxford: Oxford University Press.

Hjelmslev, L. ([1943] 1966), *Omkring Sprogteoriens Grundlæggelse*. Festskrift udgivet af Københavns Universitet november 1943; republished 1966. København: Akademisk Forlag.

—(1959), 'An introduction to linguistics', *Essais Linguistiques. Travaux du Cercle Linguistique de Copenhague*, Vol. XII. Copenhague: Nordisk Sprog- og Kulturforlag, pp. 9–20.

—(1975), *Résumé of a Theory of Language*. Copenhagen: Nordisk Sprog- og Kulturforlag.

Høysgaard, J. (1747), *Accentuered og Raisonered Grammatica*; reprinted in H. Bertelsen, *Danske Grammatikere IV*. København: Gyldendalske Boghandel, Nordisk Forlag pp. 249–488, republished as a reprint in 1979 by Det danske Sprog- og Litteraturselskab.

—(1752), *Methodisk Forsøg til en Fuldstændig Dansk Syntax*; reprinted in H. Bertelsen, *Danske Grammatikere V*. København: Gyldendalske Boghandel, Nordisk Forlag pp. 1–506, republished as a reprint in 1979 by Det danske Sprog- og Litteraturselskab.

Hudson, R. (1990), *English Word Grammar*. Oxford: Basil Blackwell.

Hulthén, L. (1948), *Studier i jämförande nunordisk syntax* II. Göteborgs högskolas årsskrift LIII 1947: 4. Göteborg: Elanders Boktryckeri.

Hurford, J. (1987), *Language and Number*. Oxford: Basil Blackwell.

—(1994), *Grammar: A Students Guide*. Cambridge: Cambridge University Press.

Ihre, J. (1745), *Föreläsningar öfver svenska språket*. Uppsala.

Jackendoff, R. (2011), 'What is the human language faculty? Two views', *Language*, 87, (3), 586–624.

—(2012), 'Response to Seuren', *Language*, 88, (1), 174–8.

Jacquette, D. (ed.) (2002), *A Companion to Philosophical Logic*. Oxford: Blackwell Publishing.

Jaworska, E. (1999), 'Prepositions and prepositional phrases', in K. Brown and J. Miller (eds) *Concise Encyclopedia of Grammatical Categories*. Oxford: Pergamon, Elsevier Science.

Jespersen, O. (1913), *Sprogets logik*. København: J. H. Schultz.

—(1924), *The Philosophy of Grammar*. London: George Allen & Unwin.

—(1937), *Analytic Syntax*. Copenhagen: Levin & Munksgaard. Ejner Munksgaard.

Johannisson, T. (1945), *HAVA ovh VARA som tempusbildande hjälpverb i de nordiska språken*. Lund: C. W. K. Glerup/Leipzig: Otto Harrassowitz.

—(1960), 'Eine syntaktische Entlehnung im Schwedischen', in *Indogermanica, Festschrift für Wolfgang Krause*. Heidelberg: Carl Winter Universitätsverlag, pp. 38–43.

Jones, W. T. (1970), *A History of Western Philosophy: The Classical Mind*. San Diego: Harcourt Brace Jovanovich.

Källström, R. (1993), *Kongruens i svenskan*. Göteborg: Acta Universitatis Gothoburgensis: Nordistica Gothoburgensia 16.

Kant, E. ([1781] 1924), *Kritik der Reinen Vernunft*. Wiesbaden: VMA-Verlag.

Kenny, A. J. P. (1981), 'Language and mind', *Philosophical Transactions of the Royal Society B, Biological Sciences*, 295, 245–51.

Koerner, E. F. and R. E. Asher (eds) (1995), *Concise History of the Language Sciences: From the Sumerians to the Cognitivists*. Oxford: Pergamon, Elsevier Science.

Koerner, F. K. (2002), *Toward a History of American Linguistics*. London: Routledge.

Kravchenko, A. V. (2010), 'Language and mind: a biocognitive view', in H. Götzsche (ed.) *Memory, Mind and Language: Proceedings from the 22nd Scandinavian Conference of Linguistics*. Newcastle: Cambridge Scholars Press.

Kripke, S. (2008), 'Frege's theory of sense and reference: some exegetical notes', *Theoria*, 74: 181–218.

Kristensen, S. A. (2001), Morfologisk syntaktiske strukturer. MA dissertation. Aalborg University.

—(2004), *Syntagmatiske Strukturer*. PhD thesis. Aalborg University.

—(2010), 'To mind or not to mind', in H. Götzsche (ed.) *Memory, Mind and Language: Proceedings from the 22nd Scandinavian Conference of Linguistics*. Newcastle: Cambridge Scholars Press, pp. 206–20.

Kristensen, S. A. and Götzsche, H. (2007), 'Kunsten at analysere en at-infinitiv', in *11. Møde om udforskningen af Dansk Sprog*. Nordisk Institut, Aarhus Universitet, pp. 259–68.

Kristeva, J. (1989), *Language the Unknown: An Initiation into Linguistics*. London: Harvester Wheatsheaf.

Lasnik, H. and M. Saito (1991), 'On the subject of infinitives', *Linguistic Inquiry* 15, 265–89.

Levinson, S. C. (1983), *Pragmatics*. Cambridge: Cambridge University Press.

—(2000), *Presumptive Meanings*. Cambridge, MA: The MIT Press.

Linguistic Typology (2005), 9, (3).

Ljunggren, R. (1934), *Supinum och dubbelsupinum. Syntaktiska studier*. Uppsala: A.-B. Lundequistska Bokhandeln.

Lorenzen, P. and O. Schwemmer (1975), *Konstruktive Logik, Ethik und Wissenschaftstheorie*. Mannheim: Bibliographisches Institut.

Ludlov, P. (2011),*The Philosophy of Generative Grammar*. Oxford: Oxford University press.

Lyons, J. (1977), *Semantics*. Cambridge: Cambridge University Press.

Madvig, J. N. ([1843] 1971), *Sprachteoretische Abhandlungen*. (posthumous edn.) København: Munksgaard/Det Danske Sprog- og Litteraturselskab.

Malmberg, B. (1969), *Introduktion till Fonetiken som vetenskap*. Stockholm: Natur och Kultur.

Malmgren, S.-G. (1985), 'Om uteläming av hjälpverbet *ha* i förbindelse med supinum', in *Svenskans beskrivning* 15. Göteborg: Göteborgs Universitet, pp. 347–58.

Mandler, G. (2007), *A History of Modern Experimental Psychology*. Cambridge, MA: The MIT Press.

McCawley, J. (1981), *Everything that Linguists Have Always Wanted to Know about Logic*, But Were Ashamed to Ask*. Oxford: Basil Blackwell.

Mikkelsen, Kr. (1911), *Dansk Ordføjningslære*. København: Lehman & Stages Forlag; reprinted 1975 by Hans Reitzels Forlag.

MIT Encyclopedia of the Cognitive Sciences (1999), Cambridge, MA: The MIT Press.

Molde, B. (1950), *Källorna till Christian III:s Bibel 1550*. Stockholm Studies in Scandinavian Philology 8. Lund: C. W. K. Gleerup, København: Rosenkilde og Bagger.

Moore, T. and C. Carling (1982), *Understanding Language: Towards a Post-Chomskyan Linguistics*. London: Macmillan.

Moro, A. (2008), *The Boundaries of Babel*. Cambridge, MA: The MIT Press.

Newmeyer, F. J. (1998), *Language Form and Language Function*. Cambridge, MA: MIT Press.

—(2005), *Possible and Probable Languages: A Generative Perspective on Linguistic Typology*. Oxford: Oxford University Press.

Novaes, C. D. (2011), 'The different ways in which logic is (said to be) formal', *History and Philosophy of Logic*, 32, 303–32.

Nydanske studier & almen kommunikationsteori (1986), vols 16–17, *Sætningsskemaet og dets stilling – 50 år efter*. København: Akademisk Forlag.

Ouhalla, J. (1994), *Introducing Transformational Grammar: From Principles and Parameters to Minimalism*, 2nd edn. London: Arnold.

Oxford Companion to Philosophy (2005), New edition, (ed.) T. Honderich. Oxford: Oxford University Press.

Pedersen, C. (1510), *Vocabularium ad usum dacorum, ordine litterario cum eorum vulgari interpretatione*. Paris.

Pettersson, G. (1988), 'Bisatsledföljden i svenskan, eller, Varifrån kommer BIFF-regeln?', *Arkiv för nordisk filologi* 103, 157–80.

Platzack, C. (1988), 'Den centralskandinaviska bisatsordföljdens framväxt', in *Studier i svensk språkhistoria*. Lund: Lunds Universitet, pp. 241–55.

Poole, G. (2005), 'Chomsky', in S. Chapman. and C. Routledge (eds) *Key Thinkers in Linguistics and the Philosophy of Language*. Edinburgh: Edinburgh University Press, pp. 53–9.

Popper, K. ([1934] 1969), *Logik der Forschung*. Tübingen: J. C. B. Mohr (Paul Siebeck).

—(1989), *Conjectures and Refutations: The Growth of Scientific Knowledge*. 5th edn. reprinted 1991. London: Routledge.

Rask, R. K. (1818), *Undersögelse om det gamle Nordiske eller Islandske Sprogs Oprindelse*. Kjöbenhavn: Paa den Gyldendalske Boghandlings Forlag.

—(1826), *Forsøg til en videnskabelig dansk Retskrivningslære med hensyn til Stamsproget og Nabosproget*. København.

Rasmussen, M. (1992), *Hjelmslevs sprogteori. Glossematikken i videnskabshistorisk, videnskabsteoretisk og erkendelsesteoretisk perspektiv*. Odense: Odense Universitetsforlag.

Rooth, M. (1992), 'A theory of focus interpretation', *Natural Language Semantics*, 1, (1), 75–116.

Sahlstedt, A. (1769), *Swensk Grammatica. Efter det nu brukliga sättet*. Uppsala.

Searle, J. (1971), 'What is a speech act?', in J. R. Searle (ed.) *The Philosophy of Language*. Oxford: Oxford University Press, pp. 37–53.

—(1992), 'Conversation', in H. Parret and J. Vershueren (eds) *(On) Searle on Conversation'*. Philadelphia, PA: John Benjamin Publishing Company, pp. 1–29.

—(1999), 'The future of philosophy', *Philosophical Transactions of The Royal Society B, Biological Sciences*, 354, 2069–80.

Serway, R. A. (1996), *Physics for Scientists and Engineers with Modern Physics*. 4th edn. Philadelphia: Saunders College Publishing.

Siewierska, A. (ed.) (1998), *Constituent Order in the Languages of Europe: EALT / EUROTYP 20-1*. Berlin: Mouton de Gruyter.

Sigurd, B. (1994), 'Generalized Word Order Grammar', in *Computerized Grammars for Analysis and Machine Translation*. Lund: Lund University Press.

Skautrup, P. (1947), *Det danske Sprogs Historie II*. København: Gyldendalske Boghandel, Nordisk Forlag.

—(1950), 'Reformationsbiblens tilblivelse og forudsætninger'. Bidrag til den danske bibels historie. Festskrift i anledning af den danske bibels 400 års jubilæum; republished in P. Skautrup: *Dansk sprog og kultur. Udvalgte afhandlnger og artikler 1921–1971*. København: Gyldendal, pp. 112–25.

—(1953), *Det danske Sprogs Historie III*. København: Gyldendalske Boghandel, Nordisk Forlag.

Stuurman, F. (1996), 'Descriptive Grammar and Formal Grammar', in K. Brown and J. Miller (eds) *Concise Encyclopedia of Syntactic Theories*. Oxford: Pergamon, Elsevier Science.

Svanlund, J. (1988), 'Två studier i äldre nysvensk syntax', in *MINS 27*. Stockholms universitet, Institutionen för nordiska språk.

Svenonius, L. (1958), 'Review of Chomsky, N. 1956, "Three Models for the Description of Language" (*Institute of Radio Engineers, Transactions on Information Theory*, vol. IT-2 no. 3, pp. 113–24)', *The Journal of Symbolic Logic*, 23, (1), 71–2.

Svenska Akademiens Grammatik (1999), Stockholm: SAG.

Tarski, A. (1937), *Die mathematische Logik. Und in die Methodologie der Mathematik*. Vienna: Verlag von Julius Springer.

Trask, R. L. (1993), *A Dictionary of Grammatical Terms in Linguistics*. London: Routledge.

Uldall, H. J. (1957), *Outline of Glossematics*, Part I: General Theory. *Travaux du Cercle Linguistique de Copenhague*, Vol. X, 1. Copenhagn: Nordisk Sprog-og Kulturforlag.

van Seuren, P. (2012), 'A reaction to Jackendoff's discussion note', *Language*, 88, (1), 174–6.

Vicente, A. (2011), 'Current physics and "the physical"', *British Journal of the Philosophy of Science* 10, 1–24.

Whitfield, F. J. (1953), *Prolegomena to a Theory of Language*, trans. of Hjelmslev (1943). Baltimore, MD: Waverly Press.

Yule, G. (2010), *The Study of Language*, 4th edn. Cambridge: Cambridge University Press.

Text sources

(HCA Dan)

Andersen, H.C. (1964), 'Historien om en Moder', in *H.C. Andersens Eventyr II: 1843–55*, critical edition by E. Dal, Det Danske Sprog- og Litteraturselskab, pp. 160–4, (*H.C. Andersens Nye Eventyr 1844–48, eventyr optagne i Eventyr 1850 samt Historier 1852–5*, Ved Erik Dal, København: Hans Reitzels Forlag, 1964).,

Swedish translation

(HCA Swe)

Backman, K. J. (1877), 'Historien om en moder', in *Sagor och Berättelser af Hans Kristian Andersen*, öfversättning från danskan af Karl Johan Backman, Stockholm: Hjalmar Linnströms Förlag 1877, Första Delen pp. 393–8.

Index